GOT LIVE ALBUM
IF YOU WANT IT!

GOT LIVE ALBUM
IF YOU WANT IT!
100 Live Recordings to Consider

Avram Mednick

iUniverse LLC
Bloomington

GOT LIVE ALBUM IF YOU WANT IT!
100 LIVE RECORDINGS TO CONSIDER

iUniverse books may be ordered through booksellers or by contacting:

iUniverse LLC
1663 Liberty Drive
Bloomington, IN 47403
www.iuniverse.com
1-800-Authors (1-800-288-4677)

ISBN: 978-1-4917-1373-0 (sc)
ISBN: 978-1-4917-1374-7 (e)

Printed in the United States of America.

iUniverse rev. date: 11/11/2013

This one is for Steven Telzak, my brother from
another mother, taken from us too soon.

I don't want to
Hang up my rock'n'roll shoes,
Something happens to me
Every time I hear the blues.

—Chuck Willis, 1958

Play that fast thing one more time,
It does something to me and it sure feels fine.

—Nick Lowe, 1980

CONTENTS

ACKNOWLEDGMENTS

I acknowledge that I did this one pretty much on my own. However, I did consult, or insult, as the case may be, the following humans: Janet Mednick (cover and author photos), Michael Abrams, Buzzy Cohen, Alan Fishman, and Lyen Steinke.

FOREWORD

When I wrote *The 100 Greatest Rock'n'Roll Albums Ever* in 2009, I intentionally excluded live albums, mainly to avoid having to compare apples with oranges. Well, I'm back, this time to consider the live album. Live albums are fun. Live albums more accurately capture the essence of a recording artist than do studio releases. Live albums can transport you to another time and place. The effect can be especially poignant when you've attended the live performance or one similar.

What to include? I've cast a wider net here. My primary focus remains the rock'n'roll era, but I've included here exemplary live recordings by artists from the blues, soul, folk, jazz, rap, and country genres. Just because an album is featured on this or that list doesn't mean that it will appear here. I pick music that I like and with which I am familiar. So there will be glaring omissions here in the opinion of others. However, if this compendium inspires one reader to reflect on his or her own favorite live albums, then I have largely accomplished my goal.

Although there certainly were excellent live recordings released prior, I first became aware of the power of the live album when *Live/Dead* came out in 1969. Having seen the Dead numerous times by then, I was aware that their studio albums released to that point did not really capture their essence. *Live/Dead* changed all that. Other rock bands, notably Jefferson Airplane, The Doors, and The Allman Brothers quickly followed suit, and the rest is history.

I've tried, for the most part, to select actual live concert recordings. They're the best. However, many live collections and/or compilations are also worthy of merit. I've limited my scope to commercially available releases, as opposed to bootlegs and tape vault collections, such as those made available to fans by the Grateful Dead, Phish, Frank Zappa, and other artists.

I've concentrated on the original releases of these live recordings, as opposed to re-releases or expanded compact disc releases, with one notable exception, *Live at Leeds* by The Who, for reasons immediately obvious to some and explained herein. Albums with some live recordings and some studio recordings (*Wheels of Fire* and *Live Cream*, *Eat a Peach*, *Bongo Fury*, *Fathers and Sons*) didn't make the cut.

Of course, release dates in this context are less significant than actual recording dates. Statistically speaking, three-quarters of the performances considered here were recorded in the 1960s and 1970s (31 percent from 1968-1971). The other 25 percent are spread fairly evenly across the decades, with 1953 being the earliest recording and 2008 (two of them) the most recent. The preponderance of selections from the '60s and '70s can be attributed most of all to my chronological age, as well as to my rock'n'roll orientation, and, sadly in retrospect, to the period of time in which the recording industry was at its apex, now inexorably in decline. For the record, I attended sixteen of the hundred live performances documented herein.

The book title derives from the name of the first live album by The Rolling Stones, *Got LIVE If You Want It!*, released in 1966. It was compiled as a result of a contractual obligation with London Records, and the Stones were not at all happy with it. They subsequently disowned it, claiming that *Get Yer Ya-Ya's Out! The Rolling Stones in Concert* (1970) was their actual live album debut.

I listened to every one of these hundred albums over the last eight or so months, some for the first time in years, some for the first time ever, having discovered them in my research. Since I couldn't possibly own them all, I borrowed a bunch from friends and public libraries and purchased a few from used record stores and the internet. I sat down to listen to each with my yellow pad and pen and took notes. It was a labor of love.

October 2013

The Allman Brothers Band – *At Fillmore East*

Released: 1971
Recorded: March 12-13, 1971, Fillmore East, NYC
Label: PolyGram
Producer: Tom Dowd
Personnel:
Duane Allman – guitar
Gregg Allman – organ, piano, vocals
Dickey Betts – guitar
Berry Oakley – bass
Jaimoe – drums, percussion
Butch Trucks – drums, percussion
Thom Doucette – harmonica
Jim Santi – tambourine

At Fillmore East is on every list of greatest albums you can get your hands on. Despite that fact, I have selected it here because it was one of the very important live albums in my musical education, along with *Live/Dead* and others. It is a double album recorded at the Fillmore East in March 1971. It marked the breakthrough success for The Allman Brothers Band and remains among the top-selling albums in their catalogue.

One of the great things about this album is that it starts out as if shot out of a cannon, with the band's great rendition of "Statesboro Blues" by Blind Willie McTell. Duane Allman takes the first solo on slide guitar, Dickey Betts answers capably with the second guitar solo. This is followed by another cover, Elmore James's "Done Somebody Wrong," featuring Thom Doucette on harmonica and blistering guitar solos by Betts and D. Allman, in that order.

An extended version of T. Bone Walker's "Stormy Monday" is next, performed about as deliberately and bluesy as can be. Gregg Allman's vocal is nuanced and his organ solo is memorably jazzy, sandwiched as it is between lengthy guitar solos by first D. Allman and then Betts. An almost twenty-minute performance of Willie Cobbs's "You Don't Love Me" completes the first album of *At Fillmore East*. It is a showcase for the guitarists to stretch out and for producer Tom Dowd, for splicing together one performance from the early show on March 12 with another from the late show on March 13 to create this recording. Sure sounds like "Joy to the World" towards the end. Thom Doucette is featured on harmonica.

"Hot 'Lanta" is an instrumental written by The Allman Brothers Band about one of their favorite places. After stating the theme, G. Allman takes the first solo on organ, followed by D. Allman and Betts, respectively, on guitar. Drummers Jaimoe and Butch Trucks are featured, but it is Berry Oakley's bass line that carries the song to its crescendo ending.

Betts's "In Memory of Elizabeth Reed" is next, an extended instrumental composition named for a headstone, a personal favorite. Betts begins with violin-like swells on his guitar and is joined by D. Allman to state the first theme on double lead guitars. The tempo picks up to a Santana-like beat, the guitars stating a secondary theme. Betts then solos to the secondary theme, leading to an organ solo from G. Allman. Throughout, drummers Jaimoe and Trucks provide a thick layer of rhythm. D. Allman then quietly starts restating the first theme, gradually building to a series of climaxes against bassist Oakley's counterpoint playing. Parts of these solos by D. Allman have been compared favorably to those by saxophonist John Coltrane and trumpeter Miles Davis. A brief percussion break follows and then the full band returns to restate the second theme and end the song abruptly.

At Fillmore East concludes with "Whipping Post," G. Allman's epic jam, twenty-three minutes in length. Beginning with Oakley's rumbling bass line, the song commences in eleven-fourths time, fairly radical for a rock'n'roll band. D. Allman takes the first guitar solo after the first verse and chorus. G. Allman returns to sing the second verse and chorus, after which Betts takes over on lead guitar for the middle part of the performance, building to a climax. The band then slows down to a tempo-less, abstract section of the piece during which the musicians experiment freely. G. Allman eventually reenters to sing a third chorus and then a fourth. D. Allman then leads the band to a violent ending . . . and the first few notes of "Mountain Jam."

Two other songs recorded during these shows, "Trouble No More" and "Mountain Jam," were later included on *Eat a Peach* (1972). These songs, along with other previously omitted tracks, were included on *The Fillmore*

Concerts (1992). In 2003, *At Fillmore East Deluxe Edition* was released on two compact discs, containing additional bonus material.

"In Memory of Elizabeth Reed" from *At Fillmore East* was one of the songs I selected to be in my book, *The 100 Greatest Rock'n'Roll Songs Ever* in 2000. I attended at least one of these shows, maybe both.

Laurie Anderson – *United States Live*

Released: 1984
Recorded: February 7-10, 1983, Brooklyn Academy of Music, NYC
Label: Warner Bros.
Producer: Laurie Anderson, Roma Baran
Personnel:
Laurie Anderson – microphone stand, violins, violin bows, harmonizer, pillow speaker, toy saxophone, Vocoder, glasses, Oberheim OB-Xa, Synclavier, tamboura, telephone, Jew's harp, voice
Peter Gordon – Prophet synthesizer, voice
Geraldine Pontius – voice
Joe Kos – voice
Chuck Fisher – clarinet, saxophone
Bill Obrecht – flute, saxophone
Anne DeMarinis – Oberheim OB-Xa, Synclavier
David Van Tieghem – drums, percussion
Roma Baran – accordion
Rufus Harley – bagpipes
Shelley Karson – soprano

United States is Laurie Anderson's magnum opus performance art piece, featuring musical numbers, spoken word pieces, and animated vignettes about life in the United States. Originally, it was presented in four parts over the course of two nights, running for eight total hours. *United States Live* is an abbreviated rendition of the performance, omitting several segments that were solely visual in nature.

It was originally released as a five-record boxed set containing no fewer than eighty-one tracks. Segments range from the humorous, such as "Yankee See," in which she wonders why Warner Bros. signed her at all, to her signature anthem, "O Superman," which somehow made it into the top ten on the British charts in 1981. She performs "Language is a virus (from outer space)," based on a phrase attributed to William S. Burroughs, which she later modified for her 1986 concert film *Home of the Brave*.

Anderson performs some of the pieces utilizing the most non-traditional "instruments," such as "Closed Circuits" for voice and amplified mike stand, "Small Voice," for speaker-in mouth, "Neon Duet," for violin and neon bow, "Odd Objects," for light-in-mouth, and a couple of tracks for Tape Bow Violin, which apparently is an electronic violin without strings, developed by Anderson in 1977. She also very effectively employs a harmonizer to raise or lower the pitch of her vocals on many of the tracks.

United States Live appropriately begins with "Say Hello," quickly conveying Anderson's quirky sense of humor in a spoken word piece, assisted by the voice of Peter Gordon. "Walk the Dog" is a personal favorite, a very strange rap by Anderson punctuated by some of her vocal chanting, harmonizer turning her voice to squeals. "Language of the Future" is an unbelievably prescient indictment of tech talk, considering that it was 1983.

As a former resident of New Jersey, I appreciate the bizarre, extended "New Jersey Turnpike." "Dance of Electricity" has a very entertaining and informative introduction by Anderson about Nikola Tesla. "From the Air" is another personal favorite, which features Chuck Fisher and Bill Obrecht on saxophones. The aforementioned "O Superman" from *Big Science* (1981) is the half-sung, half-spoken minimalist piece that brought Anderson to the attention of the public, in my case through the medium of alternative radio. It is performed brilliantly here, Obrecht assisting on flute, Ann DeMarinis on Synclavier.

In "Private Property" Anderson uses the harmonizer to lower her voice and tell the story of the time William F. Buckley, whom she dubs Mr. Private Property, was asked to leave a mall where he had hoped to give a speech because it was private property. "Let X=X" is just a great piece, warped out spoken word over swirling, hypnotic musical groove, featuring David Van Tieghem on percussion.

"Bagpipe Solo" is just that, featuring Rufus Harley. You have to love the humorous, abbreviated "Steven Weed," homage to Patty Hearst's boyfriend. "Example #22" is a wild musical romp, featuring Fisher on clarinet and soprano Shelley Karson. Another personal favorite is "I Dreamed I Had to Take a Test . . ." (in a Dairy Queen on another planet). The rousing "Dr. Miller" is co-written with installation artist Perry Hoberman.

The whole band does a spaced out rendition of "Big Science," title track from the album of the same name. "Blue Lagoon" is an example of a piece on which Anderson includes Synclavier vocal samples, with strange effect, indeed. It actually rocks out! "Mach 20" may be the most bizarre track on the album, and that's quite an accomplishment. What if sperm whales traveled at the relative speed of spermatozoa?

United States Live concludes in grand fashion with "Lighting Out for the Territories," a slight misquotation of a line from the conclusion of *The Adventures of Huckleberry Finn* by Mark Twain, in which the title character says he plans to "Light out for the Territory," referring to the unsettled frontier beyond civilization. That is clearly the direction in which Anderson hopes to point us.

The Band – *Rock of Ages: The Band in Concert*

Released: 1972
Recorded: December 28-31, 1971, Academy of Music, NYC
Label: Capitol
Producer: The Band
Personnel:
Rick Danko – bass, violin, vocals
Levon Helm – drums, mandolin, vocals
Garth Hudson – organ, piano, accordion, saxophones
Richard Manuel – piano, organ, clavinet, drums, vocals
Robbie Robertson – guitar, vocals
Howard Johnson – tuba, euphonium, saxophone
Snooky Young – trumpet, flugelhorn
Joe Farrell – saxophones, English horn
Earl McIntyre – trombones
J.D. Parran – saxophone, clarinet

The Band booked a residency at the Academy of Music in New York City for the last week of 1971, culminating in a New Year's Eve performance. Having commissioned Allen Toussaint to compose horn charts for "Life is a Carnival" on *Cahoots* earlier that year, they decided to have Toussaint write charts for a five-man horn section for the December concerts. The shows were captured on *Rock of Ages: The Band in Concert*.

The repertoire for the performances consists of tunes from all four of The Band's studio releases to date, framed on the album by covers of Marvin Gaye's 1964 single, "Don't Do It," and Chuck Willis's single, "(I Don't Want to Hang Up) My Rock'n'Roll Shoes," from 1958, quoted at the beginning of this book. Garth Hudson weaves "Auld Lang Syne" into his solo piece, "The Genetic Method," played at Midnight, December 31. Bob Dylan makes a surprise visit at the New Year's Eve show, playing four songs with The Band in the early morning of January 1, 1972, not included on the album.

Contained herein are magnificent renderings of some of The Band's best known tunes, and with a horn section! The horns are present on eleven tracks and are particularly effective on "King Harvest (Has Surely Come)" sung brilliantly by Richard Manuel, "The Unfaithful Servant," ditto Rick Danko, and most of all on "The Night They Drove Old Dixie Down" segued into "Across the Great Divide," all from The Band's 1969 eponymous second album, and on "Life is a Carnival."

Other highlights without the horn section include "This Wheel's on Fire" and "The Weight" from *Music from Big Pink* (1968), "Get Up Jake," an outtake from *The Band*, "The Shape I'm In" and "Stage Fright" from the 1970 album of the same name, and the aforementioned "The Genetic Method," which segues into "Chest Fever" from *Music from Big Pink*.

In retrospect, this project was in many ways a dry run for *The Last Waltz*, five years down the road. It was a farewell of sorts, before The Band took an extended break in 1972, ending the first stage of their career. And it was a big party, with the horn charts making the familiar and not so familiar tunes sparkle, and The Band, tight as ever, nonetheless playing like the kick-ass road warriors they were.

Originally released as a double album in 1972, it was reissued in 1980 as two separate albums, *Rock of Ages, Vol. 1* and *Rock of Ages, Vol. 2*. *Rock of Ages: The Band in Concert* was released on two compact discs in 2001, with the original album on one disc and an additional ten tracks on a second. These included the four Dylan songs and a cover of "Loving You is Sweeter Than Ever," the 1966 hit single by The Four Tops. The 2005 retrospective boxed set of The Band, *A Musical History*, includes several remixed *Rock of Ages* tracks as well as a previously unreleased performance by The Band of "Smoke Signal" from *Cahoots* from the December 28 show. I attended the December 30 concert.

The Band & various artists – *The Last Waltz*

Released: 1978
Recorded: November 25, 1976, Winterland Ballroom, San Francisco, California
April-May, 1977, MGM Sound Stage, Culver City, California
Label: Warner Bros.
Producer: Robbie Robertson
Personnel:
Rick Danko – bass, violin, vocals
Levon Helm – drums, mandolin, vocals
Garth Hudson – organ, accordion, saxophones, synthesizer
Richard Manuel – piano, organ, clavinet, dobro, drums, vocals
Robbie Robertson – guitar, piano
Howard Johnson – tuba, saxophone, clarinet, flugelhorn
Rich Cooper – trumpet, flugelhorn
Jerry Hey – trumpet, flugelhorn
James Gordon – flute, saxophone, clarinet
Charlie Keagle – clarinet, flute, saxophones
Larry Packer – violin
Paul Butterfield – harmonica, vocals
Bobby Charles – vocals
Eric Clapton – guitar, vocal
Neil Diamond – guitar, vocal
Dr. John – piano, guitar, congas, vocals
Bob Dylan – guitar, vocals
Emmylou Harris – guitar, vocals
Ronnie Hawkins – vocals
Bob Margolin – guitar
Joni Mitchell – guitar, vocals
Van Morrison – vocals
Pinetop Perkins – piano
Dennis St. John – drums
John Simon – piano
Ringo Starr – drums
Muddy Waters – vocals

Ronnie Wood – guitar
Neil Young – guitar, harmonica, vocals
The Staples Singers:
Cleotha Staples – vocals
Mavis Staples – vocals
Roebuck "Pops" Staples – guitar, vocals
Yvonne Staples – vocals

The Last Waltz was a concert by The Band, with many special guests, held on Thanksgiving Day, 1976. It was billed as the group's "farewell concert appearance." The musical director was The Band's original producer, John Simon. The event included an actual Thanksgiving dinner for 5,000 people, with ballroom dancing and a stage set for *La Traviata* borrowed from the San Francisco Opera.

The concert featured songs by The Band interspersed with the group backing up the special guests. Many of the musical guests included artists with whom The Band had worked collectively or individually, including previous employers Ronnie Hawkins and Bob Dylan and Woodstock neighbor Van Morrison. They flawlessly backed musicians as diverse as Joni Mitchell, Neil Diamond, and Muddy Waters.

The event was filmed by director Martin Scorsese and made into a documentary of the same name, released in 1978. It was the first concert film to be shot in thirty-five millimeter film, and is critically considered one of the greatest concert films ever made. In addition to the concert footage, the film includes "The Last Waltz Suite," recorded at a studio soundstage after the fact, as well as interviews by Scorsese with members of The Band.

The release of the film enabled the world at large to observe what some of us already knew, namely, that Robbie Robertson is a great, understated lead guitarist. Whether paraphrasing the guitar parts from his own tunes or trading licks with the likes of Eric Clapton on "Further On Up the Road," first released as a single in 1957 by Bobby "Blue" Bland, Robertson is always tasteful, always on the money, never over the top.

My personal favorite performances from *The Last Waltz* include the aforementioned guitar duel with Clapton, a blistering hot "Coyote" from *Hejira* (1976) by Joni Mitchell, Robertson trading leads with Garth Hudson's soprano saxophone at the end of "It Makes No Difference" from *Northern Lights – Southern Cross* (1975), and Mavis Staples putting more than a little soul into "The Weight" from *Music from Big Pink* (1968), filmed later as part of "The Last Waltz Suite."

It has come to my attention in my old age that The Band is not everyone's cup of meat. They never really had a hit record, outside of "The Weight," and their tunes aren't exactly rockers. But the songs are actually about stuff and draw from every aspect of Americana, so much so as to become part of the American tradition themselves. I would posit that from the release of *Music from Big Pink* in 1968 through 1975, when *Northern Lights – Southern Cross* came out, there was no finer songwriter in the rock idiom than Robbie Robertson, and that while some bands may have equaled The Band's impeccable musicianship, none have surpassed it.

"It Makes No Difference" from *Northern Lights – Southern Cross* was one of the songs I selected to be in my book, *The 100 Greatest Rock'n'Roll Songs Ever* in 2000. I didn't attend the concert, but I own the tee-shirt, which is now part of a quilt.

B.B. King – *Live at the Regal*

Released: 1965
Recorded: November 21, 1964, Regal Theater, Chicago, Illinois
Label: ABC, later MCA
Producer: Johnny Pate
Personnel:
B.B. King – guitar, vocals
Leo Lauchie – bass
Duke Jethro – piano
Sonny Freeman – drums
Bobby Forte – saxophone
Johnny Board – saxophone

From a tender young age, I was keenly aware of *Live at the Regal* by B.B. King. I knew that it was the definitive recording of a live blues performance, the yardstick against which all others were measured. I was a bar-mitzvah boy the year it was recorded. I never owned the album myself. But I listened to it a hundred times, thanks to Buzzy Cohen, who opened my ears to the blues. When I finally broke down and bought a compact disc player late in the previous millennium, *Live at the Regal* was among the first half dozen compact discs I purchased.

B.B. King first recorded in 1949. That winter, he and his band were performing at a dance hall in Twist, Arkansas when a lit barrel of kerosene was knocked over in a fight, setting the place on fire. King escaped with the others, but when he realized that he had left his guitar inside, he risked his life to run in to rescue his axe. He later learned that the fight had been over a woman named Lucille, so that became the name of that guitar and every one he's owned since.

King toured the "chitlin' circuit" extensively in the 1950s and '60s, setting a personal record in 1956 with 342 concerts booked. He became one of the most important artists in rhythm and blues music, with an impressive series of hits, including some performed on *Live at the Regal*. His big career break came in 1969 with the release of "The Thrill is Gone," which crossed over onto the pop charts. He gained further visibility among rock'n'roll audiences (that's me!) when he opened for The Rolling Stones on their American tour that same year.

In true blues review style, the concert opens with an introduction of King, the band playing him on stage with the first few bars of "Every Day I Have the Blues," attributed to Memphis Slim, a hit for King in 1955, and subsequently his theme song. Next is "Sweet Little Angel," an old, slow, very suggestive blues. King adapted it from "Black Angel Blues," first recorded in 1930, and had a hit with it in 1956. From that, he segues into "It's My Own Fault," a sad tale of unrequited love.

"How Blue Can You Get" was a hit for King in 1964 and quickly became a fixture in his live shows. He plays an especially mean lead guitar, in counterpoint to Bobby Forte and Johnny Board on saxophone. The tune features one of King's classic stop-time refrains: "I gave you a brand new Ford . . . ." "Please Love Me" is a funky up-tempo shuffle that features Duke Jethro on piano.

They keep things moving apace with "You Upset Me Baby," highlighting the horn section. King, ever the showman, slows things down significantly with "Worry Worry," delivering his trademark licks over the rhythm section playing in stop time. Sonny Freeman excels on drums as the audience goes wild. King also offers some free relationship advice.

The whole band swings on the way-too-short "Woke Up This Morning (My Baby's Gone)." After King introduces the band, *Live at the Regal* concludes with the one-two punch of "You Done Lost Your Good Thing Now" and "Help the Poor." The former starts out slowly and builds to a rave-up featuring the horns. The latter is a love ballad as well as a reminder to us all to help the less fortunate among us.

Many accomplished guitarists, including Eric Clapton and Mark Knopfler have acknowledged listening to *Live at the Regal* for inspiration prior to performances. In 2005, this album was selected for permanent preservation in the National Recording Registry at the Library of Congress in Washington, DC.

B.B. King & Bobby "Blue" Bland – *Together for the First Time . . . Live*

Released: 1974
Recorded: September 9, 1974, Western Recorders Studio 1, Los Angeles, California
Label: ABC
Producer: Steve Barri
Personnel:
B.B. King – guitar, vocals
Bobby "Blue" Bland – vocals
Michael Omartian – keyboards
Melvin Jackson – trumpet
Sonny Freeman – drums
Mel Brown – guitar
Ben Benay – guitar
Milton Hopkins – guitar
Joseph Burton – trombone
Ron Levy – keyboards
Louis Hubert – saxophone
Bobby Forte – saxophone
Edward Rowe – trumpet
Wilbert Freeman – bass
Charles Polk – drums
Theodore Reynolds – keyboards
Tommy Punkson – trumpet
Joseph Hardin, Jr. – trumpet
Alfred Thomas – trombone
Theodore Arthur – saxophone
Cato Walker – saxophone
Harold Potier, Jr. – drums
Leo Penn – drums

Bobby "Blue" Bland was born in 1930 in Rosemark, Tennessee. He then moved to Memphis, where he began singing in gospel groups and became a member of the Beale Streeters. In 1956, Bland began touring with Junior Parker, moonlighting when necessary as a valet. In this manner, he first met B.B. King as his driver. Bland had a few successful big-band blues singles in the late 1950s, but he really made his mark as a blues vocalist with releases such as "Cry Cry Cry," "I Pity the Fool," and the often covered "Turn on Your Love Light," all from 1961.

Bland collaborated with King on two albums in the 1970s, and they continued to tour together into the '80s. The first such collaboration was *Together for the First Time . . . Live*, a double album recorded at a soundstage in Los Angeles in 1974, featuring a big band. First up is "3 O'Clock in the Morning," King's first hit single from 1952. Bland and King exchange vocals on the twelve-bar blues. King wails on the guitar in front of the mighty horn section. Michael Omartian is featured on piano.

Interesting to compare the version of "It's My Own Fault" captured here with the one recorded ten years prior on *Live at the Regal*. This segues into a cover of Charles Brown's "Driftin' Blues," featuring outstanding vocal performances by the two headliners. "That's the Way Love Is," a hit for Bland in 1963, is a showstopper, featuring himself on vocals and the massive horn section. They slow things down significantly with an extended version of "I'm Sorry," King taking over the vocal duties.

They break out of the pure blues idiom to cover Brook Benton's ballad, "I'll Take Care of You," Bland providing the vocal. Wilbert Freeman's bass and the ample horn section are featured. "Don't Cry No More," from Bland's 1961 album *Two Steps From the Blues*, sounds an awful lot like "Turn on Your Love Light," but that's all right. It features Bland on vocal and Charles Polk on drums. King takes over vocal duties and they slow things down again with "Don't Want a Soul Hangin' Around." King's guitar playing and the horn section are featured.

They then launch into the incredible, fourteen-minute long "(Medley)" of standard blues tunes, with plenty of call-and-response, commentary, and joking added for good measure. King and Bland are clearly having a blast, sounding as relaxed as they might be in one of their living rooms. There are even brief reprises of "3 O'Clock in the Morning" and "It's My Own Fault Baby."

One of King's signature tunes, "Everybody Wants to Know Why I Sing the Blues," is next. It's performed as a funky shuffle, featuring the author on vocal and guitar as well as a solo from bassist W. Freeman. It's back over to Bland for the vocal on a cover of "Goin' Down Slow" by "St.

Louis" Jimmy Oden, featuring Omartian on organ. *Together for the First Time . . . Live*, concludes, appropriately enough, with "I Like to Live the Love." King's song expresses the artists' wish for music and love in the lives of the audience members.

In 1976, King and Bland collaborated again to create and release *Bobby Bland and B.B. King Together Again . . . Live*, recorded at the Coconut Grove in Los Angeles. Bobby "Blue" Bland died in June 2013 during the preparation of this project.

The Beatles – *Live! at the Star Club in Hamburg, Germany; 1962*

Released: 1977
Recorded: late December, 1962, Star Club, Hamburg, Germany
Label: Lingasong
Producer: Larry Grossberg
Personnel:
George Harrison – guitar, vocals
John Lennon – guitar, harmonica, vocals
Paul McCartney – bass, vocals
Ringo Starr – drums

The Beatles' five residencies in Hamburg from 1960-1962 allowed them to hone their performing skills. A new Hamburg music venue, the Star Club opened in April 1962 with The Beatles booked for the first seven weeks. The Beatles returned to Hamburg for the final time in December 1962 with a new drummer, Ringo Starr, who had replaced Pete Best that August. Some of these performances were recorded by the club's station manager using a home reel-to-reel recorder and a single microphone. The resulting double album is *Live! at the Star Club in Hamburg, Germany; 1962*. Although the sound quality is poor, it is an important document of The Beatles' club act just before the outbreak of Beatlemania.

Although these shows were comprised mostly of covers, the album starts with an original tune, "I Saw Her Standing There," with Paul McCartney on vocals. It would be the B-side to "I Want to Hold Your Hand," their breakthrough single, the following year. Chuck Berry's 1956 hit single "Roll Over Beethoven" is next, featuring George Harrison on vocals and guitar, done at breakneck speed. McCartney is back on vocals on "Hippy Hippy Shake," a hit for Chan Romero in 1959.

John Lennon sings Berry's "Sweet Little Sixteen," a hit in 1958. The Beatles really start to cook on this one, very tight and funky. Next is a cover of "Lend Me Your Comb," B-side to Carl Perkins's 1957 single, "Glad All Over." Lennon and McCartney share vocal duties. Harrison plays an excellent guitar solo. "Your Feet's Too Big," sung here by McCartney, was a hit for Fats Waller in 1939.

Lennon sings the next two songs, "Twist and Shout," the 1961 single by The Top Notes popularized by the Isley Brothers, and "Mr. Moonlight," written by Roy Lee Johnson, but with lyrics altered by Lennon. Then it's McCartney's turn to sing two, "A Taste of Honey," originally an instrumental track from the 1961 film of the same name, and "Besame Mucho," a bolero written in 1940 by Consuelo Velasquez.

A single released posthumously for Buddy Holly in 1962, "Reminiscing," written by King Curtis, features Harrison on vocals and guitar. Next is a medley of Wilbert Harrison's "Kansas City," a hit in 1959, and Little Richard's 1958 single, "Hey, Hey, Hey, Hey," sung by McCartney. Then Harrison is back on vocals on "Nothin' Shakin' (But the Leaves on the Trees)," a single for Eddie Fontaine in 1958.

They slow things down with the ballad, "To Know Her is to Love Her," Lennon on vocals, a gender reversal of the 1958 single for the Teddy Bears, written by Phil Spector. This is followed by McCartney's take on "Little Queenie," a hit for Berry in 1959. Many of us cut our teeth on The Rolling Stones' cover of this tune; actually The Beatles were doing it first. Harrison is featured on guitar solo.

"Falling in Love Again (Can't Help It)" is the English translation of the name of a song written in German by Friedrich Hollander and made famous by Marlene Dietrich in the film *The Blue Angel*. Here it is performed like a twisted waltz, vocals by McCartney. Next is another original tune, "Ask Me Why," sung by Lennon, which would be the B-side to their "Please Please Me" single the following year.

On the next two tracks, Gene Vincent's "Be-Bop-A-Lula" and Ray Charles's "Hallelujah I Love Her So," The Beatles back Star Club guest vocalists, first Fred Fascher, Star Club waiter, and then Horst Fascher, Star Club manager. This is followed by the unlikeliest cover tune of all, "Red Sails in the Sunset," first recorded by Bing Crosby in 1935, sung here with tongue planted firmly in cheek, by McCartney. Next is a personal favorite, "Everybody's Trying to be My Baby," written by Carl Perkins in 1957. It features Harrison on guitar and vocals and Starr on drums.

Lennon takes over vocal duties on the next three tracks. "Matchbox," another 1957 Perkins hit, features some interesting guitar interplay between Lennon and Harrison. The often covered "I'm Talking About You," a single for Berry in 1961, features Harrison on guitar. "Shimmy Like Kate" is based on The Olympics' 1960 arrangement of the classic "I Wish I Could Shimmy Like My Sister Kate."

The final two vocals belong to McCartney. The first is Little Richard's "Long Tall Sally," a hit in 1956, done here at super-fast speed. *Live! at the Star Club in Hamburg, Germany; 1962* concludes with the improbable "I Remember You," written by Johnny Mercer in 1941 and later popularized by Slim Whitman. Lennon is featured on harmonica.

Mike Bloomfield & Al Kooper – *The Live Adventures of Mike Bloomfield and Al Kooper*

Released: 1969
Recorded: September 26-28, 1968, Fillmore West, San Francisco, California
Label: Columbia
Producer: Al Kooper
Personnel:
Al Kooper – organ, piano
Mike Bloomfield – guitar
John Kahn – bass
Skip Prokop – drums
Carlos Santana – guitar
Elvin Bishop – guitar

The Live Adventures of Mike Bloomfield and Al Kooper is a double live album recorded at the Fillmore West in 1968. It is a follow-up to the studio album *Super Session*, which featured Bloomfield and Kooper as well as Stephen Stills, and which was a critical and commercial success earlier that year. The album is not flawless by any means, but it nonetheless documents an important, if raw, blues-rock performance of the period. It is notable for including Bloomfield's debut as a vocalist and for being one of the earliest live recordings by Carlos Santana.

The first album starts with Bloomfield's semi-coherent introduction and, improbably, "The 59th Street Bridge Song (Feelin' Groovy)" by Paul Simon. It's a great, rocking, soulful rearrangement, featuring drummer Skip Prokop, which the author liked so well that he agreed to overdub a harmony vocal on the last verse in the studio. "I Wonder Who," a cover of the Ray Charles tune, is a slow, twelve-bar blues sung by Bloomfield and featuring himself on blistering lead guitar. However, the track is faded mid-solo for no apparent reason.

Two instrumentals follow, "Her Holy Modal Highness," by Kooper and Bloomfield and Robbie Robertson's "The Weight." The former is a highlight, pun intended, on which the authors complement each other wonderfully on organ and guitar in an extended jam. John Kahn also takes a jazz-inspired solo on bass. The latter features Kooper's tasteful mastery of the Hammond organ. "Mary Ann" is another Charles cover sung by Bloomfield. Also a twelve-bar blues, this one is performed like a mid-tempo shuffle, with stop time intervals and brilliant guitar fills.

The Live Adventures of Mike Bloomfield and Al Kooper slows down a tad with "Together 'Til the End of Time," a cover of a Frank Wilson ballad. Kooper provides the vocal, as well as a studio overdub on piano under the pseudonym Roosevelt Gook. "That's All Right," the Arthur Crudup standard, is sung by Bloomfield and features Prokop on the drums. Kooper excels on "Green Onions," the Booker T. & the MG's instrumental hit.

The second album opens with an introduction, this time by Kooper, explaining, among other things, how Bloomfield's "insomnia" had caught up with him, and that local San Francisco musicians had volunteered to substitute for the missing headliner on the third scheduled night of performances. The first track is "Sonny Boy Williamson" by Jack Bruce, featuring Carlos Santana on guitar. The next, "No More Lonely Nights," is written by Williamson, and features Elvin Bishop on guitar and vocal. Steve Miller and Dave Brown also sat in that night, but did not make it onto the recording.

The album then returns to material with Bloomfield, starting with a jazzy rearrangement of "Dear Mr. Fantasy," the Traffic tune. On the last verse, Kooper's microphone fails and his vocal is picked up faintly by the audience microphone. Albert King's "Don't Throw Your Love on Me So Strong" is certainly Bloomfield's best vocal effort on the album and maybe one of the finest recordings he ever made. It is followed by the last track on the album, "Finale-Refugee," a short, staccato, guitar-dominated shuffle, on which Bloomfield is credited with "guitar dropping on floor." Confusing, or perhaps confused, as Bloomfield was not present on the final night of recording.

Blue Öyster Cult – *On Your Feet or On Your Knees*

Released: 1975
Recorded: April 27 1974, The Capitol Theater, Passaic, New Jersey
       October 5, 1974, Academy of Music, NYC
       October 12, 1974, Long Beach Arena, Long Beach, California
       October 14, 1974, Show Palace, Phoenix, Arizona
       October 18, 1974, Paramount Theater, Portland, Oregon
       October 19, 1974, Paramount North West Theater, Seattle,
           Washington
       October 21, 1974, Vancouver, British Columbia, Canada
Label: Columbia
Producer: Murray Krugman, Sandy Pearlman
Personnel:
Eric Bloom – guitar, synthesizer, vocals
Donald "Buck Dharma" Roeser – guitar, vocals
Allen Lanier – guitar, keyboards
Joe Bouchard – bass, vocals
Albert Bouchard – drums, guitar, vocals

On Your Feet or On Your Knees is Blue Öyster Cult's first live album. It contains three songs from each of the band's first three albums, an original instrumental that remains a staple of their live shows to this day, and two covers, "I Ain't Got You" by the Yardbirds, albeit with modified lyrics, and "Born to be Wild" by Steppenwolf. It is the band's highest charting album.

It starts with an elongated version of "Subhuman" with excellent interplay between Donald Roeser and Allen Lanier on guitar. "Harvester of Eyes" is a serious boogie, strangely evocative of Steely Dan's "Black Friday." "The Red and the Black" is a personal favorite, a speeded up version of "I'm On the Lamb But I Ain't No Sheep" from the eponymous first album, again featuring the guitarists.

"Buck's Boogie" is Roeser's signature song and showcases him as the guitar virtuoso that he is. There's great keyboard playing by Lanier as well. "Last Days of May" is another favorite, a ballad sung by Roeser about a failed drug deal. "ME 262" is noteworthy for the section during which all five band members play guitar. "Before the Kiss (A Redcap)" is a very interesting and complicated song featuring a surprisingly jazzy jam in the middle.

It's been documented that, as a young man, I had two housemates who were certifiable lunatics and Blue Öyster Cult mavens. Forty years later, they have the following to say about *On Your Feet or On Your Knees*, proving them still certifiable:

Alan Fishman, 62, from Ft. Lauderdale, opines: "The album was a way to take advantage of the tight and exciting live performances of BOC. There are some gems to be sure, exceptional extended versions of "Last Days of May," "Subhuman," and the previously unreleased "Buck's Boogie." Conveying the new heavy metal sound live onto vinyl seemed to be easier said than done, and the overproduction, particularly the fade-in/fade-outs of the crowd noises and stage announcements are tricks that are more annoying than welcomed. Still, the fire in Allan Lanier's and particularly Don Roeser's guitars is never less than satisfying and at times ferocious."

Michael Abrams, 61, from San Francisco, adds: "If you had not seen Blue Öyster Cult perform live when their eponymous first album was released in 1972, you would have had no clue as to their true identity. From the jazzy and rhythmic changes in "Before the Kiss, A Red" to the country lean of "Redeemed" to the ethereal dirge of "She's As Beautiful As a Foot" to the sinister, psychedelic boogie of "Screams" you would think this was an art-rock band, more Roxy Music than Black Sabbath. The song titles alone set them apart from the standard rock tripe. Only "Cities on Flame With Rock'n'Roll" allowed a hint to their actual personality.

When their second effort was released, *Tyranny and Mutation*, there was little confusion as to the direction they were taking. Filled with blindingly tasteful riffs and sci-fi imagery, side one is a tour-de-force unmatched by any of Blue Öyster Cult's contemporaries. And yet the follow-up third release, the near perfect *Secret Treaties*, again blurred the lines. Once the double live LP, *On Your Feet or On Your Knees* hit the record shops, everything became clear.

Live recording technology was in its infancy and capturing the BÖC blitzkrieg provided fidelity challenges. That said, as one of their later songs asked, are you ready to rock? The song and the band most emphatically answered, yes I am. BÖC pulled no punches. The gatefold packaging featured a cover of a limousine with an aerial flag depicting the BÖC logo, letting you know these are the hard rock VIPs. The vehicle, standing before a gothic church, was inviting you in for a heavy metal mass.

The back cover depicted an opened bible held by leather-gloved hands and listing the song titles. And once the needle hits the grooves the sermon is loud and forceful. Seeing them on consecutive New Years Eves at the Academy of Music in Manhattan back in 1973-74, my friends and I took the subway home, and in our youthful exuberance proudly proclaimed we couldn't hear the train. Blue Öyster Cult provided a sonic storm."

My wife, Janet, went to the Academy of Music show with Abrams and Fishman. She met a friend who worked there and who took her on a tour of the backstage area. On the way back to her seat, she witnessed a guy falling out of the balcony. He landed in the orchestra aisle, got up, and walked back to the lobby, where he collapsed. She and others informed the authorities as to what had transpired, so that they wouldn't treat him as just another drug catastrophe.

The Blues Project – *Live at the Café Au Go Go*

Released: 1966
Recorded: November 24-27, 1965, Café Au Go Go, NYC
            January 29-30, 1966, Café Au Go Go, NYC
Label: Verve Folkways
Producer: Jerry Schoenbaum
Personnel:
Danny Kalb – guitar, vocals
Al Kooper – keyboards, vocals
Steve Katz – guitar, harmonica, vocals
Roy Blumenfeld – drums
Andy Kulberg – bass
Tommy Flanders – vocals

Live at the Café Au Go Go is the debut album by the Blues Project, recorded at the Café Au Go Go in New York City in November 1965 as part of an event called The Blues Bag. Other participants were Muddy Waters, John Lee Hooker, and Otis Spann. However, vocalist Tommy Flanders left the band immediately following the shows and the record label decided it wouldn't be wise to feature him on a majority of the tracks. So the band returned to the Café Au Go Go as a quintet in January to play two afternoon concerts to college students who had won tickets. More than likely, side one (tracks one through six) was recorded at the afternoon shows; side two (tracks seven through eleven) at The Blues Bag.

The concert is comprised mainly of an eclectic bunch of cover tunes with one original and one traditional song included for good measure. The album begins with an up-tempo cover of Muddy Waters's "Goin' Down Louisiana." It features Steve Katz on harmonica and Danny Kalb on guitar and vocal, singing "Lou-EEZ-iana, like a New Yorker (I should know). This is followed by Willie Dixon's "You Go, I'll Go With You," done as a funky shuffle. Kalb handles the vocals and excels on guitar, as does Al Kooper on organ.

Steve Katz takes over vocal duties on Donovan's "Catch the Wind," featuring interesting interplay between Kalb on guitar and Kooper on organ. Chuck Berry's "I Want to Be Your Driver" is next, sung by Kooper (channeling Bob Dylan, with whom he had worked on *Highway 61 Revisited*, released only three months prior) and featuring solos by Kalb on guitar. Kalb's vocal performance on the traditional "Alberta" is both moody and jazzy, and his guitar figures match perfectly.

"The Way My Baby Walks" is an instrumental written by bassist Andy Kulberg. A twelve-bar blues with a twist, it's a vehicle for Kalb, the author, and Kooper to solo on guitar, bass, and organ, respectively. Next is an unapologetic cover of Eric Anderson's "Violets of Dawn," a psychedelic folk song featuring Flanders on the vocal and Roy Blumenfeld's drumming.

Dixon's "Back Door Man" is next, sung by Flanders, on which Kalb plays perhaps his most ambitious guitar solo on the album. The band gets down and dirty on "Jelly Jelly Blues," written by Billy Eckstein and Earl Hines. Kalb is featured on vocal and guitar, as is Kooper on piano. A third Dixon cover, "Spoonful," done up-tempo style, follows. Flanders's vocal is bluesy and Kalb wails on guitar.

Live at the Café Au Go Go concludes with Howlin' Wolf's "Who Do You Love." The entire band is featured with Flanders on vocal. Once again, the influence of Dylan is recognized in the arrangement of the classic blues tune. Six additional tracks recorded at The Blues Bag, including alternate versions of "Alberta" and "Who Do You Love" were included on *The Blues Project Anthology* (1997). All of the tracks were included on a 2004 compact disc reissue.

James Brown & The Famous Flames – *Live at the Apollo*

Released: 1963
Recorded: October 24, 1962, Apollo Theater, NYC
Label: King, later Polydor
Producer: James Brown
Personnel:
James Brown – vocals
Lucas "Fats" Gonder – organ, vocals, MC
Les Buie – guitar
Al "Brisco" Clark – saxophones
St. Clair Pinckney – saxophone
Clifford "Ace King" MacMillan – saxophone
William "Po' Devil" Burgess – saxophone
Louis Hamlin – trumpet
Teddy Washington – trumpet
Roscoe Patrick – trumpet
Dickie Wells – trombone
Hubert Perry – bass
Clayton Fillyau – drums
George Sims – drums
The Famous Flames:
Bobby Byrd – keyboards, vocals
Bobby Bennett – vocals
"Baby" Lloyd Stallworth – vocals

James Brown booked the Apollo Theater in Harlem from October 19-25, 1962. He wanted to record a live album, as Ray Charles had done twice. However, King Records did not support his idea, believing that a live album featuring no new songs wouldn't sell. So *Live at the Apollo*, captured October 24, was recorded at Brown's own expense. To the record label's surprise, the album was a rapid seller, peaking at number two on the Billboard charts.

The album begins with Master of Ceremonies Fats Gonder introducing James Brown & the Famous Flames, then the band plays them onstage with a few bars of the instrumental "The Scratch," and we're off and running. The concert seems to flow seamlessly, each song leading into the next. The first track is "I'll Go Crazy," the 1960 single, featuring guitarist Les Buie and the horn section. When Brown and the Famous Flames do their call-and-response part of the song, it's the audience that goes crazy. This track was itself issued as a single in 1966.

Brown then drops right into the ballad "Try Me," originally titled "Try Me (I Need You)" when it was released as a single in 1958. The band takes a back seat as Brown and the Famous Flames deliver fabulous four-part harmony vocals in true doo-wop tradition. The rhythm section of Hubert Perry on bass and Clayton Fillyau on drums is featured. The band then plays the first of three snippets of "Hold It," designed to be an instrumental bridge between tracks.

"Think" is next, one of my favorites, a cover of the 1957 single by The "5" Royals, released as a single by Brown in 1960. It's super hot, featuring the horn section in a rhythmic attack that anticipates Brown's later funk music. This track was itself released as a single in 1964. After a little bit more of "Hold It," the band shifts into "I Don't Mind," released as a single in 1961. Brown's vocal is off the charts, the Famous Flames' harmony vocals are impeccable, and Buie excels on guitar.

After one last bit of "Hold It," we are treated to an amazing extended version of "Lost Someone," originally released as a single in 1961. It's a tour-de-force for Brown's vocalizing, not to mention his screaming and growling, while the band vamps behind him. The audience reaction is not to be believed. An abbreviated version of this track was itself released as a single in 1966.

The centerpiece of *Live at the Apollo* is next, a medley of Brown's hits, beginning and ending with "Please, Please, Please," the 1956 single. As Brown moves effortlessly from tune to tune, changing the rhythm and the mood at will, the audience gasps with recognition. Organist Gonder is featured on "I Love You, Yes I Do," while guitarist Buie solos tastefully on "Strange Things Happen." An abbreviated version of this track was also released as a single in 1966.

The last track on the album is "Night Train," released by Brown in 1962 just prior to the run of shows at the Apollo. It's a twelve-bar blues, a cover of an instrumental first recorded by Jimmy Forrest in 1951. Brown, of course, adds his own lyrics, a shouted list of cities on his touring itinerary (with radio stations he hoped would play his music) and many repetitions of the song's title.

Because the master recordings had been misplaced and available copies were not of good quality, *Live at the Apollo* was not reissued on compact disc until 1990. A deluxe edition was released in 2004 that included four bonus tracks, alternate takes of "Think," "Medley: I Found Someone/Why Do You Do Me/I Want You So Bad," "Lost Someone," and "I'll Go Crazy."

Brown went on to record several more albums at the Apollo over the course of his career: *Live at the Apollo, Vol. II* (1968), *Revolution of the Mind: Recorded Live at the Apollo, Vol. III* (1971), and *Live at the Apollo 1995*.

Johnny Cash – *At Folsom Prison*

Released: 1968
Recorded: January 13, 1968, Folsom State Prison, Folsom, California
Label: Columbia
Producer: Bob Johnston
Personnel:
Johnny Cash – guitar, harmonica, vocals
June Carter – vocals
Marshall Grant – bass
W.S. Holland – drums
Carl Perkins – guitar
Luther Perkins – guitar
The Statler Brothers:
Lew DeWitt – vocals
Don Reid – vocals
Harold Reid – vocals
Phil Balsley – vocals

Ever since the release of his 1955 single, "Folsom Prison Blues," Johnny Cash had been interested in performing at a prison. His idea was put on hold, however, until 1967, when Columbia Records put Bob Johnston in charge of producing Cash's material. After several years of limited commercial success, Cash had recently taken control of his drug abuse problem and was looking to turn his career around.

Backed by June Carter, whom he married later the same year, Carl Perkins and the Tennessee Three, and the Statler Brothers, Cash performed two shows at Folsom State Prison in California on January 13, 1968. The resulting double album, *At Folsom Prison* consists of fourteen tracks from the first show and two from the second. Despite little investment from Columbia, the album was a hit, reaching number one on the country charts and the top fifteen nationally.

The album begins, predictably, with "Folsom Prison Blues," an edited version of which became a hit single all over again for Cash in 1968. (Edited due to the assassination of Robert Kennedy on June 5.) Cash hits all the really low notes, Carl Perkins excels on solo guitar, and the audience is, well, captive. This is followed by a cover of Merle Travis's "Dark as a Dungeon," about the hazards of coal mining. Cash interrupts himself to admonish audience members for laughing during the song.

After a humorous introduction, Cash launches into "I Still Miss Someone," written with his bother Roy, from *The Fabulous Johnny Cash* (1958). This leads to a cover of "Cocaine Blues," written by T.J. "Red" Arnall in 1947. A comical reworking of the traditional "Miss Sadie," it is very well received by the prisoners. The comic theme continues with the gallows humor of "25 Minutes to Go" by Shel Silverstein, about a man awaiting his own execution.

"Orange Blossom Special," about the passenger train of the same name, written by Ervin T. Rouse in 1938, features Cash on the harmonica. Cash's vocal performance is outstanding on "Long Black Veil," the country ballad originally recorded by Lefty Frizell in 1959. After some back-and-forth between Cash and the audience, side two of *At Folsom Prison* begins with two prison songs, "Send a Picture of Mother" from *Old Golden Throat* (1968), and "The Wall" from *Orange Blossom Special* (1965).

Cash then says he intends to do two love songs, both written by Jack Clement, and promptly dedicates "Dirty Old Egg Sucking Dog" to his dog and "Flushed from the Bathroom of Your Heart" to no one in particular. The crowd howls in approval. Cash then brings June Carter on stage to perform with him on a cover of "Jackson" by Billy Edd Wheeler and Jerry Leiber and on Cash's own "Give My Love to Rose."

This is followed by another prison song, "I Got Stripes" from *Songs of Our Soil* (1959), featuring the Statler Brothers on backing vocals. They are also prominent on a cover of the Tom Jones hit from 1965, "Green, Green Grass of Home." The album concludes dramatically with "Greystone Chapel" written by Folsom Prison inmate Glen Sherley, who was in the front row, unaware that his song would be played. C. Perkins is featured on lead guitar.

At Folsom Prison was critically acclaimed and helped revitalize Cash's career, leading to the release of a second prison album, *At San Quentin*, in 1969. The album was re-released with three additional tracks, "Busted," "Joe Bean," and "The Legend of John Henry's Hammer," in 1999. In 2008, it was reissued on two compact discs and one digital video disc, containing both concerts uncut and re-mastered.

Cheap Trick – *Cheap Trick at Budokan*

Released: 1979
Recorded: April 28, 30, 1978, Nippon Budokan, Tokyo
Label: Epic
Producer: Cheap Trick
Personnel:
Robin Zander – guitar, vocals
Rick Nielsen – guitar, vocals
Tom Petersson – bass, vocals
Bun E. Carlos – drums

Having found early success in Japan, Cheap Trick recorded *Cheap Trick at Budokan* in Tokyo in 1978 in front of an audience of 12,000 screaming fans. It was originally intended for release only in Japan, but an estimated 30,000 import copies were sold in the United States and it was released domestically in 1979. It peaked at number four on the Billboard charts and became Cheap Trick's best selling album. "I Want You to Want Me" and "Ain't That a Shame" also charted as hit singles.

The show begins with "Hello There" from *In Color* (1977), as did all Cheap Trick concerts of the period. And it's a perfect opener, a kick-ass hard rock party song. It features Bun E. Carlos on drums, who then segues into "Come On, Come On," also from *In Color*. This is your basic mid-tempo rock love song, featuring Robin Zander on vocals and Rick Nielsen on guitar.

"Lookout" is next, from *Cheap Trick [1977]*, a very infectious rocker, featuring Tom Petersson on bass and backing vocals. A drum introduction by Carlos ushers in "Big Eyes" from *In Color*, a driving rocker with Zander at the helm with an inspired vocal. Nielsen is featured on solo guitar. The crowd goes wild in a paroxysm of screams. Cheap Trick then perform an extended version of "Need Your Love," a new song at the time that would appear on *Dream Police* in 1979. It's a complicated composition with many interesting changes in time signature. Nielsen takes one of his most distinctive guitar solos on the album. At times, the band is barely audible above the screaming.

Next is their great cover of "Ain't That a Shame," the hit single for Fats Domino in 1955, itself a hit for Cheap Trick in 1979. With its distinctive introduction featuring Carlos on drums and Nielsen on guitar, it ultimately showcases Zander's snarling, growling vocal performance. Reportedly the Fat Man's favorite cover of his classic tune, it was actually played as part of a two-song encore.

This is followed by "I Want You to Want Me" from *In Color*. This song was released as a single in 1977 but failed to chart in the United States, although it was number one in Japan. This version, however, from *Cheap Trick at Budokan*, became the biggest selling single of their career. Much more up-tempo than the original, it features the band with some remarkable ensemble playing and especially Nielsen on guitar. The audience is so into it, that they actually mimic the echo effect from the studio version's refrain, "Cryin', cryin, cryin' . . . ."

The hits keep on coming with "Surrender," Cheap Trick's first big hit in 1978 from *Heaven Tonight*. A definite teen anthem of it's time, it is a power pop classic. During the final chorus of the song, "We're all all right," repeated four times, the excited audience shouts along in unison. "Goodnight Now" or "Goodnight," also from *Heaven Tonight*, was written as a companion piece to "Hello There." Utilized as a show-closer by Cheap Trick for many years, it basically announces that the concert is over.

Cheap Trick at Budokan concludes with "Clock Strikes Ten" from *In Color*, played as part of an encore. Starting with Nielsen playing guitar notes to sound like Big Ben's chimes, it's a song about living for the weekend and going nuts on Saturday night. It has similarities to "Rock Around the Clock" by Bill Haley & His Comets, but it mostly reminds me of "Rip it Up" by Little Richard. A great way to end the show.

Budokan II was released in 1994 as a sequel to *Cheap Trick at Budokan*, consisting of the remaining tracks from the concert not included on the original album plus three tracks recorded on Cheap Trick's 1979 tour. *At Budokan: The Complete Concert* was issued in 1998 on two compact discs, which included all of the tracks in the order in which they were played. Cheap Trick played this version of the album in its entirety in Chicago on April 30, 1998, to coincide with its release. A 30th anniversary collectors edition was released in 2008 as a four compact disc set, including all of the above plus a compact disc and digital video disc of the April 1998 concert.

The Clash – *From Here to Eternity: Live*

Released: 1999
Recorded: April 30, 1978, Victoria Park, East London, England
         July 27, 1978, Music Machine, London, England
         December 28, 1978, Lyceum Theater, London, England
         February 18, 1980, Lewisham Odeon, London, England
         June 13, 1981, Bonds International Casino, NYC
         September 7-8, 1982, The Orpheum, Boston, Massachusetts
         October 13, 1982, Shea Stadium, NYC
Label: Epic
Producer: The Clash
Personnel:
Mick Jones – guitar, vocals
Paul Simonon – bass, guitar, vocals
Joe Strummer – guitar, bass, vocals
Topper Headon – drums
Terry Chimes – drums
Mickey Gallagher – organ
Mikey Dread – vocals

Although The Clash's live performances were legendary, they did not release an official live album until 1999, long after their demise as a band. *From Here to Eternity: Live* was recorded at various venues between 1978 and 1982. It works exceptionally well as a concert album because the performances are sequenced according to the date of the song, not the date of the performance. Consequently, it has the genuine momentum and flow of a real set-list and it is impossible to tell when each song was recorded.

The first six tracks originate on The Clash's eponymous 1977 debut album. *From Here to Eternity: Live* begins with "Complete Control," a vicious condemnation of record companies, the band's reaction to having "Remote Control" released by CBS Records without their permission. The song includes the earliest usage of the phrase "guitar hero" and features guitar hero Mick Jones with two excellent solos. This is followed by

"London's Burning," about isolated, alienated life in London, which the band performs with reckless abandon.

"What's My Name" is a short blur of a punk song. "Clash City Rockers" is the band's attempt at writing some of their own mythology. It features a riff reminiscent of The Who's debut single, "I Can't Explain." "Career Opportunities," a personal favorite, features a spirited vocal by Joe Strummer with a "take this job and shove it" theme. "(White Man) In Hammersmith Palais," about Strummer's visit to an all-night reggae show, may be the first song to merge punk and reggae.

"Capital Radio" is next, from the *Capital Radio Extended Play* disc. It's an indictment of London's only legal commercial radio station at the time, even parodying one of their jingles. "City of the Dead" from *Black Market Clash* (1980) is one of The Clash's more melodic tunes, featuring Jones on guitar and Paul Simonon on bass. This is followed by The Clash's great cover of "I Fought the Law," a hit single for the Bobby Fuller Four in 1965.

"London Calling," from the 1979 album of the same name, is a powerful post-punk anthem and a signature song for The Clash. Strummer delivers a snarling vocal performance apropos of the strident lyrics. They finally slow things down a bit with "Armagideon Time," a cover of a tune by Willie Williams and Coxsone Dodd from *Black Market Clash*. It's an extended foray into dub-style reggae, featuring Mickey Gallagher and Mikey Dread sitting in on organ and vocals, respectively.

"Train in Vain," another personal favorite, is from *London Calling*, as is the following song, "Guns of Brixton." The former is one of those great rock songs with all the elements: great playing, infectious hooks, and interesting lyrics, referencing Robert Johnson in the title and Ben E. King in the chorus. Jones is featured on vocals. The latter carries a strong political message and features Simonon on vocals and guitar and Strummer on bass.

"The Magnificent Seven" is from *Sandinista!*. Inspired by old school hip hop acts from New York City, it's the first attempt by a rock band to write and perform original rap music and an early example of hip hop music with political content. "This is a public service announcement . . . with guitars!" So begins "Know Your Rights" from *Combat Rock* (1982) continuing the social commentary. This one is a facetious look at the rights of the poor and disenfranchised. Terry Chimes is featured on drums.

Also from *Combat Rock*, "Should I Stay or Should I Go" features Jones on vocals and guitar and Strummer on Spanish translation. It became The

Clash's only number one single a decade after it was released. *From Here to Eternity: Live* concludes with an extended, emotional performance of "Straight to Hell" from *Combat Rock*. Like many of The Clash's songs, it shines a light on various forms of injustice in society.

"Train in Vain" from *London Calling* was one of the songs I selected to be in my book, *The 100 Greatest Rock'n'Roll Songs Ever* in 2000.

Joe Cocker – *Mad Dogs and Englishmen*

Released: 1970
Recorded: March 27-28, 1970, Fillmore East, NYC
Label: A&M
Producer: Denny Cordell, Leon Russell
Personnel:
Joe Cocker – vocals
Leon Russell – keyboards, guitar, vocals
Chris Stainton – keyboards
Don Preston – guitar, vocals
Carl Radle – bass
Jim Gordon – drums, percussion
Chuck Blackwell – drums, percussion
Jim Keltner – drums, percussion
Sandy Konikoff – drums, percussion
Bobby Keys – saxophones
Jim Price – trumpets
Rita Coolidge – vocals
Donna Washburn – vocals
Claudia Lennear – vocals
Denny Cordell – vocals
Daniel Moore – vocals
Nicole Barclay – vocals
Bobby Jones – vocals

The title of Joe Cocker's *Mad Dogs and Englishmen* is drawn from the 1931 Noel Coward song of the same name. The album is mostly comprised of covers, drawing equally from rock'n'roll (The Rolling Stones, Traffic, Bob Dylan, The Beatles) and soul (Ray Charles, Sam & Dave, Otis Redding). Accompanying Cocker is a huge choir, a two-piece horn section, and several drummers.

I listened to this album a lot back in the day. In retrospect, it was truly unique; big-band rock'n'roll with almost three dozen players backing the singer. And it was very well recorded, equally capturing quieter moments like the beginning of Leonard Cohen's "Bird on the Wire" as well as the band going all-out on Arthur Hamilton's "Cry Me a River." Then as now, I always thought Leon Russell was the unsung hero of this project.

Mad Dogs and Englishmen begins with a French-accented introduction of Cocker, which leads into the Stones' *Honky Tonk Woman*, Russell making his presence felt early on piano. Dave Mason's *Feelin' Alright* is certainly an early highlight, this time featuring Russell on guitar. Rita Coolidge does a nice job handling the vocal on *Superstar*, co-written by Russell. Cocker's interpretation of Ray Charles's *Let's Go Get Stoned*, with the band and the choir wailing behind him is just about as good as it gets.

The centerpiece of the concert is a medley of three blues ballads, Charles's "I'll Drown in My Own Tears," "When Something is Wrong With My Baby," popularized by Sam & Dave, with a little help from Bobby Jones on vocals, and Otis Redding's "I've Been Loving You Too Long." Cocker is soulful throughout, the choir is gospel-tinged, and the big band works out. Carl Radle rocks steady on the bass.

After Bob Dylan is acknowledged in the audience, Cocker and Russell deliver a short, sweet, soulful rendition of Dylan's "Girl from the North Country." "Space Captain" was always a favorite of mine, with its refrain of "Learning to live together" and Russell as funky as can be on piano. Cocker's cover of the Box Tops' "The Letter" is fun, Jim Price and Bobby Keys getting a chance to solo on trumpet and saxophone, respectively. This leads into the raucous concert finale, Russell's "Delta Lady."

It's been documented that the tour from which this album was drawn just about wiped Cocker out. The music was presented on such a vast scale, and his own contribution was so overshadowed by Russell's work as arranger and bandleader, that he never really bounced back. However, although he may have been a hijacking victim of sorts, the music, nonetheless, still shines brightly today.

In 2005, *Mad Dogs and Englishmen* was released as a two-disc deluxe edition set to commemorate the album's 35th anniversary. In 2006, it was re-released as a six-disc boxed set under the title *The Complete Fillmore East Concerts*. This included both early and late shows from both nights in their entirety. I attended one of these shows. No way I remember which one.

John Coltrane – *Live at the Village Vanguard*

Released: 1962
Recorded: November 2-3, 1961, Village Vanguard, NYC
Label: Impulse!
Producer: Bob Thiele
Personnel:
John Coltrane – saxophones
Eric Dolphy – clarinet
McCoy Tyner – piano
Reggie Workman – bass
Jimmy Garrison – bass
Elvin Jones – drums

John Coltrane was born in 1926 in North Carolina, but by 1943 he was a resident of Philadelphia, a city with a vibrant music scene. In 1949, he joined the last Dizzy Gillespie big band and stayed on when the trumpeter downsized to a sextet. Coltrane left Gillespie in 1951, playing in a variety of bands until deciding, in 1955, to join a new quintet being formed by trumpeter Miles Davis. Coltrane stayed with Davis for the better part of five years (stepping out briefly to join the Thelonious Monk Quartet), developing an innovative approach to the tenor saxophone as featured soloist that helped establish Davis as the principal voice in modern jazz.

By 1960, when Coltrane left Davis to form his own quintet, the tenor saxophone had been supplanted by the rarely played soprano saxophone as his primary horn. Recordings such as *Blue Train* (1957) and *Giant Steps* (1960) had established him as a leader in the development of the music. The band that arrived in New York City for a two-week stay at the Village Vanguard grew out of the quartet with which Coltrane regularly worked: McCoy Tyner on piano, Elvin Jones on drums, and Reggie Workman on bass.

At the Vanguard, Workman was joined by Jimmy Garrison, who would take his place a month later. Most significant, however, was the recent addition of multi-instrumentalist Eric Dolphy to the band. The tape rolled for four of the last five nights of the run. In all, twenty-two takes of nine different titles were recorded, up to four versions of some of the tunes. Three performances were selected for the album, one pop standard, an adaptation of a Negro Spiritual, and "Chasin' the Trane," one of the most important recordings in the history of jazz.

"Spiritual" is first, featuring the quintet of Coltrane on saxophones, Dolphy on bass clarinet, Tyner, Jones, and Workman, recorded November 3. It's based on "Nobody Knows de Trouble I See," published in *The Book of American Negro Spirituals* by James Weldon Johnson. Coltrane starts the melody on tenor saxophone over Dolphy's clarinet counterpoint. Dolphy then takes a reflective solo, followed by Tyner. Coltrane, now on soprano saxophone, returns to restate the theme with great emotion.

"Softly as in a Morning Sunrise," the standard by Sigmund Romberg and Oscar Hammerstein II, starts with the trio of Tyner, Jones, and Workman, with Jones on brushes. Tyner's solo builds and builds until he brings on Coltrane's soprano saxophone. With Jones now swinging on sticks, Coltrane takes the composition apart and puts it back together again. This was recorded November 2.

The extended "Chasin' the Trane" takes up all of side two of *Live at the Village Vanguard*. Also recorded November 2, it is the jewel of the collection and features Coltrane on tenor saxophone, Jones, and Garrison. On the surface, it is a free-form jam session, without a theme and completely improvised. Coltrane takes solo after abstract solo, rooted both in the blues and the classics, unlike anything else he ever recorded. In a 1966 interview, Coltrane recalled that he had "listened to [Sun Ra Arkestra saxophonist] John Gilmore kind of closely before I made 'Chasin' the Trane'."

Two additional recordings taken from these shows, "India" and "Impressions," appeared on the album *Impressions* (1963). In 1997, Impulse! released a boxed set, *The Complete 1961 Village Vanguard Recordings*, with the sets from November 1, 2, 3, and 5, 1961, chronologically on four compact discs.

Sam Cooke – *Live at the Harlem Square Club, 1963*

Released: 1985
Recorded: January 12, 1963, Harlem Square Club, Miami, Florida
Label: RCA
Producer: Hugo Peretti and Luigi Creatore
Personnel:
Sam Cooke – vocals
King Curtis – saxophone
Clifton White – guitar
Cornell Dupree – guitar
Jimmy Lewis – bass
Albert "June" Gardner – drums
Tate Houston – saxophone
George Stubbs – piano

Sam Cooke was born Samuel Cook in Clarksdale, Mississippi, in 1931. He began his career with his siblings in a group called The Singing Children when he was nine years old. He became the lead singer in the Highway QC's at fourteen. In 1950, Cooke replaced R.H. Harris as lead singer in the gospel group The Soul Stirrers. The group signed with Specialty Records and released many gospel tracks in the early 1950s.

His first pop single was "Lovable," released in 1956 under the pseudonym Dale Cook in order not to alienate his gospel fan base. In 1957, he released "You Send Me," which spent six weeks at the top of the Billboard charts. In the early '60s, he had a series of hit singles, including "Cupid," "Another Saturday Night," and "Twistin' the Night Away." He also released two critically acclaimed albums, *Night Beat* (1963) and *Ain't That Good News* (1964).

Cooke recorded *Live at the Harlem Square Club, 1963* in Miami's historically African American neighborhood of Overtown with a merged band that included guitarist Clifton White and drummer Albert "June" Gardner from his regular touring group and saxophonist King Curtis and his band. The recording reveals a rougher, rawer side to Cooke that his singles only hinted at, as great as they were. It was originally to be released at the time as *One Night Stand*, but did not come out until 1985.

The concert begins with Curtis's saxophone growling out the first few notes of "Soul Twist" and the club's master of ceremonies introducing Cooke. After Cooke acknowledges the audience, he launches into "Feel It (Don't Fight It)," the 1961 feel good single, featuring the rhythm section of Gardner on drums and Jimmy Lewis on bass. "Chain Gang," the 1960 single, is next, but stripped down to its bare bones. Cooke eventually gets the crowd to grunt along with him, while Gardner continues to amaze on drums.

This is followed by the 1961 single, "Cupid," on which Cooke delivers a brilliant, nuanced vocal performance. White is featured on guitar. After a lengthy introduction, Cooke sings a medley of "It's All Right" and "(I Love You) For Sentimental Reasons," released as singles in 1961 and 1957, respectively. Cooke gets the audience to sing along with the standard written by Deke Watson and William Best.

"Twistin' the Night Away," the 1962 smash hit single, takes off like a rocket ship and only gets better, fueled by Curtis's saxophone solos. They slow things down a bit with "Somebody Have Mercy," also released as a single in 1962. Cooke is at his smoothest, delivering an emotional gospel-tinged vocal. Curtis is impeccable on saxophone.

"Bring it On Home to Me," a single in 1962, is just about a perfect song as performed here. The entire band is featured. By this point, the audience, especially the female members thereof, are worked up to a frenzied state. Cooke doesn't disappoint with "Nothing Can Change This Love," also released in 1962, featuring White on guitar and Curtis on saxophone. *Live at the Harlem Square Club, 1963* concludes, appropriately, with "Having a Party," yet another 1962 single. The band and the audience eagerly sing along with Cooke, as if wishing that the party could go on.

An entire generation of singers, Solomon Burke, Wilson Pickett, Bobby Womack, Otis Redding, Smokey Robinson, Teddy Pendergrass, Al Green, Aretha Franklin, Rod Stewart, and Steve Perry, among others, has acknowledged the influence of Sam Cooke. In 2000, *Live at the Harlem Square Club, 1963* was included as the second half of compact disc four in the boxed set *The Man Who Invented Soul*.

Cream – *Live Cream, Volume II*

Released: 1972
Recorded: March 9-10, 1968, Winterland Ballroom, San Francisco, California
               October 4, 1968, Oakland Coliseum, Oakland, California
Label: Atco
Producer: Felix Pappalardi
Personnel:
Jack Bruce – bass, harmonica, vocals
Eric Clapton – guitar, vocals
Ginger Baker – drums

It's hard to believe that the great power trio, Cream, only really existed for 29 months, from their first studio sessions in London to their last performance in 1968, considering the influence they had on rock'n'roll music. It was clearly their stage performance that defined them. Fully fifty percent of their recorded output was culled from live performances, beginning with *Wheels of Fire* in 1968, a two-record set, one of which was live.

Goodbye (1969) featured a side of live selections from The LA Forum, recorded in October 1968. *Live Cream* was released in 1970, despite the band having stopped performing two years prior. Inexplicably, however, one track, "Lawdy Mama," is an outtake from the *Disraeli Gears* (1967) sessions and cannot be considered a live performance. It is "Strange Brew" with alternate lyrics.

Live Cream, Volume II was released with little promotion or reaction in 1972, four years after Cream last performed. Perhaps the listening public and Eric Clapton fans had moved on to Derek & the Dominoes. This is unfortunate, as this album perhaps best represents an actual Cream concert more than any other. It features their two most recognized tunes as well as material from every phase of their short-lived career.

It opens with "Deserted Cities of the Heart," a seldom played live cut, one of my personal favorite Cream tunes. Its changing time signatures demonstrate what a truly gifted drummer Ginger Baker is. The jamming is hard and fast and straight ahead, Clapton's guitar and Jack Bruce's bass communicating in counterpoint. "White Room," their mega-hit is next, just a little slower, funkier, and heavier than the familiar version on *Wheels of Fire*.

"Politician," a blues with a twist, gives Bruce the opportunity to stretch his vocal performance with a double-entendre laden observation on the political situation as he sees it. Eric Clapton reminds us with his guitar that all politics are local. "Tales of Brave Ulysses" is the gem in this collection, an almost perfect song, and great in every way. Note Bruce's vocal, Baker's rock steady back beat, and Clapton soaring on guitar with his wah-wah pedal.

"Sunshine of Your Love," their other mega-hit, starts out somewhat true to the original on *Disraeli Gears*, but takes off during the extended instrumental break. This is essential power trio jamming, Clapton brilliant on guitar. "Steppin' Out" is a really long jam that starts out as a twelve-bar blues and evolves into an atonal improvisation. It was incorrectly identified on the original album cover as "Hideaway."

Cream reunited momentarily on the occasion of their induction in the Rock and Roll Hall of Fame in Cleveland, Ohio, in 1993. It was the first time they had performed in 25 years. They reunited in May 2005 for four shows at the Royal Albert Hall in London, the site of their final concerts in 1968. These concerts led to three more shows at Madison Square Garden in New York City in October 2005. Despite many rumors, no more Cream reunions are in the works.

Crosby, Stills, Nash & Young – *4 Way Street*

Released: 1971
Recorded: June 2-7, 1970, Fillmore East, NYC
        June 26-28, 1970, The Forum, Los Angeles, California
        July 5, 1970, The Chicago Auditorium, Chicago, Illinois
Label: Atlantic
Producer: David Crosby, Stephen Stills, Graham Nash, Neil Young
Personnel:
David Crosby – guitar, vocals
Stephen Stills – guitar, keyboards, vocals
Graham Nash – guitar, keyboards, vocals
Neil Young – guitar, harmonica, keyboards, vocals
Calvin "Fuzzy" Samuels – bass
Johnny Barbata – drums

4 Way Street is a double album by Crosby, Stills, Nash, & Young documenting performances from their 1970 summer tour. The album includes material from the various groupings as well as the individual work of the principals. Two songs each by David Crosby ("The Lee Shore," "Triad") and Graham Nash ("Chicago," "Right Between the Eyes") had not yet been officially released by the authors.

The album begins with the last few seconds of Steven Stills's "Suite: Judy Blue Eyes," as performed by Crosby, Stills, & Nash, after which Nash brings Neil Young up on stage to join the rest and perform his "On the Way Home." We get our first taste of their exquisite four-part harmonies as well as Young's acoustic lead guitar. This is followed by Nash's popular "Teach Your Children," sans Jerry Garcia on pedal steel guitar, which turns into an exuberant audience sing-along.

Crosby sings his somewhat controversial "Triad," recorded by Jefferson Airplane on *Crown of Creation* (1968). It is a brilliant solo performance, Crosby accompanying himself on acoustic guitar. He then does the eerily beautiful "The Lee Shore," with a little harmony help from his famous friends. This is followed by two new songs by Nash. His political "Chicago" would appear one month later on his *Songs for Beginners* album. It features the author on vocal and piano. "Right Between the Eyes" is a delicate little song about honesty, featuring some of the sweetest harmonies on the album.

It being Young's turn, he delivers a memorable solo performance of "Cowgirl in the Sand." After some self-deprecatory remarks, he sings "Don't Let it Bring You Down" in his falsetto voice to the delight of the audience. Not to be outdone, Stills launches into "49 Bye-Byes"/"America's Children," with a little "For What It's Worth" thrown in for good measure, accompanying himself on piano, with rhythmic hand clapping by the crowd. When the applause finally dies down, he switches to guitar to lead the band on a spirited "Love the One You're With."

The second album of *4 Way Street* features electric instruments and a rhythm section comprised of Calvin "Fuzzy" Samuels on bass and Johnny Barbata on drums, beginning with Nash's "Pre-Road Downs." Stills is featured on lead guitar. This is followed by Crosby's "Long Time Gone," featuring Young on guitar and Stills on organ. A much extended version of Young's "Southern Man" follows, featuring great harmonies and Stills and the author trading guitar riffs.

Young's "Ohio" is a highlight, the events at Kent State University still fresh in everyone's mind at the time of the concerts. The performance is emotional, the audience reaction electric. Stills's "Carry On" is another extended jamming vehicle, featuring great guitar interplay between Young and the writer. *4 Way Street* concludes with Stills's "Find the Cost of Freedom," performed acoustically, featuring the band's signature four-part harmonies.

At the time of this recording, tensions among band members were high, their dressing room fights becoming legendary, as referenced by Frank Zappa and the Mothers of Invention on *Fillmore East – June 1971* (1971). They dissolved as a band before the album was released, not to reunite until *CSN* (1977). *4 Way Street* was released in expanded form for compact disc in 1992. The expanded edition includes solo acoustic performances by each member. Additional tracks from the tour appeared on Young's *The Archives Vol.1 1963-1972*, released in 2009. I attended one of the shows at the Fillmore East.

Miles Davis – *Miles Davis at Carnegie Hall*

Released: 1962
Recorded: May 19, 1961, Carnegie Hall, NYC
Label: Columbia
Producer: Teo Macero
Personnel:
Miles Davis – trumpet
Hank Mobley – saxophone
Wynton Kelly – piano
Paul Chambers – bass
Jimmy Cobb – drums
The Gil Evans Orchestra:
Gil Evans – piano
Ernie Royal – trumpet
Bernie Glow – trumpet
Johnny Coles – trumpet
Louis Mucci – trumpet
Jimmy Knepper – trombone
Dick Hixon – trombone
Frank Rehak – trombone
Julius Watkins – French horn
Paul Ingraham – French horn
Bob Swisshelm – French horn
Bill Barber – tuba
Romeo Penque, Jerome Richardson, Eddie Caine, Bob Tricarico, Danny
    Bank – reeds and woodwinds
Janet Putnam – harp
Bobby Rosengarden – percussion

In 1948, Miles Davis left the Charlie Parker Quintet and began looking for a new project. At about the same time, arranger Gil Evans began holding informal jam sessions at his apartment, located close to the jazz clubs on 52nd Street in New York City. The two men met and collaborated to form what was to become the Miles Davis Nonet, recording

Birth of the Cool in 1950. Davis and Evans would then work together on *Miles Ahead* (1957), *Porgy and Bess* (1959), and *Sketches of Spain* (1960). *Miles Davis at Carnegie Hall* captures one of the only two occasions on which Miles Davis performed with the Gil Evans Orchestra.

The concert begins with an extended version of the Davis classic, "So What," the first and arguably the most distinctive piece from *Kind of Blue* (1959), one of the landmarks of modern music. All twenty-one musicians, the Miles Davis Quintet as well as the Gil Evans Orchestra, perform on this track, with remarkable results. Paul Chambers leads the way with the familiar bass introduction, Davis takes the first solo on trumpet, Hank Mobley follows on saxophone, and Evans swings on piano. A lush arrangement of "Spring is Here," the Rodgers and Hart tune, is next, performed by the orchestra with Davis as trumpet soloist and also featuring Wynton Kelly on piano. On both of these pieces, Evans pays homage with his arrangements to pianist, composer, and namesake Bill Evans.

The quintet then takes over for three tunes, beginning with an extended version of "No Blues." Called "Pfrancing" on *Someday My Prince Will Come* (1961), it contains arguably the best solo ever recorded by saxophonist Mobley, sandwiched among tasteful solos by Davis on trumpet, Kelly on piano, and Chambers on bass. This is followed by "Oleo," the frenetic, be-bop influenced Sonny Rollins composition that first appeared on *Bags' Groove* (1954). Davis is at his best here, delivering barrages of notes, the rhythm section swinging behind him. "Someday My Prince Will Come," from the album of the same name, is a brilliant interpretation of the popular song from Walt Disney's 1937 animated movie *Snow White and the Seven Dwarfs*. It features Davis's muted horn and drummer Jimmy Cobb's excellent brushwork.

We next hear again from the Gil Evans Orchestra performing "The Meaning of the Blues"/"Lament" from *Miles Ahead*. It is a very spiritual tune, featuring Davis's intelligent trumpet solo soaring above the rest. *Miles Davis at Carnegie Hall* concludes with "New Rhumba," also from *Miles Ahead*, also performed by the orchestra. It's an excellent showcase for Evans's arranging and Davis's playing.

A double compact disc of the complete concert was released in 1998. This edition has the entire first half of the concert on compact disc number one, including "Teo" from *Someday My Prince Will Come* and "Walkin'" from the 1954 album of the same name; and the complete second half on compact disc number two, including "I Thought About You" from *Someday My Prince Will Come* and "En Arranjuez Con Tu Amor" from *Sketches of Spain*.

Miles Davis – *Black Beauty: Miles Davis at Fillmore West*

Released: 1973
Recorded: April 10, 1970, Fillmore West, San Francisco, California
Label: CBS
Producer: Teo Macero
Personnel:
Miles Davis – trumpet
Steve Grossman – saxophones
Chick Corea – piano
Dave Holland – bass
Jack DeJohnette – drums
Airto Moreira – percussion, cuica

Shortly after *Bitches Brew* was released in 1970, Miles Davis lost saxophonist Wayne Shorter to Weather Report, replacing him with young Steve Grossman to fill out his sextet. *Black Beauty: Miles Davis at Fillmore West* is a double album recorded by the band at the Fillmore West in April of that year. It was first released in 1973 in Japan with album sides named "Black Beauty – Parts I-IV" by producer Teo Macero. Only on the 1997 compact disc reissue are the names of the compositions and composers identified.

To say that the performances captured on this album are abstract is an understatement, even by the standards established on *In a Silent Way* (1969) and *Bitches Brew*. Most of the tracks are lengthy, complicated jams. Melody is extinct and harmony is absent, but the rhythm and the groove are undeniable. The total effect is that of one long suite of music that pauses at points but doesn't really stop.

"Black Beauty – Part I" begins with a cover of the Joe Zawinul composition, "Directions." After taking an outrageous trumpet solo, Davis, with a little three-note pattern, gives saxophonist Grossman the freedom to take off into deep space, barely supported by the rhythm section of Dave Holland on bass and Jack DeJohnette on drums. By comparison, "Miles Runs the Voodoo Down" is almost structured in nature, with a discernible melody and groove. The band is tight behind Davis's blues figures and pianist Chick Corea's distorted chords.

"Black Beauty – Part II" kicks off with "Willie Nelson," a shorter piece, which is built around a funky riff established by bassist Holland. Davis's trumpet dances in and out of the groove, the tune going nowhere and everywhere at once. This is followed by a very brief snippet of "I Fall in Love Too Easily" by Sammy Cahn and Julie Styne, an odd choice indeed for the program, during which time temporarily stands still. As on *Bitches Brew*, Shorter's reworked ballad "Sanctuary" is next, Davis playing the theme and the rest of the band falling in.

"Black Beauty – Part III" commences with "It's About That Time" from *In a Silent Way*. It features Davis, Grossman, and Corea trading extended solos on trumpet, saxophone, and piano, respectively. The title track from *Bitches Brew* follows seamlessly, ushered in by Corea's keyboard introduction. Holland on bass and then DeJohnette on drums gradually add their voices to the mix before Davis on trumpet and then Grossman on saxophone enter the fray. This track features outstanding unconscious interplay between Davis and Corea.

"Black Beauty – Part IV" starts with the distinctive introduction to Shorter's "Masqualero" from *Sorcerer* (1967). The soloists each have an opportunity to take apart and then reconstruct the Spanish-favored theme. Corea particularly excels on piano, as does DeJohnette on the drums. *Black Beauty: Miles Davis at Fillmore West* concludes with "Spanish Key"/"The Theme," a mesmerizing groove. Davis on trumpet and then Grossman on saxophone trade incredible licks with Corea on piano, Holland's bass providing the foundation. The audience reacts as if stunned.

Delaney & Bonnie & Friends – *On Tour with Eric Clapton*

Released: 1970
Recorded: December 7, 1969, Fairfield Halls, Croydon, England
Label: Atco
Producer: Jimmy Miller, Delaney Bramlett
Personnel:
Bonnie Bramlett – vocals
Delaney Bramlett – guitar, vocals
Eric Clapton – guitar, vocals
Dave Mason – guitar
George Harrison – guitar
Bobby Whitlock – keyboards, vocals
Carl Radle – bass
Jim Gordon – drums, percussion
Tex Johnson – percussion
Doug Bartenfeld – guitar
Bobby Keys – saxophone
Jim Price – trumpet, trombone
Rita Coolidge – vocals

On Tour with Eric Clapton features Delaney and Bonnie Bramlett's best known touring band, including Eric Clapton and George Harrison appearing under the pseudonym "L'Angelo Misterioso." It was a significant group of players, to be sure, many of whom would work with Harrison on his post-Beatles debut album, *All Things Must Pass* (1970). Bobby Whitlock, Carl Radle, and Jim Gordon formed Derek & the Dominoes with Clapton for *Layla and Other Assorted Love Songs* (1970). The horn players, Bobby Keys and Jim Price, appeared on The Rolling Stones' albums *Sticky Fingers* (1971) and *Exile on Main St.* (1972) and toured with them in 1972.

The album cover is interesting in and of itself. As no pictures of Delaney and Bonnie were found suitable, the cover is a photograph of a Rolls Royce Silver Dawn out in the desert, supposedly taken by tour manager Barry Feinstein when he was working as a photographer covering Bob Dylan in 1966. According to mythology, Dylan's feet are hanging from the car window in the photograph. And in the interest of full disclosure, I listened to this album a lot. For one thing, it was chance to hear another side of Clapton, apart from Cream and Blind Faith.

D. Bramlett exhorts the crowd with "Come on, everybody!" and the concert begins with "Things Get Better." We are immediately served up a heaping portion of blue-eyed soul, both Bramletts on vocals, Radle rock steady on bass, and Clapton absolutely tearing it up on guitar. It is strangely evocative of the Coca Cola commercial jingle. To the best of my ability to ascertain, the slogan "Things go better with Coke" originated in 1963. Eddie Floyd wrote "Things Get Better" with Steve Cropper and Wayne Jackson in 1966.

The following gospel-tinged medley is dedicated to Robert Johnson. Dave Mason's "Only You Know and I Know" is performed as a funky shuffle, Mason sharing vocal duties with B. Bramlett. Clapton shines on guitar, as does the horn section. This is followed by "I Don't Want to Discuss It," a fast-driving rocker, featuring the refrain, "You're my girl!" and Clapton's brilliant guitar work. They slow things down significantly with the torch song, "That's What My Man Is For," very ably performed by B. Bramlett with an assist from Rita Coolidge.

"Where There's a Will There's a Way" is an anthem of positive thinking, on which the Bramletts sing incredible harmony vocals. It contains some interesting changes and affords drummer Gordon the opportunity to stretch out. Clapton takes over vocal duties on "Comin' Home," co-written with the Bramletts. It features Radle on bass and the horn section.

After band member introductions, the concert concludes with a raucous medley of Little Richard tunes, done at super-fast speed. The band engages in full-out jamming between verses, first Clapton and then Keys taking extended solos on guitar and saxophone, respectively. There is little question that a certain Mr. Penniman would have been pleased.

On Tour with Eric Clapton was reissued in 2010 as a four compact disc boxed set containing the complete performance from the Royal Albert Hall in London, a composite of the following night's show in Bristol, and both early and late shows from Fairfield Halls in Croydon. As Harrison joined the tour after the Royal Albert Hall concert, he appears on three of the four compact discs.

Derek and the Dominoes – *In Concert*

Released: 1973
Recorded: October 23-24, 1970, Fillmore East, NYC
Label: Polydor
Producer: Derek and the Dominoes
Personnel:
Eric Clapton – guitar, vocals
Carl Radle – bass
Bobby Whitlock – piano, organ, vocals
Jim Gordon – drums, percussion

Derek & the Dominoes went on tour in 1970 to promote the release of their album, *Layla & Other Assorted Love Songs*. However, band member Duane Allman only appeared at a small handful of live performances, so the touring band became, in essence, the Eric Clapton Band. Not that there's anything wrong with that! Six of the double album's nine tracks subsequently appeared on the 1994 album *Live at the Fillmore*. The other three songs, "Why Does Love Got to Be So Sad," "Let It Rain," and "Tell the Truth" are included on the later release, but from different sets than the ones appearing here.

Starting with drummer Jim Gordon, one of the best live introductions ever conjured up leads into "Why Does Love Got to Be So Sad," my favorite rearrangement on the album. It's slowed down just enough to make it funky, and they swap major chords for some fancy ones on the choruses. The result is very pleasing, indeed, Clapton smooth as silk on several extended solos.

This is followed by the optimistic "Got to Get Better in a Little While," featuring Clapton playing guitar with a wah-wah pedal. It is probably his strongest vocal performance on the album, supported by Bobby Whitlock's capable harmony vocal. "Let it Rain" is the longest jam by far on *In Concert*. It is from Clapton's eponymous studio album released in 1970 and written in collaboration with Bonnie Bramlett. It features Carl Radle's bass line, Whitlock on organ, and an extended drum solo from Gordon.

"Presence of the Lord," from Clapton's Blind Faith days, with its interesting time signature changes, features Whitlock on gospel piano and Clapton's wah-wah pedal. "Tell the Truth" is one of the great songs on *Layla & Other Assorted Love Songs* and it does not disappoint here. Clapton and Whitlock share vocal duties and Whitlock excels on piano in a version that's a little slower and a great deal more soulful than the studio track.

"Bottle of Red Wine" is another track from *Clapton* co-written with Bramlett. It is performed here as an up-tempo shuffle with Clapton on guitar and Whitlock on organ trading licks. "Roll it Over" is a rocking blues that would appear on *Eric Clapton's Rainbow Concert*, which took place the same month that *In Concert* was released. "Blues Power" is yet another track from *Clapton*, this time co-written with Leon Russell, featuring Whitlock's boogie-woogie piano playing.

It segues into the final track on *In Concert*, "Have You Ever Loved a Woman," the 1960 Freddie King single. Clapton had been playing this tune since 1965 from his days with John Mayall & the Bluesbreakers, and it appears on *Layla & Other Assorted Love Songs*. It is a highlight here, Clapton playing and singing his heart out about unrequited love.

I attended one of these performances. Asking me which one can only lead to irresponsible speculation. "Have You Ever Loved a Woman" from *Layla & Other Assorted Love Songs* was one of the songs I selected to be in my book, *The 100 Greatest Rock'n'Roll Songs Ever* in 2000.

The Doors – *Absolutely Live*

Released: 1970
Recorded: July 21-22, 1969, Aquarius Theater, Hollywood, California
　　　　　January 17-18, 1970, Felt Forum, Madison Square Garden, NYC
　　　　　April 10, 1970, Boston Arena, Boston, Massachusetts
　　　　　May 1-2, 1970, The Spectrum, Philadelphia, Pennsylvania
　　　　　May 8, 1970, Cobo Arena, Detroit, Michigan
Label: Elektra
Producer: Paul A. Rothchild
Personnel:
Jim Morrison – vocals
Ray Manzarek – organ, keyboard bass, vocals
Robby Krieger – guitar
John Densmore – drums

Many concerts were recorded during The Doors' 1970 tour to create *Absolutely Live*. Producer Paul Rothchild carefully edited the album from the various shows to create one cohesive performance. The album is notable, among other reasons, for containing two original songs, "Universal Mind" and "Build Me a Woman," that are not found on any studio albums.

After some typically annoying announcements by the house announcer, The Doors are introduced, apparently in Philadelphia, and John Densmore's drums kick start an extended cover of "Who Do You Love," Jim Morrison putting his personal vocal stamp on the Bo Diddley classic tune. The band then performs a medley of four songs, beginning with the "oom-pah-pah" of "Alabama Song (Whiskey Bar)," featuring Ray Manzarek on organ. This segues into a screaming rendition of "Backdoor Man," featuring Robbie Krieger on solo guitar, which seamlessly becomes a brief version of "Love Hides." The medley concludes with a deliberate performance of "Five to One," featuring Morrison's vocal and Krieger's guitar.

The aforementioned "Build Me a Woman" is next, a fairly straightforward twelve-bar blues tune, in which Morrison admits, "I've got the poontang blues." This is followed by a sixteen-minute version of

"When the Music's Over," one of The Doors' signature anthems, on which they pull out all the stops, building to a number of crescendos, Krieger and Manzarek trading solos on guitar and organ, respectively, Morrison telling noisy audience members to "shut up."

Manzarek then does a rare vocal performance on a cover of Willie Dixon's "Close to You," featuring Krieger on guitar. The haunting and jazzy "Universal Mind" is next, the other previously unreleased original. It's a highlight in this collection, as refreshing as it is quirky. It leads into Morrison's blood-curdling recitation of "Petition the Lord with Prayer," which, in turn, ushers in a medley of two tunes. The insane "Dead Cats, Dead Rats," featuring Densmore's drumming, segues neatly into "Break on Through (to the Other Side) No.2," which features Manzarek's organ and keyboard bass.

Absolutely Live continues with a rare and memorable fourteen-minute version of "Celebration of the Lizard," Morrison's epic performance piece in seven sections. Performed in its entirety at only a handful of concerts by The Doors, it is comprised of a series of poems, musical sections, spoken verse, and storytelling. One of the musical passages, "Not to Touch the Earth," appeared on *Waiting for the Sun* (1968). The album and concert conclude with an extended, rocking performance of "Soul Kitchen," featuring Manzarek's organ.

As a teenager, I was a counselor at a sleep-away summer camp in the Catskill Mountains of New York. Buzzy Cohen, six years my senior, was the head of the waterfront, meaning that he was the chief lifeguard at the camp's man-made lake. Taking his job seriously, he insisted on basic safety precautions at the lake, such as swimming with a "buddy." He'd blow his whistle regularly, asking that the buddies call out their designated numbers in order. When some poor kid forgot his number or forgot to call out when it was their turn, Cohen would make the unfortunate youngster climb up on the lifeguard's tower and recite "Petition the Lord with Prayer" through a megaphone before anyone could resume swimming.

Absolutely Live and 1983's *Alive, She Cried* were both repackaged and released as a two compact disc set in 1991 called *In Concert*. *Absolutely Live* was subsequently issued by itself on compact disc in 1996 with all tracks in their original sequence. Ray Manzarek died in May 2013 during the preparation of this project.

Bob Dylan – *Live 1966: The "Royal Albert Hall" Concert*

Released: 1998
Recorded: May 17, 1966, Manchester Free Trade Hall, Manchester, England
Label: Columbia
Producer: Jeff Rosen
Personnel:
Bob Dylan – guitar, harmonica, piano, vocals
Rick Danko – bass, guitar, vocals
Garth Hudson – organ
Mickey Jones – drums
Richard Manuel – piano
Robbie Robertson – guitar

In the spring of 1966, Bob Dylan, accompanied by The Hawks, later renamed The Band, went on a world tour that began in Australia and wound through western Europe and the United Kingdom, culminating in London, England. Dylan's move to electric music continued to be controversial and his United Kingdom audiences were particularly disruptive.

Live 1966: The "Royal Albert Hall" Concert was actually recorded in Manchester that May. It was extensively bootlegged for decades, finally being released officially in 1998, Vol. 4 of *The Bootleg Series*. The concert consisted of two parts: The first set is Dylan alone on stage performing acoustic compositions, warmly greeted by the audience. The second set is Dylan playing an electric set of songs with The Hawks, with heckling before and after each song.

As was the practice in those days, recording was done using two tape machines, one starting several minutes after the first, so nothing would be lost if a tape ran out mid-song. And as it happened, the master tapes ran out twice. The last verse of "Desolation Row" and the last two lines of "Visions of Johanna" are from the secondary tape source. This can be detected by a slight shift in the sound of the hall ambience.

The first song in the acoustic set is "She Belongs to Me" from *Bringing it All Back Home* (1965). Dylan, accompanying himself on guitar and harmonica, is in fine voice as he sings about a woman, maybe Joan Baez, who, ironically, belongs to no man. This is followed up with "Fourth Time Around," from the soon-to-be-released *Blonde on Blonde* (1966). This song, suggestive of a young romance, is evocative of and may even have been a response to The Beatles' "Norwegian Wood."

"Visions of Johanna," which would also appear on *Blonde on Blonde*, is one of my all-time favorite Dylan compositions, and this version is one of the best. It was written in the fall of 1965, when the author lived in the Chelsea Hotel in New York City, where "the heat pipes just cough." While it's difficult to say what this song, rich in subtlety, is all about, it nonetheless pits the carnal Louise against the unattainable Johanna in the singer's thoughts. The audience reacts as if stunned.

Dylan delivers a remarkably nuanced vocal performance on "It's All Over Now, Baby Blue," which is only surpassed by the great harmonica solos he plays. Originally performed with Spike Lee's father on bass on *Bringing it All Back Home*, this song is one of the most often covered in contemporary music. "Desolation Row," Dylan's eleven minute tour-de-force from *Highway 61 Revisited* (1965) is next. He sings effortlessly of characters from history, from fiction, from the Bible, and from his own imagination, woven into a series of interconnected vignettes. His harmonica solo is as unique and wonderful as any he recorded. The audience doesn't know what hit them. How does he remember the words?

It's difficult for me to imagine a more perfect rendering of "Just Like a Woman," which would also appear on *Blonde on Blonde*, than the version here. Dylan's singing, guitar playing, and harmonica soloing are all excellent. The set ends with his signature "Mr. Tambourine Man" from *Bringing it All Back Home*. This track is distinguished by Dylan's bizarre enunciation and by two fabulous extended harmonica solos. The crowd goes wild.

The electric set stands as an important document in rock history, Dylan at his most controversial and hard-rocking. He burns through "Just Like Tom Thumb's Blues," "Ballad of a Thin Man," and "Like a Rolling Stone" from *Highway 61 Revisited*, his first electric album. He performs radically rearranged electric versions of songs that had originally been recorded acoustically, such as Rev. Gary Davis's "Baby Let Me Follow You Down" from his eponymous 1962 debut album, "One Too Many Mornings" from *The Times They Are A-Changin'* (1964), and "I Don't Believe You (She Acts Like We Never Have Met)" from *Another Side of Bob*

Dylan (1964). He previews *Blonde on Blonde* with "Leopard-Skin Pill-Box Hat." There's even the hard rocking "Tell Me, Momma," never recorded in the studio.

The Hawks are tight, Robbie Robertson is playing great guitar solos, but the audience is uneasy from the start. Dylan introduces "I Don't Believe You (She Acts Like We Never Have Met)" with, "It used to be like that, now it goes like this." Dissenters in the crowd start a slow hand clap, but Dylan ignores them and sings a song from his first album. Then there are cat-calls and more slow clapping, drowned out by Robertson's guitar introduction to a brand new bluesy rocker.

After more yelling by the audience, Dylan tells a barely audible story and kick starts "One Too Many Mornings," sung with a little help from bassist Rick Danko. After "Ballad of a Thin Man," the lyrics of which are a direct challenge to the unhappy audience members, someone famously calls out, "Judas!" Then some clapping and more heckling, including a man shouting, "I'm never listening to you again, ever!" To which Dylan responds, "I don't believe you," and after a pause, "You're a liar." He then turns to the band and yells, "Play it fucking loud," as they begin the last tune, "Like a Rolling Stone." They do.

"Visions of Johanna" from *Blonde on Blonde* was one of the songs I selected to be in my book, *The 100 Greatest Rock'n'Roll Songs Ever* in 2000.

Bob Dylan and The Band – *Before the Flood*

Released: 1974
Recorded: January 30, 1974, Madison Square Garden, NYC
  February 13-14, 1974, The Forum, Los Angeles, California
Label: Asylum
Producer: Bob Dylan and The Band
Personnel:
Bob Dylan – guitar, harmonica, piano, vocals
Rick Danko – bass, violin, vocals
Garth Hudson – organ, clavinet, piano, synthesizer, saxophone
Levon Helm – drums, mandolin, vocals
Richard Manuel – piano, organ, drums, vocals
Robbie Robertson – guitar, vocals

Before the Flood is a double album that was recorded during Bob Dylan and The Band's American reunion tour of 1974. All the tracks but one were recorded in February at The Forum in Los Angeles. The remarkable thing about this album is the degree to which Dylan rearranges and reinterprets some of his best known songs, something he could only accomplish with a group as familiar with his material as The Band. The album was a commercial and critical success.

The concert opens with The Band backing Dylan on a series of songs, the first of which is "Most Likely You Go Your Way (And I'll Go Mine)," from *Blonde on Blonde* (1966). It's done as an up-tempo rocker, featuring Robbie Robertson on guitar solo, and with Dylan shouting out the last word of each verse for emphasis. This is followed by a rearranged "Lay Lady Lay" from *Nashville Skyline* (1969), also featuring Robertson on guitar.

Next is a raucous version of "Rainy Day Women #12 & 35," also from *Blonde on Blonde* and also featuring Robertson on guitar, as well as Garth Hudson on organ. "Knockin' on Heaven's Door" is the only track on *Before the Flood* recorded in New York City. It's one of Dylan's strongest vocal performances on the album and features all of the backing vocalists and Hudson's swirling synthesizer.

"It Ain't Me, Babe" from *Another Side of Bob Dylan* (1964) is so completely rearranged that it's a little scary sounding. Robertson's guitar fills are tasteful and understated as usual. "Ballad of a Thin Man" from *Highway 61 Revisited* (1965), is about as acerbic as possible under the circumstances. This time it is Hudson who provides the perfect fills on organ.

At this point, Dylan leaves the stage and The Band take over for five tunes. The first is "Up on Cripple Creek" from The Band's 1969 eponymous second album. Levon Helm handles the vocals and yodeling; Hudson gets that wild sound by playing the clavinet with a wah-wah pedal. "I Shall Be Released" is next, from *Music from Big Pink* (1968), with Richard Manuel breathtakingly excellent on lead vocals.

Illustrating The Band's versatility, Rick Danko takes over vocal duties on the obscure rocker, "Endless Highway," but it's Robertson who steals the show with his fabulous guitar playing. This is followed by their Civil War classic, "The Night They Drove Old Dixie Down" from *The Band*, sung by Helm with help from the rest. This section of the concert ends with the title track from *Stage Fright* (1970), with Danko on lead vocals. Written by Robertson about a problem he once had, it features Hudson on organ solo and the author on guitar.

Dylan then takes the stage to perform three songs alone. "Don't Think Twice, It's All Right" from *The Freewheelin' Bob Dylan* (1963), "Just Like a Woman" from *Blonde on Blonde*, and "It's Alright, Ma (I'm Only Bleeding)" from *Bringing it All Back Home* (1965). The performances are vintage, Dylan singing his classic tunes brilliantly, accompanying himself on acoustic guitar and harmonica.

Dylan leaves again and The Band returns to the stage for three more songs, the first of which is "The Shape I'm In" from *Stage Fright*, an oddity in that it's a rocker sung by Manuel. Hudson is featured on organ solo. This is followed by a personal favorite, the quirky "When You Awake," sung in fine fashion by Danko, from *The Band*. They then perform their signature tune, "The Weight," from *Music from Big Pink*, Helm handling the vocals on all but the fourth verse, sung by Danko.

Dylan then returns again to play four more numbers with The Band. They begin with "All Along the Watchtower" from *John Wesley Harding* (1968). Robertson's guitar is on fire throughout; Hudson plays a short synthesizer solo. The title track from *Highway 61 Revisited* follows, barely recognizable from the rearranging. Dylan's vocal is mesmerizing, Robertson's guitar playing is outstanding.

"Like a Rolling Stone," also from *Highway 61 Revisited*, is next. The crowd goes wild as Dylan and The Band blaze through the classic tune. Manuel is featured on piano, Hudson on organ. Dylan enunciates the verses and the audience screams out the choruses. *Before the Flood* concludes with another classic Dylan tune, "Blowin' in the Wind" from *The Freewheelin' Bob Dylan*, performed as an encore. It is actually two performances, from the afternoon shows on February 13 and 14, spliced together.

I attended the January 30 show at Madison Square Garden.

Either/Orchestra & Guests – *Ethiopiques 20: Live in Addis*

Released: 2004
Recorded: January 21, 2004, Ethiopian Music Festival, Addis Ababa, Ethiopia
Label: Buda Musique
Producer: Francis Falceto, Russ Gershon
Personnel:
Either/Orchestra:
Russ Gershon – saxophones
Jeremy Udden – saxophone
Henry Cook – saxophone, flute
Joel Yennior – trombone
Tom Halter – trumpet
Colin Fisher – trumpet
Greg Burk – piano
Rick McLaughlin – bass
Harvey B. Wirht – drums
Vicente Lebron – congas, percussion
Guests:
Bahta Gebre-Heywet – vocals
Getatchew Mekurya – saxophone
Mulatu Astatqe – vibes, percussion
Tsedenia Gebre-Marqos – vocals
Michael Belayneh – vocals

The story of the *Ethiopiques* series of compact discs is much too complicated and important to be done justice on these pages. Suffice it to say that there was a thriving music scene in Ethiopia in the 1960s and 1970s with many artists performing live in clubs and recording on Amha, Kaifa, and Philips-Ethiopia Records. However, all of this ceased in 1974 when Emperor Haile Selassie I was deposed by a military junta that outlawed the music scene altogether. The artists had to either leave the country to perform, or quit performing to take regular jobs.

A remarkable man named Francis Falceto took it upon himself to locate Amha Eshete, owner of Amha Records, in the United States and to convince him to reissue his collection, the master tapes of which were hunted down and located in Greece. In 1993, the rule of the military junta in Ethiopia ended, and music returned to the streets of Addis Ababa.

In addition to re-releasing material from the so-called golden age, Falceto has been able, over time, to get some of the original artists to return, perform, and record in Ethiopia. *Ethiopiques Volume 1: The Golden Years of Modern Ethiopian Music* was released in 1998. As of 2013, there have been twenty-eight volumes released. I recommend them highly; they're all I buy these days.

Either /Orchestra was founded in Boston in 1986 by saxophonist Russ Gershon. After being influenced by Ethiopian music, especially the material that would later be released as *Ethiopiques 13*, Gershon revamped Either/Orchestra in 1997 and began playing "The Ethiopian Suite," a reinterpretation of three original Ethiopian compositions, which was released on *More Beautiful Than Death* (2000).

This came to the attention of Francis Falceto, who invited Either/Orchestra to perform at the third Ethiopian Music Festival in Addis Ababa in January 2004, with local Ethiopian musicians sitting in. The resultant recording is *Ethiopiques 20: Live in Addis*. Either/Orchestra was the first big band from the United States to play in Ethiopia since Duke Ellington's in 1973, and certainly no other American artist had ever traveled to Addis Ababa to play Ethiopian music for an Ethiopian audience.

The album begins with the first section of "The Ethiopian Suite," actually entitled "Amlak Abet Abet," an extended instrumental adventure that's a little difficult for the Western ear to fathom. It features Colin Fisher on trumpet solo and Jeremy Udden on saxophone solo. Gershon's saxophone introduction indicates that the middle part of the "Suite" is next, "Muziqawi Silt," a little more accessible with its funky Afro-jazz feel. Rick McLaughlin is featured on bass solo as well as Henry Cook on saxophone solo. "Feqer Aydelem Wey," another difficult composition, completes the "Suite," featuring Gershon on saxophone solo.

"Altchalkoum" is next, a hauntingly beautiful song featuring the entire horn section, notably Gershon on solo saxophone. This is followed by "Yezemed Yebada," co-arranged by guest percussionist Mulatu Astatqe. It is a composition in several distinct parts, each with a different time signature, featuring Joel Yennior on trombone solo and Udden on saxophone solo.

"Soul Tezeta" is a personal favorite in this collection, a very soulful tune featuring guest vocalist Michael Belayneh, who gets an enthusiastic reaction from the audience, and Gershon on saxophone solo. "Eyeye" is a brief but gorgeous performance of an elegant composition, featuring the horn section playing banks of chords. "Antchim Endelela" is some kind of strange Semitic tango, bringing together all kinds of musical traditions. It features guest vocalist Bahta Gebre-Heywet as well as Yennior on trombone solo.

"Keset Eswa Betcha" is another extended composition that is not so easy to grasp, except for the outstanding section featuring drummer Harvey Wirht, percussionist Vicente Lebron, and guest percussionist Astatqe. Tom Halter also excels on trumpet solo. Bassist McLaughlin plays a lengthy introduction to "Bati," which features the incredible range of guest vocalist Tsedenia Gebre-Marqos as well as a trumpet solo by Fisher.

"Shellela," with its marching band cadence, is a vehicle for guest artist Getatchew Mekurya to riff out on the saxophone, to the delight of the crowd. This is about as authentic as it gets. *Ethiopiques 20: Live in Addis* concludes with an extended encore performance of the lively "Embi Ba (Gourague)," also featuring Mekurya on saxophone as well as Gregory Burk on piano solo.

Duke Ellington – *Ellington at Newport*

Released: 1956
Recorded: July 7, 1956, Newport Jazz Festival, Newport, Rhode Island
Label: Columbia
Producer: George Avakian
Personnel:
Duke Ellington – piano
Harry Carney – saxophone
Willie Cook – trumpet
Paul Gonzalves – saxophone
Jimmy Hamilton – clarinet
Johnny Hodges – saxophone
Quentin "Butter" Jackson – trombone
William "Cat" Anderson – trumpet
Ray Nance – trumpet
Russell Procope – clarinet, saxophone
John Sanders – trombone
Clark Terry – trumpet
Jimmy Woode – bass
Britt Woodman – trombone
Sam Woodyard – drums

Many big bands had folded completely by the mid-1950s, but Duke Ellington had kept his band working, often supporting the musicians himself. *Ellington at Newport* was recorded in the summer of 1956 at the Newport Jazz Festival. His band was the first and last to play. The first, short set was played without a few of the band members who could not be located. After performances by the other groups, the missing members were located and the real concert began.

Columbia Records recorded the concert and the album soon followed. Ellington appeared soon after on the cover of *Time* magazine and his resurgent popularity lasted the rest of his life. However, in 1996 a tape was discovered in the Voice of America archives that changed everything. It turned out that the 1956 album had been fabricated with studio performances mixed with some live recordings and artificial applause. Indeed, Ellington had been unhappy with the performance and had the band enter the studio immediately after the festival to cut studio tracks.

The album begins with a new composition written for the festival, a suite in three pieces by Ellington and Billy Strayhorn. The first is entitled "Festival Junction." Jimmy Hamilton states the theme and takes the first solo on clarinet. The band then swings into action, backing solos by Willie Cook on trumpet, Paul Gonzalves on tenor saxophone, Britt Woodman on trombone, Harry Carney on baritone saxophone, Butter Jackson on trombone, Russell Procope on alto saxophone, and, finally, Cat Anderson on trumpet.

The second part is called "Blues to Be There," a delightfully slow, twelve-bar blues, effortlessly driven by the rhythm section of Jimmy Woode on bass and Sam Woodyard on drums. Ellington takes the first solo on piano, followed by Procope on clarinet and Ray Nance on trumpet. The third section, appropriately entitled "Newport Up," is a swinging, up-tempo composition on which Hamilton blows the first solo on clarinet, followed by Clark Terry on trumpet, and Gonzalves on tenor saxophone. The three of them then exchange lines, playing one extended solo in a circular fashion, to the great delight of the audience.

"Jeep's Blues" is another deliberate blues tune, featuring lush chording by the horn section as well as a moving solo by Johnny Hodges on alto saxophone, backed by Ellington's piano and the rhythm section. Ellington then steps to the microphone and announces that the band would be playing "some of our 1938 vintage," a pair of blues, "Diminuendo in Blue" and "Crescendo in Blue," joined by an improvised interval, which would be played by saxophonist Gonzalves.

Ellington is believed to have told Gonzalves to play as long as he felt like playing when the solo came around, and the rest is history. "Diminuendo in Blue" begins innocuously enough, with an Ellington piano introduction. The horn section then states the theme and improvises collectively for a while, leading to a piano solo from Ellington. And then it happens, Gonzalves steps up and takes an amazing twenty-seven-chorus solo, backed only by Woode on bass, Woodyard on drums, and Ellington on piano. Band members call out their encouragement while the crowd dances wildly in the aisles.

When Gonzalves finishes, collapsed in exhaustion, Ellington takes over for two choruses of piano solo before the band returns for "Crescendo in

Blue." This part is a swinging up-tempo shuffle, with a solo by Hodges on alto saxophone and a rousing finale section featuring trumpeter Anderson. After this performance, pandemonium ensues.

On the 1999 reissue on two compact discs, *Ellington at Newport (Complete)*, the Voice of America live recording and the live Columbia tapes were meticulously spliced together to create a stereophonic recording of the concert. (Stereophonic long playing records were not mass produced until 1957, the year after this recording.) Now Gonzalves's solo can be clearly heard, as opposed to on the original album, where he had been playing into the wrong microphone and was completely inaudible.

The Flying Burrito Brothers – *The Last of the Red Hot Burritos*

Released: 1972
Recorded: Fall 1971, Union College, Schenectady, New York
            Dartmouth College, Hanover, New Hampshire
            Antioch College, Yellow Springs, Ohio
Label: A&M
Producer: Jim Dickson
Personnel:
Chris Hillman – bass, mandolin, vocals
Rick Roberts – guitar, vocals
Al Perkins – guitar, pedal steel guitar
Kenny Wertz – guitar, banjo, vocals
Michael Clarke – drums
Byron Berline – fiddle
Roger Bush – bass, guitar, vocals
Spooner Oldham – piano

The Last of the Red Hot Burritos is exactly that, the final album by the first incarnation of The Flying Burrito Brothers, recorded on tour in 1971 and released as a contractual obligation in 1972, after all of the original members except Chris Hillman had departed. However, Hillman assembled an excellent band for this album reflecting his bluegrass sensibilities, the songs are great, and the musicianship is tastefully outstanding.

The album begins with "Christine's Tune," otherwise known as "Devil in Disguise," from *The Gilded Palace of Sin* (1969). It's a song about a not very nice woman, featuring Hillman on vocals and Al Perkins on pedal steel guitar. "Six Days on the Road" may not have been the first song about truck driving, but it certainly is the most popular. A single for Dave Dudley in 1963, this performance features Byron Berline on fiddle. This is followed by "My Uncle," also from *The Gilded Palace of Sin*. A personal favorite, it features Perkins on pedal steel guitar.

The band then performs a three song acoustic bluegrass mini-set. "Dixie Breakdown," the classic instrumental written Jimmy Lunceford and Don Reno, features Kenny Wertz on banjo, Berline on fiddle, and Roger

Bush on bass. Bush then takes over the vocals on "Don't Let Your Deal Go Down," made famous by Flatt and Scruggs, which showcases Berline's fiddle playing. "Orange Blossom Special," about the passenger train of the same name, was written by Ervin T. Rouse in 1938. Known as "the fiddle player's national anthem," it is no surprise that this tune is a vehicle for Berline to demonstrate his virtuosity.

Hillman resumes vocal duties on "Ain't That a Lot of Love," a cover of the 1966 single by Homer Banks. The band really rocks out on this one, led by Perkins on guitar. "High Fashion Queen" first appeared on *Burrito Deluxe* in 1970. It's a mellow, mid-tempo rocker with some interesting changes about a trendy chick, featuring Perkins on guitar and Spooner Oldham with a piano overdub in the studio.

This is followed by a cover of "Don't Fight It," a hit single for Wilson Pickett in 1965. The band finds a funky groove and locks it in. Perkins is featured with two tasty guitar solos. "Hot Burrito #2" is next, from *The Gilded Palace of Sin*. It's a bluesy ballad featuring Perkins with an extended solo on pedal steel guitar. *The Last of the Red Hot Burritos* concludes with a swinging cover of "Losing Game," a single for James Carr in 1967. It features Perkins on guitar and Oldham with another studio overdub on piano.

By the time the album was released, this band had dissolved. The Flying Burrito Brothers toured Europe until 1973, led by Rick Roberts, and then called it quits. Original members Chris Ethridge and "Sneaky" Pete Kleinow reformed the band in 1975. In 2008, *The Last of the Red Hot Burritos* was reissued on compact disc with three bonus tracks: the Everly Brothers' "Wake Up Little Susie," Jesse Stone's "Money Honey," and Gram Parsons's "One Hundred Years From Now" from *Sweetheart of the Rodeo* (1968) by The Byrds.

Marvin Gaye – *Marvin Gaye Live!*

Released: 1974
Recorded: January 4, 1974, Oakland Coliseum, Oakland, California
Label: Tamla
Producer: Marvin Gaye
Personnel:
Marvin Gaye – vocals
James Jamerson – bass
Joe Clayton – congas
Ed Greene – drums
David T. Walker – guitar
Ray Parker – guitar
Joe Sample – keyboards
John Arnold – percussion
Ernie Watts – saxophone
George Bohanon – trombone
Paul Hubinon – trumpet
Jack Shulman – violin
James Getzoff – violin
Charles Burns – vocals
Dwight Owens – vocals
Eric Dolen – vocals
Michael Torrance – vocals
Wally Cox – vocals, MC

Largely as a result of the success of *Let's Get It On* (1973), Marvin Gaye interrupted a two-and-a-half year sabbatical from touring to record *Marvin Gaye Live!* in early 1974 in Oakland, California. According to the album, the concert was divided into three sections: The Beginning, Fossil Medley, and Now. Gaye performs with a seventeen-piece orchestra, conducted by Gene Page and Lesley Drayton.

The Beginning section of the concert starts with an introduction of Gaye by Master of Ceremonies Wally Cox. Then the orchestra plays "Overture" while Gaye takes the stage. The first song Gaye performs is an extended performance of "Trouble Man" from the 1972 album of the same name. It immediately sets the tone for the show and a very high bar, indeed. The orchestra lays down a heavy groove behind Gaye, anchored by the great James Jamerson on bass.

This is followed by "Flyin' High (In the Friendly Sky)" segued into "Mercy Mercy Me (The Ecology)." Both songs originally appeared on *What's Going On* (1971) and both feature Gaye's incredible vocal range. From the same album, the very funky "Inner City Blues (Make Me Wanna Holler)" features the horn section and the backing vocalists.

Then a remarkable thing happens. The orchestra starts playing "Theme from Trouble Man" from *Trouble Man*, and as they segue into a slower paced version of "Distant Lover," women in the audience begin shrieking, which continues as Gaye does his show-stopping performance of the song. It is one of the highlights of Gaye's career; he would always subsequently perform "Distant Lover" in a similar fashion. Ernie Watts is featured on saxophone

Gaye follows that up with a new song, "Jan," which he dedicates to his girlfriend, Janis Hunter. It is a sweet ballad, featuring Joe Sample on piano and Jack Shulman and James Getzoff on violin. This is followed by Gaye's only live performance of "Keep Gettin' It On," the sequel to the title track of *Let's Get It On*, featuring Watts on saxophone.

The horn section announces that the Fossil Medley part of the concert has begun. It's an eleven minute romp through some of Gaye's hits from the 1960s. First is "I'll Be Doggone," a hit single in 1965, featuring Ray Parker on guitar. Next is "Try it Baby" from 1964, which gets a big response from the audience. "Can I Get a Witness" is from 1963 and features the horn section. This is followed by "You're a Wonderful One" from 1964, which segues, with a roar of the crowd, into "Stubborn Kind of Fellow," Gaye's first hit single from 1962. Finally, we are treated to "How Sweet It Is (To Be Loved By You)," a personal favorite, a hit single in 1964. They do it nice and slow and funky.

After Gaye thanks the orchestra, he launches into the Now portion of the program with "Let's Get it On" from the album of the same name. It's a superb reading of the song, featuring Ed Greene on drums and the backing vocalists. *Marvin Gaye Live!* concludes beautifully, with "What's Going On" Gaye's signature single from 1971. A commentary on the troubles and problems of the world, it features the backing vocalists, George Bohanon on trombone, and Watts on saxophone.

"How Sweet It Is (To Be Loved By You)" was one of the songs I selected to be in my book, *The 100 Greatest Rock'n'Roll Songs Ever* in 2000.

Grateful Dead – *Live/Dead*

Released: 1969
Recorded: January 26, 1969, Avalon Ballroom, San Francisco, California
February 27, March 2, 1969, Fillmore West, San Francisco,
California
Label: Warner Bros.
Producer: Grateful Dead, Bob Matthews, Betty Cantor
Personnel:
Tom "T.C." Constanten – keyboards
Jerry Garcia – guitar, vocals
Mickey Hart – drums, percussion
Bill Kreutzmann – drums, percussion
Ron "Pigpen" McKernan – organ, congas, vocals
Phil Lesh – bass, vocals
Bob Weir – guitar, vocals

Grateful Dead formed in 1965 as a quintet. They expanded to six pieces in 1967 with the addition of a second drummer, Mickey Hart. They went to a septet in 1968 when keyboardist Tom "T.C." Constanten joined on. At this point, the Dead were experimenting with a long composition they were calling "Dark Star," with lyrics by Robert Hunter, jamming into a number of different songs. Shortly thereafter, "St. Stephen" took form, requiring some of Constanten's more sophisticated keyboard work.

The Dead played the Avalon Ballroom in January 1969 and on the third night of the run recorded versions of "The Eleven" and Bobby "Blue" Bland's "Turn on Your Lovelight" that would later appear on *Live/Dead*. Back from their February tour, they scheduled four nights at the Fillmore West, February 27-March 2. They made specific plans for recording the shows, drastically limiting the number of tunes they would perform. They planned a first set around "The Other One" and a Pigpen number or two, and then a second set with some variation of the "Dark Star/St. Stephen" suite.

The February 27 show started with equipment problems but produced one of my favorite ever versions of "That's It For the Other One" in the first set, and the "Dark Star" into "St. Stephen" that was to become the first disc of *Live/Dead* in the second. Grateful Dead mavens usually pick the March 1 show as the one to bring to the proverbial desert island, despite the worst version of "Hey Jude" in recorded history as an encore. March 2 produced the versions of Reverend Gary Davis's "Death Don't Have No Mercy" and the traditional "We Bid You Goodnight" that completed *Live/Dead*.

The next day, March 3, the Dead bid farewell to their old neighborhood, ravaged by overpopulation and bad drugs, by playing, literally, on Haight Street. Photographs from that concert are the centerfold of *Live/Dead*. It was a transformational moment in their lives. Soon after, they would all move to Marin County, guitarist Jerry Garcia and Hunter becoming housemates and embarking on the collaboration which would result in the tunes that would appear on *Workingman's Dead* and *American Beauty*. Twelve days after the Haight Street performance, Grateful Dead and Jefferson Airplane opened the Carousel Ballroom.

I've already mentioned in the foreword that *Live/Dead* was a big deal to me. Having seen the Dead live, I was of the opinion that their music went to places that other bands would never even know existed. But the studio albums, great as they were, fell short; *Live/Dead* fully documented and captured the Dead's live performance thing. The so-called suite, despite being spliced together from several sources, is a monumental compositional and improvisational accomplishment, unparalleled before or since. It wasn't until the advent of the compact disc, however, that the whole thing could be heard seamlessly, without jumping up to turn over the albums.

Live/Dead was re-mastered and released with bonus tracks as part of the 2001 boxed set *The Golden Road (1965-1973)* and subsequently as a stand-alone album in 2003.

Grateful Dead – *Grateful Dead*

Released: 1971
Recorded: March 24, 1971, Winterland Ballroom, San Francisco, California
        April 5-6, 1971, Manhattan Center, NYC
        April 26-29, 1971, Fillmore East, NYC
Label: Warner Bros
Producer: Grateful Dead, Bob Matthews, Betty Cantor
Personnel:
Jerry Garcia – guitar, vocals
Bill Kreutzmann – drums
Ron "Pigpen" McKernan – organ, harmonica, vocals
Phil Lesh – bass, vocals
Bob Weir – guitar, vocals
Merl Saunders – organ

Tom "T.C." Constanten left the Dead in 1970, as did Mickey Hart in 1971, leaving the original quintet to record *Grateful Dead*. It is also referred to as "Skull and Roses," due to its iconic cover art, and "Skull Fuck," the name the band originally wanted, but which was rejected by Warner Bros. Records. This album has the first acknowledgment by the Dead of its loyal fans, referred to as "Dead Heads" in an invitation to contact the band.

For the three new original tunes, "Bertha," "Playing in the Band," and "Wharf Rat," the band invited Merl Saunders to overdub an organ part, unfortunately burying Pigpen's contributions on organ in the mix. "Playing in the Band" received a fair amount of FM radio airplay at the time, and would gradually evolve into the Dead's next major improvisational vehicle after "Dark Star." The closing segue of "Not Fade Away" into "Goin' Down the Road Feeling Bad" became an instant concert favorite.

Sides one and three contain shorter songs, while sides two and four contain longer compositions, designed to resemble the two sets of a typical Dead show. I was always of the opinion that the San Francisco and New York City shows were a cut above the rest, that the Dead seemed to make every tune sparkle. These performances were no exceptions, the pared-down band showing their true chops as interpreters and as improvisers.

Taping Grateful Dead shows was in its nascent stage; it had not yet become a cottage industry. The first widely distributed Dead tape on the east coast was the WNEW-FM radio broadcast from the Felt Forum at Madison Square Garden, New York City, on December 5, 1971. Since *Live/ Dead* had been uncharacteristically focused on the longer compositions only, *Grateful Dead* was really the first opportunity for most of us to hear a "good old Grateful Dead show" in the comfort of home.

And, boy, did I hear it. I played this album as often or more so than any other in my lifetime. In retrospect, it's steeped in pure Americana. Their original tunes notwithstanding, just look at who they chose to cover: Merle Haggard, Noah Lewis, John Phillips, Kris Kristofferson, Chuck Berry, Buddy Holly, and, indirectly, Elvis. Impossible to pick a favorite here, but I'll mention guitarist Jerry Garcia's harmony vocals on "Mama Tried" and "Me & Bobby McGee," Pigpen's organ sounding like church on "Wharf Rat," and Bob Weir's rhythm guitar on "Not Fade Away" into "Goin' Down the Road Feeling Bad."

For some reason, I always found those last two tunes, especially the way they segue from one into the other, to be moving, almost inspirational. In the '70s and '80s, I listened to them to get psyched up before big basketball or softball games; in the '90s and '00s, I played them as background when I exercised. I was present at some of the Manhattan Center and Fillmore East shows represented here. I certainly can't remember which ones. "That's It For the Other One" from *Anthem of the Sun* (1968) was one of the songs I selected to be in my book, *The 100 Greatest Rock'n'Roll Songs Ever* in 2000.

Grateful Dead – *Europe '72*

Released: 1972
Recorded: April 8, 1972, Wembley Empire Pool, Wembley, England
April 14, 1972, Tivolis Koncertsal, Copenhagen, Denmark
April 26, 1972, Jahrhundert Halle, Frankfurt, Germany
May 4, 1972, Olympia Theater, Paris, France
May 10, 1972, Concertgebouw, Amsterdam, the Netherlands
May 23, 24, 26, 1972, Lyceum Theatre, London, England
Label: Warner Bros.
Producer: Grateful Dead
Personnel:
Jerry Garcia – guitar, vocals
Bill Kreutzmann – drums
Ron "Pigpen" McKernan – organ, harmonica, vocals
Phil Lesh – bass, vocals
Bob Weir – guitar, vocals
Keith Godchaux – piano
Donna Jean Godchaux – vocals

Grateful Dead added a second keyboardist again later in 1971 when Keith Godchaux joined the band to play piano alongside Pigpen's organ. His wife, backing vocalist Donna Jean Godchaux's first show was that New Year's Eve, and the Dead were once again a septet. While the Dead had played Europe before, two dates in England in 1970 and one in France in 1971, the twenty-two shows they performed in April and May 1972 represented their most extensive foreign tour and their most ambitious undertaking to date.

Although the Dead were abroad, their concerts were, nonetheless, once again steeped in Americana, especially the Jerry Garcia-Robert Hunter tunes which made their first appearances on vinyl on *Europe '72*. These include "He's Gone," "Jack Straw," "Brown-Eyed Women," "Ramble On Rose," and "Tennessee Jed." We're also treated to a brilliant version of "Truckin'" and an equally excellent "Chinacat Sunflower" into the traditional "I Know You Rider," one of their signature segues.

There's also "Epilogue" at the end of "Truckin'" and "Prologue" prior to "(Walk Me Out in the) Morning Dew." These are not really songs, per se, but the extended jam that connected the two structured compositions. The piece could not be presented in its entirety, due to the time limitations of records; it can be heard seamlessly on compact disc. Garcia's guitar playing and vocal on "(Walk Me Out in the) Morning Dew" just may be the highlight of the album.

Europe '72 opens with "Cumberland Blues," one of my favorite concert tunes, really three songs in one. Phil Lesh sets the tone with his booming bass introduction and we're off and running. "Jack Straw" features some great tempo changes. Garcia does a smile-inducing cover of Hank Williams's "You Win Again." "Brown-Eyed Women" is nothing short of brilliant. Pigpen makes his presence known in a limited role with a bluesy cover of "It Hurts Me Too" by Elmore James and "Mr. Charlie," a funky original, written with Hunter.

"Sugar Magnolia" seems out of place mid-concert, not having yet migrated to its rightful place as show-stopper. Similarly, "One More Saturday Night" was apparently played on a Friday night! In the interest of full disclosure, "Ramble On Rose" and "Tennessee Jed" were two of my least favorite Dead songs to catch in concert, but the versions captured here are among the best I've heard.

Grateful Dead were around for thirty years, and many of us felt that that wasn't nearly long enough. However, most would agree that the Dead were in their prime from about 1968 or so until they took a hiatus at the end of 1974. They were certainly at the peak of their powers during their 1972 European tour, despite the recent addition of Keith and Donna Godchaux and Pigpen's failing health.

Following the *Europe '72* tour, Pigpen's condition had deteriorated to the point that he could no longer tour. His final concert appearance was June 17, 1972, at the Hollywood Bowl. He died in March 1973. *Europe '72: The Complete Recordings* was released as a limited edition boxed set in 2011, purportedly capturing every note played at all twenty-two shows on the tour.

Buddy Guy – *This is Buddy Guy*

Released: 1969
Recorded: June 11-13, 1968, The Orleans House, Berkeley, California
Label: Vanguard
Producer: Samuel Charters
Personnel:
Buddy Guy – guitar, vocals
George Alexander – trumpet
Leslie Crawford – saxophone
Bobby Fields – saxophone
Tim Kaihatsu – guitar
Jack Myers – bass
Norman Spiller – trumpet
A.C. Reed – saxophone
Glenway McTeer – drums

George "Buddy" Guy was born in Louisiana in 1936 and first learned to play on a homemade two-stringed instrument made of wire and tin cans. Eventually graduating to acoustic guitar, Guy started playing professionally in Baton Rouge as a sideman for John "Big Poppa" Tilley. In 1957, Guy cut a demo tape at a local radio station, sent a copy to Chess Records, and bought a one-way train ticket to Chicago.

Guy's first single for Chess, "First Time I Met the Blues" (1960), was a critical and modest commercial success, but he was used by the label mostly as a sideman for artists such as Muddy Waters, Koko Taylor, Howlin' Wolf, Little Walter, and others. His first album for Chess, *I Left My Blues in San Francisco* was released in 1967. However, when his contract expired, Guy signed with Vanguard in 1968 and released *A Man and the Blues*.

The first track on *This is Buddy Guy* is "I Got My Eyes on You," co-written with Willie Dixon. It's an up-tempo bluesy shuffle, featuring the entire band swinging behind Guy's vocal and guitar. They slow things down quite a bit on "The Things I Used to Do," a cover of a tune by Eddie "Guitar Slim" Jones. Guy had seen and was influenced by Guitar Slim in his Baton Rouge days. He is impressive as he takes one great guitar solo after another.

Guy then performs the popular "(You Give Me) Fever," popularized by Peggy Lee in 1958, but, frankly, this version might have frightened Ms. Lee. Guy sounds more like Screamin' Jay Hawkins as he trades shouts with the horn section. The band makes it very funky with a cover of "Knock on Wood," the 1966 Eddie Floyd single he co-wrote with Steve Cropper. The rhythm section of Jack Myers on bass and Glenway McTeer on drums is featured. The Berkeley crowd goes wild.

The band returns to the blues form on "I Had a Dream Last Night," a Guy original. The horn section is featured: George Alexander and Norman Spiller on trumpet as well as Leslie Crawford, Bobby Fields, and A.C. Reed on saxophone. Guy then performs the up-tempo, traditional "24 Hours of the Day," once again featuring the horn section, this time chiming the hours on a clock.

Two more Guy originals follow. "You Were Wrong" is a deliberate twelve-bar blues on which Guy delivers his strongest vocal performance on the album and absolutely shreds his guitar solo. *This is Buddy Guy* concludes with "I'm Not the Best," an extended showcase for the band. It features interesting interplay between Guy on lead and Tim Kaihatsu on rhythm guitar.

After a long career as a largely underappreciated journeyman guitarist, Guy finally achieved commercial success with his first album on Silvertone Records, *Damn Right, I've Got the Blues* (1991), followed rapidly by *Feels Like Rain* in 1993 and *Slippin'* the following year. Guy is now considered one of the greatest blues guitarists of his generation, one who embodied Chicago blues while embracing rock'n'roll. Few guitarists of any genre have enjoyed the respect of his peers as has Guy, with artists such as Eric Clapton, Jimi Hendrix, Jeff Beck, Keith Richards, Stevie Ray Vaughn, and Mark Knopfler citing him as a personal favorite.

George Harrison & Friends – *The Concert for Bangladesh*

Released: 1971
Recorded: August 1, 1971, Madison Square Garden, NYC
Label: Apple
Producer: George Harrison, Phil Spector
Personnel:
George Harrison – guitar, vocals
Ravi Shankar – sitar
Bob Dylan – guitar, harmonica, vocals
Leon Russell – piano, bass, vocals
Ringo Starr – drums, tambourine, vocals
Billy Preston – organ, vocals
Eric Clapton – guitar
Ali Akbar Khan – sarod
Alla Rakha – tabla
Kamala Chakravarty – tamboura
Jesse Ed Davis – guitar
Klaus Voorman – bass
Jim Keltner – drums
Pete Ham – guitar
Tom Evans – guitar
Joey Molland – guitar
Mike Gibbins – tambourine, maracas
Don Preston – guitar, percussion, vocals
Carl Radle – bass
Jim Horn – saxophones
Chuck Findley – trumpet
Jackie Kelso – saxophones
Allan Beutler – saxophones
Lou McCreary – trombone
Ollie Mitchell – trumpet
Claudia Linnear – vocals
Jo Greene – vocals
Jeanie Greene – vocals

Martin Greene – vocals
Dolores Hall – vocals
Don Nix – vocals

After being made aware of the seriousness of the situation in what was then known as East Pakistan by friend and musician Ravi Shankar, George Harrison, in June 1971, began organizing two fundraising concerts at Madison Square Garden in New York City to aid the war-ravaged and disaster-stricken nation. Harrison then headlined the UNICEF benefit concerts, backed by a twenty-four piece all-star band, on August 1.

The shows were a groundbreaking charity event, in aid of homeless Bengali refugees, which was to become the model for future multi-artist rock benefits, such as *Live Aid* (1985) and *The Concert for New York City* (2001). *The Concert for Bangladesh* is a triple album documenting the performances. On release, it was a huge critical and commercial success, and its sales continue to benefit the George Harrison Fund for UNICEF.

After introductory remarks by Harrison and Shankar, setting the tone, the concert begins with "Bangla Dhun," a sitar and sarod duet, performed by Shankar and Ali Akbar Khan, with Alla Rakha on tabla and Kamala Chakravarty on tamboura. The forty-five minute piece is unfortunately edited down to less than seventeen minutes for the album. Harrison then sings three of his tunes, "Wah-Wah," "My Sweet Lord" done acoustically, and "Awaiting on You All."

Billy Preston then does his gospel-tinged "That's the Way God Planned It" in remarkable fashion, starting out slowly, but working himself and the audience into a frenzy before it's over. Out comes Ringo Starr to perform his hit, "It Don't Come Easy," only forgetting some of the words. Harrison then performs "Beware of Darkness," with help from Leon Russell on vocals and featuring Jim Horn on saxophone.

After introducing the band, Harrison performs "While My Guitar Gently Weeps" in fine fashion, featuring Eric Clapton on solo guitar, as he was on *The Beatles* (1968). In post-production, Harrison double-tracked his lead vocal. Next is a medley of "Jumpin' Jack Flash" into "Youngblood," with vocals by Russell and featuring Carl Radle on bass and Don Preston on lead guitar and backing vocal. These tracks were significantly reworked in the studio by Russell after the fact.

Harrison then performs "Here Comes the Sun" acoustically, with assistance from Badfinger's Pete Ham on a second acoustic guitar. Bob

Dylan is then introduced, to the audible approval of the audience. He performs five of his tunes, "A Hard Rain's A-Gonna Fall," "It Takes a Lot to Laugh, It Takes a Train to Cry," "Blowin' in the Wind," "Mr. Tambourine Man," and "Just Like a Woman," accompanied by Harrison on guitar, Russell on bass, and Starr on tambourine.

When everyone has recovered from what had just transpired, Harrison takes the stage again to perform a moving rendition of "Something." This is followed by the last track on *The Concert for Bangladesh*, appropriately enough called "Bangla Desh." Harrison had written the song during the hurried preparations for the concerts to call further attention to the Bengalis' cause and rush released it as a charity single four days before the shows. It features Harrison's vocal and Horn's saxophone.

Saul Swimmer's concert documentary film of the same name opened in 1972. The album was first issued on compact disc in 1991 in a two-disc set with significant editing of the breaks between songs. In 2005, *The Concert for Bangladesh* was re-mastered and re-released, with the addition of Dylan's afternoon performance of "Love Minus Zero/No Limit" as a bonus track. In 2011, to mark the fortieth anniversary of the album's release, the George Harrison Fund for UNICEF raised $1.2 million in emergency relief for children in famine-stricken areas of the Horn of Africa.

My friends and I took turns waiting in the line outside Madison Square Garden for two days and nights in order to get tickets to this concert. I had the night shift, sleeping on the sidewalk, shaving and washing in a Penn Station bathroom before going to work each morning. I think we were, collectively, fifth in line. It was all worth it, as we got seats in the very first row available to non-press and non-posers.

Jimi Hendrix – *Jimi Plays Monterey*

Released: 1986
Recorded: June 18, 1967, Monterey Pop Festival, Monterey, California
Label: Reprise
Producer: Alan Douglas
Personnel:
Jimi Hendrix – guitar, vocals
Noel Redding – bass
Mitch Mitchell – drums

The Monterey International Pop Music Festival was a three-day concert event held June 16-18, 1967, at the Monterey County Fairgrounds. It was the first widely promoted and heavily attended rock festival, attracting as many as 90,000 people at the event's peak. The festival is noteworthy for the first major American appearances by Jimi Hendrix, The Who, and Ravi Shankar, the first large public appearance by Janis Joplin, and the introduction of Otis Redding to a large, predominantly white audience. Monterey became the template for future music festivals such as The Woodstock Music and Art Fair in 1969.

Jimi Plays Monterey is a posthumous album by Jimi Hendrix, released in 1986. It documents the performance by the Jimi Hendrix Experience at the Monterey Pop Festival on June 18. *Jimi Plays Monterey* is also the name of a short film directed by D.A. Pennebaker documenting the same performance. It's notable for several interviews with rock stars and for containing an art piece by Denny Dent during the performance of "Can You See Me."

The album and concert begin with a cover of Howlin' Wolf's "Killing Floor." The audience clearly doesn't know what hit them, as they are assaulted by the essence of power trio excellence, not to mention when Hendrix takes his first feedback-laced guitar solo. "Foxy Lady," from *Are You Experienced* (1967), is next, psychedelic and deeply funky at the same time. Hendrix takes two guitar solos to the delight of the crowd. How does he do that on a right-handed guitar played upside-down?

What can one say about Hendrix's cover of Bob Dylan's "Like a Rolling Stone?" That it's the greatest Dylan cover ever? No, that's Hendrix doing "All Along the Watchtower." That it's one of the best reinterpretations of another artist's composition? Well, maybe. With a nod to the author's grandmother, he apologetically only does three of the four verses, but who cares? Hendrix's remarkable vocal performance is surpassed only by his work on guitar.

A cover of B.B. King's "Rock Me Baby" is next, done at break-neck speed, a vehicle for some of the heaviest jamming on the album, featuring Noel Redding on bass. They slow things down a tad out of necessity with "Hey Joe," their 1966 debut single, featuring Mitch Mitchell simulating gunfire on the drums. Hendrix delivers a soulful vocal and plays one guitar solo with his teeth and another with the guitar held behind his head. The above-mentioned "Can You See Me" is next, a hard-driving power trio composition which opens the Pennebaker film.

They slow things down even further with the ballad, "The Wind Cries Mary," released as a single in 1967. It's a showcase for Hendrix's guitar virtuosity without the pyrotechnics and ear-splitting volume, a highlight of the collection. "Purple Haze," another 1967 single, is next, done in extended fashion. The band is never tighter than on this tune, a just about perfect performance, which is played over the closing credits in the Pennebaker film.

Hendrix then thanks the crowd for coming and states that he intends to "sacrifice something important." *Jimi Plays Monterey* concludes with a cover of The Troggs' "Wild Thing," arguably one of the most notable live performances ever, in which Hendrix sets his guitar on fire and then smashes it at the end of the song. Audience members are visibly wigged out.

"Like a Rolling Stone" from *Monterey Pop Festival* (1970) was one of the songs I selected to be in my book, *The 100 Greatest Rock'n'Roll Songs Ever* in 2000.

Jimi Hendrix – *Band of Gypsys*

Released: 1970
Recorded: January 1, 1970, Fillmore East, NYC
Label: Capitol
Producer: Jimi Hendrix
Personnel:
Jimi Hendrix – guitar, vocals
Billy Cox – bass, vocals
Buddy Miles – drums

Band of Gypsys is the eponymous live album by the band that was formed after the dissolution of the Jimi Hendrix Experience. Hendrix is backed by bassist Billy Cox and drummer Buddy Miles. Two shows per night were recorded at the Fillmore East on December 31, 1969 and January 1, 1970, with songs from the two January 1 shows appearing on the album. Released just six months before his death, this was the last album authorized by Hendrix. It is arguably his best work ever recorded.

Inspired by the new rhythm section, Hendrix took these concerts as an opportunity to showcase his new material, a seamless combination of rock, funk, and rhythm and blues, and with a new lyrical direction as well. Plagued in the past by equipment problems, everything worked perfectly for Hendrix at the Fillmore shows, remarkable considering that he was combining new foot pedals on stage for the first time.

The album begins with "Who Knows," an extended bluesy jam driven by Cox's bass line. Miles is featured on vocals, while Hendrix tears it up throughout on guitar. This is followed by an even longer version of "Machine Gun," written in protest of the Vietnam War. Hendrix takes some of the most outstanding guitar solos of his meteoric career, as well as simulating the sounds of a battlefield with percussive riffs and controlled feedback, effectively redefining what could be done with an electric guitar.

Side two of *Band of Gypsys* kicks off with "Changes," the title track from Miles's first solo album (1970). Hendrix is absolutely brilliant on guitar, wah-wah pedal in effect. The rhythm section of Cox on bass and Miles on drums rocks out mightily, driving the crowd into a clapping, screaming frenzy. "Power of Love" is next, a heavy metal rocker, Hendrix and Cox hammering home the theme over and over again.

"Message to Love" is basically a vehicle to showcase Hendrix's singing and incredible guitar playing. And incredible it is. The album and concert conclude with another Miles composition, "We Gotta Live Together." It features Miles on vocals and interesting interplay between Hendrix on guitar and Cox on bass, the band building to a mighty crescendo. After a disastrous show at Madison Square Garden in New York City on January 28, 1970, Band of Gypsys broke up.

I attended the early show on December 31. I had tickets to the late show, also, but that's a long story. Having been there, however, I can attest that although *Band of Gypsys* may be one of the greatest live albums ever recorded, the six songs it contains only scratch the surface of what was performed. The band played an average of twelve songs over each of the four shows.

Apparently Hendrix was under a contractual obligation to produce an album of new material for Capitol Records, so the album couldn't include any of his concert favorites from the Jimi Hendrix Experience era. A 1991 European and Japanese re-release of *Band of Gypsys* includes "Hear My Train," "Foxy Lady," and "Stop." *Live at the Fillmore East* (1999) contains "Wild Thing," "Voodoo Child (Slight Return)," and "Stone Free."

John Lee Hooker – *Live at the Café Au Go Go*

Released: 1967
Recorded: August 30, 1966, Café Au Go Go, NYC
Label: Bluesway
Producer: Bob Thiele
Personnel:
John Lee Hooker – guitar, vocals
Muddy Waters – guitar
Sammy Lawhorn – guitar
Luther Johnson – guitar
Otis Spann – piano
Francis Clay – drums
Mac Arnold – bass

John Lee Hooker was born in Mississippi in 1917, son of a sharecropper and Baptist minister. His parents separated in 1921, his mother marrying William Moore a year later. Hooker's stepfather was a local blues guitarist who taught young Hooker to play guitar and was his first major blues influence. Throughout the 1930s, Hooker lived in Memphis, Tennessee, where he worked on Beale Street and performed at house parties. He drifted during World War II, ending up in Detroit on 1948, where his popularity grew and he bought his first electric guitar.

Hooker released his first single, "Boogie Chillen'" in 1948 and it was a hit. Despite being illiterate, Hooker was a prolific lyricist. He'd go from studio to studio recording songs under a variety of pseudonyms. Hooker rarely played on a standard beat, making it difficult to find musicians who could back him. As a result, in addition to playing guitar and singing, he often was recorded stomping along with the music on a wooden pallet. From 1949-1962, he recorded and toured with guitarist Eddie Kirkland.

In August 1966, Hooker recorded *Live at the Café Au Go Go* in New York City's Greenwich Village, backed by Muddy Waters and his band (minus harmonica player George Smith, who is credited on the album but goes unheard). Hooker and Waters were no strangers: They had recorded together at Chess Records in the 1950s and toured together at that time.

By the mid-'60s, both men had become icons of British invasion bands such as The Rolling Stones and The Animals.

The concert begins with Hooker doing an absolutely evil, almost intimidating reading of "I'm Bad Like Jesse James." It depicts the seamier side of the blues spectrum, retribution for the untrustworthy friend, drowned in the river for his indiscretions. Otis Spann is featured on piano. "She's Long, She's Tall (She Weeps Like a Willow Tree)" is next, joyful by comparison despite its title. It features Spann on piano and interesting interplay among Hooker and the other guitarists.

"When My First Wife Left Me," as Hooker states at its conclusion, is "real blues." It's sad, reflective, and philosophical, featuring a dynamic conversation between Hooker's guitar and Spann's piano. Hooker then says, "I'm going to stay in soulville for a little while," and launches into "Heartaches and Misery," another profoundly sad tale. It contains the line, "Singing for the people who feel the same way I do."

"One Bourbon, One Scotch and One More Beer," one of Hooker's signature tunes, is next, performed as an up-tempo funky shuffle. The rhythm section of Francis Clay on drums and Mac Arnold on bass is featured. This track was first recorded by Amos Milburn in 1953 and then famously covered by George Thorogood and the Delaware Destroyers in 1977. "I Don't Want No Trouble" is mesmerizingly slow, featuring brilliant piano fills by Spann.

"I'll Never Get Out of These Blues Alive" is even sadder and bleaker if that's possible. Hooker's vocal performance is remarkable, Spann's piano solo is tasteful, and the guitarists collectively predict man's fate. *Live at the Café Au Go Go* concludes with "Seven Days," called "Seven Days and Seven Nights" on *Hooker & the Hogs* (1965). It is equally despairing, but at least the situation seems only to be temporary. The entire ensemble is featured.

Hooker recorded *Live at Soledad Prison* on June 11, 1972, released that same year. In 1996, a compact disc was released entitled *Live at the Café Au Go Go (and Soledad Prison)*, which contained all of the tracks from *Live at the Café Au Go Go* plus the five tracks on which Hooker appears on *Live at Soledad Prison*. (The other two tracks feature John Lee Hooker, Jr.)

Hot Tuna – *Hot Tuna*

Released: 1970
Recorded: September 16-24, 1970, New Orleans House, Berkeley, California
Label: RCA
Producer: Al Schmitt
Personnel:
Jorma Kaukonen – guitar, vocals
Jack Casady – bass
Will Scarlett – harmonica

It's been well documented that Jorma Kaukonen and Jack Casady have been partners for fifty years now and that the latter followed the former from Washington, DC to San Francisco and Jefferson Airplane. And how Hot Tuna evolved from Kaukonen's and Casady's love for the blues. And that they took their tunes from hotel rooms to onstage with the Airplane to forming their own band. And that I have always been a huge Hot Tuna fan.

It takes balls to put out a live album as one's first effort, but Kaukonen and Casady were no newcomers. They added local Bay Area harmonica player Will Scarlet, booked six nights at a tiny club in Berkeley, California, and worked through their blues repertoire. The result was their eponymous first album. Kaukonen credits guitarist Ian Buchanan, whom he had met during his college years in Ohio, with first teaching him many of the songs on the album.

Hot Tuna reflects the band's affinity for classic acoustic blues including traditional tunes and compositions by Jelly Roll Morton and Reverend Gary Davis, the latter having an especially profound influence on Kaukonen. Kaukonen has said of Davis's style, "There's a spiritual quality, and it was just right for me, something in his personality and his voice."

As great as all of these songs are, and as well as Hot Tuna performs them, I have always considered the traditional "Hesitation Blues" to be their signature song. Their performance here is the gold standard against which all other versions are compared. Kaukonen and Casady immediately demonstrate the unique and masterful interplay between guitar and bass that has made them infamous. They handle Leroy Carr's eight-bar "How

Long Blues" as if they were sitting on your back porch. Likewise the traditional "Uncle Sam's Blues," this time in twelve bars.

Scarlett makes his presence felt on harmonica for the first time on Morton's "Don't You Leave Me Here," adding another texture to the tapestry. This is followed by the Davis classic, "Death Don't Have No Mercy," the centerpiece of the set. Here, Kaukonen emulates the finger-picking style of his hero, while he and Casady engage in an extended musical conversation. This song, as well as the next, the traditional "I Know You Rider," featuring Scarlett, were also staples of the Grateful Dead's sets for the better part of thirty years.

"Oh Lord, Search My Heart" is another cover in which Kaukonen becomes Reverend Gary Davis. "Winin' Boy Blues" by Morton, is a Hot Tuna concert favorite on which Scarlett is particularly effective on harmonica. *Hot Tuna* concludes with two original Kaukonen compositions. "New Song (For the Morning)," a mellow groove featuring Scarlett, and "Mann's Fate," dedicated to fellow guitarist and friend Steve Mann. Casady is absolutely brilliant here on bass, playing the lead against Kaukonen's rhythm guitar.

Hot Tuna (the album) established Hot Tuna (the band) as a musical entity that existed independent of Jefferson Airplane. It freed up Kaukonen to return to the accomplished finger-picking style he had developed before joining the Airplane and it allowed Casady to dispense with keeping time in favor of contrapuntal bass soloing. Hot Tuna are still going strong. I saw them at the Fillmore in San Francisco in January 2012 and the chemistry and interplay between Kaukonen and Casady were as electric as ever. Also on the bill was David Bromberg, another student of Reverend Gary Davis.

Howlin' Wolf – *Live and Cookin' (At Alice's Revisited)*

Released: 1977
Recorded: January 1972, Alice's Revisited, Chicago, Illinois
Label: Chess
Producer: Leonard Chess
Personnel:
Howlin' Wolf – harmonica, vocals
Hubert Sumlin – guitar
Sunnyland Slim – piano
Fred Below – drums
L.V. Williams – guitar
Dave Myers – bass
Eddie Shaw – saxophone

Chester Arthur Burnett, named after the 21st President of the United States, was born in Mississippi in 1910. He got the name Howlin' Wolf from his grandfather. In 1930, he met Charley Patton, the most popular Delta bluesman at the time, who taught him to play the guitar. He learned the harmonica from Sonny Boy Williamson, who married his half-sister.

During the 1930s, Howlin' Wolf performed throughout the South as a solo act and with a number of blues musicians. After serving in World War II, he returned home to help with the farming. Howlin' Wolf settled in Chicago in 1952. Within a year, he enticed guitarist Hubert Sumlin to leave Memphis and join him in Chicago. Sumlin remained with Howlin' Wolf for the rest of his career, perfectly complimenting the singer's huge voice.

He had several hits in the '50s, including "Smokestack Lightning." His eponymous 1962 album was very influential, containing classics such as "Wang Dang Doodle," "Goin' Down Slow," "Spoonful," and "Little Red Rooster," all written by Willie Dixon. His *Howlin' Wolf London Sessions* (1970), recorded with Eric Clapton and other British rockers, was a critical and commercial success.

By 1972, Howlin' Wolf was on the downside of his illustrious career with various health problems. But his performance at Alice's Revisited in

Chicago, remarkably his only live album, nonetheless captures the blues giant at his growling best. *Live and Cookin' (At Alice's Revisited)* opens with "When I Laid Down I Was Troubled," evocative of the traditional "Rollin' and Tumblin'," featuring Sumlin's guitar riffs and Dave Myers's bass.

"I Didn't Know" is done up-tempo style. Howlin' Wolf is exceptional on vocal and harmonica, Eddie Shaw excels on saxophone, and Sumlin's guitar sings. A cover of Muddy Waters's "Mean Mistreater" is next, performed in Howlin' Wolf's unmistakable vocal style. The rhythm section of Myers on bass and Fred Below on drums is featured. "I Had a Dream" is an up-tempo shuffle that features the entire band swinging behind Howlin' Wolf.

"Call Me the Wolf" is primal Howlin' Wolf on the prowl, spoken rather than sung, eliciting exuberant audience reaction. Shaw is featured on saxophone as is Sunnyland Slim on piano. "Don't Laugh at Me" resides in the same musical neighborhood as "Killing Floor," one of Howlin' Wolf's signature tunes. It features Myers on base and interesting interplay between Sumlin and L.V. Williams on guitars.

"Just Passing By" is a mid-tempo twelve bar blues, featuring the vocal and harmonica stylings of Howlin' Wolf. The album concludes with "Sitting on Top of The World," the only big hit included thereon. It is performed in deliberate fashion, Howlin' Wolf calling out directions on the fly, and featuring Shaw on saxophone and Sunnyland Slim on piano.

After Howlin' Wolf died in 1976, Sumlin and Shaw kept his legacy going as the nucleus of the Wolf Gang band that worked around Chicago for several years. *Live and Cookin' (At Alice's Revisited)* was re-released on compact disc in 1992 with two bonus tracks, "The Big House" and "Mr. Airplane Man."

The Jam – *Dig the New Breed*

Released: 1982
Recorded: September 11, 1977, the 100 Club, London, England
February 16, 1979, Reading U., Reading, England
December 13, 1979, the Rainbow Club, London England
December 14, 1981, Hammersmith Palais, London, England
March 21, 1982, Bingley Hall, Birmingham, England
April 6, 1982, Edinburgh Playhouse, Edinburgh, Scotland
April 8, 1982, Glasgow Apollo, Glasgow, Scotland
Label: Polydor
Producer: Peter Wilson
Personnel:
Rick Buckler – drums
Bruce Foxton – bass, vocals
Paul Weller – guitar, keyboards, vocals

Dig the New Breed was the final album released by The Jam before they split up in December 1982. It is an overview of the band's work presented in a collection of live performances, from small club dates in 1979 to much larger venues in 1982. It goes a long way to demonstrate that The Jam's reputation as a live act without parallel was well earned.

The album begins with "In the City," the hit single from the 1977 album of the same name. Influenced by and borrowing the title from The Who, it is a celebration of youth in the big city. And it is pure, raw, power trio rock'n'roll. Bruce Foxton's bass line is fierce. This is followed by another title track, this time from *All Mod Cons* (1978). It is social commentary with harmony vocals from Paul Weller and Foxton and unbelievable drumming by Rick Buckler.

"All Mod Cons" segues into "To Be Someone (Didn't We Have a Nice Time)," a scathing portrayal of fame and its pitfalls, a personal favorite. Drummer Buckler never stops playing as the band slips into "It's Too Bad" from *All Mod Cons*. Weller is featured on vocals and guitar. "Start!" from *Sound Affects* (1980) is a crowd pleaser, despite Foxton's bass line being lifted from "Taxman" by The Beatles.

"Big Bird" by Eddie Floyd and Booker T. Jones is the only cover tune on the album. It features call-and-response vocals by Weller and Foxton and overdubbed horns. The extended "Set the House Ablaze" from *Sound Affects* is appropriately hot, making it difficult to believe there are only three musicians on stage. "Ghosts" from *The Gift* (1982) is a beautiful song, with lots of building tension and a superb vocal by Weller. It absolutely sparkles, despite the overdubbed brass.

You can hear The Who's influence on "Standards" from *This is the Modern World* (1977), which is next. Foxton is once again outstanding on bass. "In the Crowd" from *All Mod Cons* is another personal favorite, and apparently I'm not alone, as the audience sings the lyrics knowingly along with Weller. From Foxton's first notes on the bass, the crowd recognizes "Going Underground" from *Setting Sons* (1979). The band is captured here on fire with punk energy blended with a pop-ish appeal.

"Dreams of Children," also from *Setting Sons*, is a departure from The Jam's usual approach, featuring a more psychedelic sound. The dreams take on a nightmarish quality as Weller faces his demons alone. This is followed by "That's Entertainment," a truly great song from *Sound Affects*. Weller strings along a series of quintessential British images, leading to the inevitable conclusion that we each find entertainment where we may. *Dig the New Breed* concludes with a shocking extended version of "Private Hell" from *Setting Sons*. It is a very disturbing song about lost youth or slipping into depression or some such, and it is played with the appropriate raw edge.

"Going Underground" from *Setting Sons* was one of the songs I selected to be in my book, *The 100 Greatest Rock'n'Roll Songs Ever* in 2000.

Jefferson Airplane – *Bless Its Pointed Little Head*

Released: 1969
Recorded: October 24-26, 1968, Fillmore West, San Francisco, California
            November 28-30, 1968, Fillmore East, NYC
Label: RCA Victor
Producer: Al Schmitt
Personnel:
Marty Balin – bass, vocals
Jack Casady – bass, guitar
Spencer Dryden – drums, percussion
Paul Kantner – guitar, vocals
Jorma Kaukonen – guitar, vocals
Grace Slick – vocals

Bless Its Pointed Little Head is supposedly the favorite Jefferson Airplane album of each member of Jefferson Airplane. Their first live album, recorded at the Fillmores West and East in 1968, it captures the raw, unadulterated sound of the Airplane live on stage, with no studio post-production. Five songs on the album had not appeared on any of the band's four previous studio recordings. The songs that did previously appear were completely reworked and much more rocking.

Like an Airplane show at the time, the album opens with the audio track to the last scenes from *King Kong*. The concert audience is actively booing the dive-bombing airplanes and cheering for the ape. "Oh, no, it wasn't the airplanes; it was beauty killed the beast." With that, drummer Spencer Dryden kicks off the introduction to "3/5's of a Mile in 10 Seconds" and we're off. This first song immediately sets the tone for what is to come, the incredible interplay between Jorma Kaukonen's guitar and Jack Casady's bass, Grace Slick's and Marty Balin's unequaled harmony vocals.

"Somebody to Love" is completely rearranged and funkified. Slick is at her best here, reinterpreting her own vocal performance. More brilliance from Kaukonen and Casady. "Fat Angel" appeared on Donovan's *Sunshine Superman* album in 1966, including the lyric, "Fly Jefferson Airplane, gets you there on time." Returning the tribute, the Airplane covers it here, with Paul Kantner comfortable in the role of "Captain High." A great opportunity for the band to stretch out instrumentally, it features Balin on bass, Casady on rhythm guitar, and Kaukonen and Kantner trading guitar solos.

"Rock Me Baby" was my personal favorite part of an Airplane show, a first look at what would become Hot Tuna, the band Kaukonen and Casady would form in two years. Slick and Balin leave the stage and the remaining four players rock the blues, Kaukonen on vocal. Kantner takes over vocal duties on the cover of his hero Fred Neil's "The Other Side of This Life." The Airplane turns this folk song into something else entirely. The two main vocalists return to kick much ass on "It's No Secret" and "Plastic Fantastic Lover," both Airplane staples by Balin, both radically rearranged. They each contain a tight jam, once again featuring the textured interplay between Kaukonen on guitar and Casady on bass.

I'm not a big fan of "Bear Melt," the extended group improvisation which is the last track on the album, named for Owsley "Bear" Stanley, the designer chemist. The first half features Slick, vamping in front of the band, not unlike Pigpen with the early Grateful Dead. It morphs into a free-form jam that is definitely spaced out, if a little disjointed. At its conclusion, Slick intones, "You can move your rear ends now."

Bless Its Pointed Little Head was an important album in Jefferson Airplane's discography, clearly demonstrating early in their career that their live sound was distinctly different from their studio recordings. I was present at one of the Fillmore East shows represented here, probably Friday, November 29, the day after Thanksgiving Day, 1968.

Janis Joplin – *In Concert*

Released: 1972
Recorded: March 2, 1968, The Grande Ballroom, Detroit, Michigan
         April 12, 1968, Winterland Ballroom, San Francisco, California
         June 23, 1968, Carousel Ballroom, San Francisco, California
         April 4, 1970, Fillmore West, San Francisco, California
         June 28, 1970, CNE Stadium, Toronto, Ontario, Canada
         July 4, 1970, McMahon Stadium, Calgary, Alberta, Canada
Label: Columbia
Producer: Elliot Mazer
Personnel:
Janis Joplin – vocals
Nick Gravenites – vocals
Big Brother & the Holding Company:
James Gurley – guitar
Sam Andrew – guitar
Peter Albin – bass
Dave Getz – drums
Full Tilt Boogie Band:
John Till – guitar
Richard Bell – piano
Ken Pearson – organ
Brad Campbell – bass
Clark Pierson – drums

In Concert is a double live album by Janis Joplin released posthumously. The first record contains performances with Big Brother & the Holding Company recorded at various venues in 1968 and 1970. The second record was recorded with the Full Tilt Boogie Band during the Festival Express concert tour in the summer of 1970. Staged in three Canadian cities, the musicians, including the Grateful Dead and The Band, traveled on a chartered Canadian National Railways train between shows. The concerts and the endless jam sessions on the train were captured in Bob Smeaton's 2003 documentary, *Festival Express*.

The first album begins in rocking fashion, driven by drummer Dave Getz, with "Down on Me." In addition to Joplin's distinctive vocal style, we are immediately treated to the outstanding interplay between guitarists Sam Andrew and James Gurley, considered by many to be the first psychedelic guitarists in rock'n'roll. They slow things down a bit with "Bye, Bye Baby," with its interesting changing time signatures.

Joplin credits Moondog, a blind New York City street person, with the authorship of "All is Loneliness," a very strange poem set to music on which the other band members add their voices to Joplin's. This is followed by the classic, "Piece of My Heart," a single for Aretha Franklin's older sister Emma in 1967, and which Joplin made her own on *Cheap Thrills* the following year. She tears it up on this live version, as does Andrews on solo guitar.

"Road Block," written by bassist Peter Albin, is another strange tune, more of a chant than a song, which seems to get the loudest audience response of any track on *In Concert*. "Flower in the Sun" is an interesting song, written by Andrews, and featuring himself on guitar. "Summertime" follows, where Big Brother meets the Gershwin brothers. Gurley and Andrews trade guitar leads and Joplin's vocal is truly phenomenal. The first album concludes with "Ego Rock," an autobiographical 12-bar blues co-written with Nick Gravenites, who sits in on guest vocal.

The Full Tilt Boogie Band performances on the second album begin with "Half Moon" by John and Johanna Hall from the band Orleans. Joplin's vocal is inspiring and John Till excels on guitar. "Kozmic Blues" is next, from Joplin's days with the Kozmic Blues Band, and popularized when she performed it at the Woodstock Music and Art Fair. Richard Bell is featured on piano.

"Move Over," which would become the opening track on *Pearl* in 1971, is a show-stopper as performed here. The entire band rocks out behind Joplin, especially Ken Pearson on organ and the rhythm section of Brad Campbell on bass and Clark Pierson on drums. After inviting the entire Toronto audience to her place in San Francisco, Joplin launches into "Try (Just a Little Bit Harder)." She wails this one out in her unmistakable style, taking it up, bringing it down, and taking it up once again. Bell is outstanding on piano.

After Joplin tells the crowd how much fun they were all having on the train, Bell leads the band into "Get It While You Can," another great song that would eventually appear on *Pearl*. Joplin delivers another moving vocal performance on a song with a message that, in retrospect, sums up her brief, meteoric career. *In Concert* concludes with an extended version of "Ball and Chain," Joplin's classic cover of the Big Mama Thornton tune that she popularized at the Monterey Pop Festival and that appeared on *Cheap Thrills*. It's an outstanding version, featuring Till on guitar, reminding us that there will never be another Janis Joplin.

King Crimson – *USA*

Released: 1975
Recorded: June 28, 1974, the Casino, Asbury Park, New Jersey
         June 30, 1974, the Palace Theatre, Providence, Rhode Island
Label: Island
Producer: King Crimson
Personnel:
Robert Fripp – guitar, mellotron
John Wetton – bass, vocals
David Cross – violin, viola, mellotron, piano
Bill Bruford – drums, percussion
Eddie Jobson – violin, piano

USA is a concert recording documenting King Crimson's 1974 tour of North America, which, at the time, was to be their last. So insistent was he that the band would not be resurrected, songwriter/guitarist Robert Fripp concluded the album's liner notes with "R.I.P." The album was recorded mostly in Asbury Park, New Jersey, except for "21st Century Schizoid Man," recorded in Providence, Rhode Island, two nights later. Multi-instrumentalist Eddie Jobson added overdubs to that track and two others in the studio.

The concert begins with a tiny instrumental snippet called "Walk On . . . No Pussyfooting" from *No Pussyfooting* (1973) by Fripp and Brian Eno. The audience is immediately jolted upright by the start of "Larks' Tongues in Aspic (Part II)," a mighty instrumental from the 1973 album of the same name. The whole band is featured, enhanced by a violin overdub by Jobson.

"Lament" from *Starless and Bible Black* features John Wetton on bass and vocal, as well as an electric piano overdub by Jobson. It is a very introspective song, a jaundiced view of King Crimson's (Fripp's) experiences in the music business. They then launch into an extended version of "Exiles" from *Larks' Tongues in Aspic*. It's definitely a highlight and features Wetton's excellent vocal performance, David Cross on violin, and Fripp on guitar.

Every King Crimson concert on the 1974 tour featured one or two improvisations, and the appropriately titled "Asbury Park" is the one selected for this collection. It's an unbridled, free-form jam, featuring Bill Bruford on drums and Fripp's guitar. "Easy Money" from *Larks' Tongues in Aspic* is a personal favorite. It's performed here more slowly and in more bizarre fashion than the original, featuring Wetton on the vocal.

USA concludes with "21st Century Schizoid Man" from King Crimson's first album, *In the Court of the Crimson King* (1969). It has been their signature tune from their beginning quite literally into the 21st century. This version does not disappoint, ranging from heavy metal to classical and back again. There is amazing interplay among the musicians, notably between Fripp on guitar and Wetton on bass. Jobson adds a violin overdub in the studio.

Two bonus tracks, "Fracture" from *Starless and Bible Black* (1974) and "Starless" from *Red* (1974) are included on the 30th anniversary compact disc edition of *USA* released in 2002. King Crimson, of course, did not cease to exist in 1974. Fripp re-formed the band with a new lineup in 1981 for about three years before breaking up again for about a decade. They started up again in 1994; their current status is ambiguous.

Throughout his long career, Fripp has always pushed the boundaries of popular music and dabbled in many experimental musical ideas. He was the founder and leader of King Crimson, leading their several incarnations in new and different directions each time out. He pursued many side projects with the likes of Brian Eno, David Bowie, Peter Gabriel, and Daryl Hall. He invented "Frippertronics," a technique of layering guitars and tape loops. He released a series of solo albums, from *Exposure* in 1979 to *That Which Passes* in 1997. In 1985, he began teaching guitar, calling his students and school "the League of Crafty Guitarists."

Albert King – *Live Wire/Blues Power*

Released 1968
Recorded: June 26-27, 1968, Fillmore Auditorium, San Francisco, California
Label: Stax
Producer: Al Jackson, Jr.
Personnel:
Albert King – guitar, vocals
Willie James Exon – guitar
James Washington – organ
Roosevelt Pointer – bass
Theotis Morgan – drums

Albert King was born Albert King Nelson in 1923 on a cotton plantation in Indianola, Mississippi. During his childhood, he sang in a family gospel group at a church where his father played the guitar. He began working as a professional musician with In The Groove Boys in Osceola, Arkansas. Moving to St. Louis, he briefly played drums for Jimmy Reed's band in the early 1950s and appeared on several early recordings by Reed.

Influenced by Blind Lemon Jefferson and Lonnie Johnson, King adopted the electric guitar as his instrument, his preference being the Gibson Flying V, which he nicknamed "Lucy." He earned his own nickname, "The Velvet Bulldozer," as he drove one of them for a living in the 1950s. He had a hit in 1961 with the release of "Don't Throw Your Love on Me So Strong," included on his debut album, *The Big Blues*, the following year.

In 1966, King moved to Memphis, where he signed with Stax Records and recorded dozens of important tracks with Booker T. & the MG's, produced by Al Jackson, Jr. *Live Wire/Blues Power* was King's first live recording, recorded at the Fillmore Auditorium in San Francisco in June 1968. Leftover tracks from these performances were released in 1990 as *Wednesday Night in San Francisco* and *Thursday Night in San Francisco*.

There are only six tracks on *Live Wire/Blues Power*. The first is a cover of Herbie Hancock's "Watermelon Man," which King turns into an up-tempo, funky shuffle. About half way through the song, the band brings it down a bit while King greets the crowd and leads them in rhythmic clapping. Willie James Exon excels on rhythm guitar as does Theotis Morgan on drums.

An extended version of the title track, King's "Blues Power" is next. A twelve-bar blues done in deliberate style, King preaches more than sings the verses, which are about the many ways one can get the blues, exhorting the crowd with "Can you feel it?" But he does his serious talking with his guitar, laying down solo after dynamic solo. This tune also features James Washington on organ and Roosevelt Pointer on bass.

"Night Stomp" is an up-tempo twelve-bar blues, co-written with Jackson, Jr. It is a showcase for King's guitar mastery, his solos soaring above the steady, swinging backbeat of the band. This is followed by an extended performance of "Blues at Sunrise," another slow composition, a signature tune for King. He sings the verses with great emotion, and his guitar playing is at once emotional, effortless, and dynamic. The rhythm section of Pointer on bass and Morgan on drums is featured, as is Washington on organ. For my money, this is one of the greatest blues performances ever recorded live.

"Please Love Me" is next, an up-tempo shuffle with a killer bass line provided by Pointer. King makes short shrift of the verses and then launches into some of the best guitar soloing on the album. *Live Wire/ Blues Power* concludes way too quickly with "Look Out," a mid-tempo instrumental that features King's virtuoso solo guitar playing with the band vamping behind him.

The Kinks – *One for the Road*

Released: 1980
Recorded: March 3, 1979, The Barn, Rutgers U., New Brunswick, New Jersey
March 6, 1979, Lowell Memorial Auditorium, Lowell, Massachusetts
September 23, 1979, Providence Civic Center, Providence, Rhode Island
November 11, 1979, The Volkhaus, Zurich, Switzerland
March 4, 1980, Syracuse Area Landmark Theater, Syracuse, New York
March 6, 1980, U. of Massachusetts, Amherst, Massachusetts
March 7, 1980, SE Massachusetts U., North Dartmouth, Massachusetts
Label: Arista
Producer: Ray Davies
Personnel:
Ray Davies – guitar, harmonica, keyboards, vocals
Dave Davies – guitar, vocals
Ian Gibbons – keyboards, vocals
Mick Avory – drums
Jim Rodford – bass, vocals
Nick Newell – keyboards

The Kinks, the most British of the British invasion bands, never really hit it as big in the United States initially as did some of their peers. They did, however enjoy an up-swing of popularity in the late 1970s and early 1980s. *One for the Road* is a double album recorded by The Kinks at various venues in 1979 and 1980. It is an important document of a band that paved the way for heavy metal and punk, but never met a pop song they wouldn't attempt.

The album begins with "Opening," a short instrumental tease of "You Really Got Me," The Kinks' signature song. Then the band launches into a kick-ass version of "The Hard Way" from *The Kinks Present Schoolboys in*

Disgrace (1975). Supposedly about one of Dave Davies's school headmasters, it features him on lead guitar and Mick Avory on drums.

"Catch Me Now I'm Falling" is next, from *Low Budget* (1979). Vocalist Ray Davies personifies the once great United States as it drifts inexorably into decline. Timely. The much underrated D. Davies is featured on solo guitar. This is followed by "Where Have All the Good Times Gone" from *The Kink Kontroversy* (1965). It's about how nostalgia for the good old days can quickly turn to generation gap resentment.

At this point, they play a "Lola" tease and then the real thing, from *Lola vs. Powerman and the Moneygoround* (1970). A personal favorite, it is the story of an encounter between a straight man and a transvestite. The fact that it was accepted by the public in 1970 is a tribute to R. Davies's skill as a songwriter. There's lots of audience participation. "Pressure" from *Low Budget* is a very short, proto-punk tune, with a rockabilly introduction.

"All Day and All of the Night," The Kinks' second hit single from their 1964 debut album, *Kinks*, is next. They do a fairly straightforward reading, save for D. Davies's psychedelic guitar playing. This is followed by an extended performance of "20th Century Man" from *Muswell Hillbillies* (1970). In a strong vocal performance, R. Davies complains about living in the modern world. D. Davies excels on guitar, referencing "Born to Be Wild" during his solo.

"Misfits," from the 1978 album of the same name, is a gorgeous ballad sung by R. Davies that features D. Davies with an equally gorgeous guitar solo as well as Ian Gibbons on piano. "Prince of the Punks" from *Sleepwalker* (1977) is supposedly an angry message from R. Davies to ex-protégé Tom Robinson. "Stop Your Sobbing" is from *Kinks* and was coincidentally a hit for The Pretenders in 1979. This performance pays homage to the Shirelles' "Then He Kissed Me" and features D. Davies on backing vocals.

The next four tracks are from *Low Budget*, released just a few months prior to the concerts captured on *One for the Road*. The title track refers to the oil crisis of the late 1970s and the need to tighten all of our belts. Prescient. "Attitude" is social commentary with tongue in cheek in a mid-tempo rocker, reminiscent of The Kinks' British invasion days. "(Wish I Could Fly Like) Superman" is much harder edged than the disco-friendly studio version. Did I hear the "Batman Theme?" "National Health" is a veiled endorsement of a healthy lifestyle rather than drugs to combat nervous tension.

"Till the End of the Day" from *The Kink Kontroversy* is performed here with a reggae flavor, featuring the band on backing vocals behind R. Davies. This is followed by an extended version of "Celluloid Heroes," a truly great song from *Everybody's in Show-Biz* (1972). It features D. Davies on guitar and Gibbons on keyboards, and demonstrates the influence of British dancehall music on R. Davies's songwriting.

D. Davies then provides a psychedelic guitar introduction to "You Really Got Me," the first big hit from *Kinks*, the one everyone's been waiting for, and the crowd goes nuts. They are rewarded with a rousing rendition of "Victoria" from *Arthur (Or the Decline and Fall of the British Empire)* (1969). *One for the Road* concludes with "David Watts," performed pretty much as it sounds on *Something Else by The Kinks* (1967), famously covered by The Jam in 1978.

A compact disc version of *One for the Road* was released in 1989, but omitted "20th Century Man" due to time restraints. A two compact disc set was issued in 1999, which reinstated "20th Century Man" and which includes twenty minutes of video footage from the September 23 show in Providence. "Lola" from *Lola vs. Powerman and the Moneygoround* was one of the songs I selected to be in my book, *The 100 Greatest Rock'n'Roll Songs Ever* in 2000.

Fela Kuti & the Africa '70 with Ginger Baker – *Live!*

Released: 1971
Recorded: early 1971, Abbey Road, London, England or Batakota, Lagos,
        Nigeria
Label: Regal Zonophone
Producer: Jeff Jaratt
Personnel:
Fela Kuti – organ, percussion, African drums, congas, vocals
Ginger Baker – drums, percussion, African drums
Tony Allen – drums, percussion
Tunde Williams – trumpet
Eddie Faychum – trumpet
Igo Chiko – saxophone
Lenkan Animashaun – saxophone
Peter Animashaun – guitar
Maurice Ekpo – bass
Henry Koffi – percussion
Friday Jumbo – percussion
Akwesi Korranting – percussion
Tony Abayumi – percussion
Isaac Olaleye – percussion

Ginger Baker first met Fela Kuti in the mid-1960s when the latter played trumpet alongside fellow Nigerian Remi Kebaka at The Flamingo Club in London. In 1970, Baker traveled to Ghana to visit master drummer Guy Warren. While there, he became fascinated with Nigerian music and contacted Kuti once again, with whom he traveled in Nigeria in a Land Rover to get in touch with the country's rhythms. Baker liked the capital, Lagos, so well, that he built a sixteen-track mobile recording studio there, called Batakota Studios, with Kuti's and Kebaka's help.

At the same time, Baker agreed to do some recording with Kuti and his Africa '70 band. Supposedly, this occurred in early 1971, but there are two schools of thought as to where. One school believes that *Live!* was recorded at Batakota Studios, which Baker subsequently sold to Polygram Nigeria in 1976. The other school asserts that 150 lucky people were crammed into a large studio at Abbey Road in London with colored spotlights projected on the walls to give it the feel of a live show, and it was recorded there. Either way, *Live!* contains only four pieces, interesting artifacts from the Kuti-Baker collaboration.

The concert begins with "Let's Start," a blatant invitation to have graphic, explicit sex. Kuti sings in Yoruba with some broken English explanations: "Let us start what we've come into the room to do." The band is incredibly tight and funky, evocative of James Brown in the late '60s. Kuti is also featured on organ, as is Igo Chico on tenor saxophone.

The remaining tracks are extended performances, all exceeding eleven minutes in length. "Black Man's Cry" is about identity. It is aimed at those black people who feel inferior to whites and who use chemicals to bleach their skin. Kuti sings in Yoruba: "Who says black is not beautiful! There is nothing as beautiful as the black skin! Look at me! Look at me very well!" A hypnotic shuffle, it features Chico on tenor saxophone, Lenkan Animashaun on baritone saxophone, Kuti on organ, and Maurice Ekpo on bass.

"Ye Ye De Smell" translates from the Yoruba as "Bullshit stinks." It's about people getting what they deserve or reaping what they sow, implying that if you give people bullshit expect to get the same in return. It's a wild percussive ride, featuring Baker and Tony Allen on drums, trumpeters Tunde Williams and Eddie Faychum, Kuti on organ, and Chico on tenor saxophone

The final track on *Live!* is "Egbe Mi O (Carry Me I Want to Die)." In this very funky song, Kuti sings in Yoruba about the various things that can happen to you while you dance: you can go into a trance, a woman's beads can break, or a man could lose his hat. Kuti ends the track with a general chorus of the band and the audience, calling everyone together.

The 2001 compact disc reissue of *Live!* includes a bonus track, a sixteen-minute drum duet between Baker and Allen recorded at the 1978 Berlin Jazz Festival.

Led Zeppelin – *How the West Was Won*

Released: 2003
Recorded: June 25, 1972, Los Angeles Forum, Los Angeles, California
          June 27, 1972, Long Beach Arena, Long Beach, California
Label: Atlantic
Producer: Jimmy Page
Personnel:
John Bonham – drums, percussion, vocals
John Paul Jones – bass, keyboards, mandolin, vocals
Jimmy Page – guitar, mandolin, vocals
Robert Plant – vocals, harmonica

How the West Was Won is a triple album recorded by Led Zeppelin on their 1972 tour of the United States, specifically in Los Angeles and Long Beach, California, but not released until 2003. For many years, live recordings of these two concerts circulated among fans in the form of bootlegs. The songs from the two shows underwent extensive editing by producer Jimmy Page at Sarm West Studios in London before being released on the album. Page has been quoted as saying that these gigs represent Led Zeppelin at their artistic peak.

The album begins with "LA Drone," a brief snippet of tape created by guitarist Page and bassist John Paul Jones. This segues into the first tune, "Immigrant Song" from *Led Zeppelin III* (1970). One of Led Zeppelin's few single releases, it's written from the point of view of Vikings rowing west in search of new conquests. Right away, it's apparent that the band is at the top of their game. Robert Plant's unmistakable vocal is amazing, Page is outstanding on lead guitar, and the rhythm section of John Bonham on drums and Jones on bass is rock solid.

This segues into "Heartbreaker" from *Led Zeppelin III*, which is a vehicle for Page to demonstrate some of his virtuoso guitar technique in an extended, unaccompanied solo. "Black Dog" is next, from the untitled 1971 album usually referred to as *Led Zeppelin IV* or ⚒♨⚙◎. It is blisteringly hot, with Plant wailing away and the rest of the band responding in kind. Page's brilliant guitar introduction initiates "Over the Hills and Far Away," which would appear the following year on *Houses of the Holy*. Page also takes an excellent guitar solo, but it is the tight interplay between Bonham on drums and Jones on bass that makes the song so effective.

They mellow things out considerably with "Since I've Been Loving You," a slow blues from *Led Zeppelin III*. Page's guitar solo is among the strongest on the album. Jones is featured on organ, using the bass pedals for the bass line. This is followed by their classic signature tune, "Stairway to Heaven" from *Led Zeppelin IV*. There's not much that hasn't already been written about this song. This performance is certainly dynamic and vigorous despite being overly familiar.

From the same album, "Going to California" is performed acoustically. Supposedly about Joni Mitchell, it features Page on acoustic guitar and Jones on mandolin. Keeping things quiet, the band performs "That's the Way" from *Led Zeppelin III*, showcasing Plant's remarkable vocalizing and Page's understated guitar prowess. "Bron-Yr-Aur Stomp," named for the house in Wales where the band wrote *Led Zeppelin III*, is another acoustic number, a real crowd pleaser, featuring Bonham on spoons and castanets.

Next is a twenty-five minute performance of "Dazed and Confused." It was written by Jake Holmes, covered by the Yardbirds, and reworked by Led Zeppelin on their eponymous 1969 debut album. Any track this long is bound to have highlights as well as moments of pure self-indulgence, and this is no exception. The band also make reference to "Walter's Walk," which wasn't released until *Coda* (1982) and to "The Crunge," destined to be on *Houses of the Holy*, during the extended jam.

This is followed by "What Is and What Should Never Be" from *Led Zeppelin II* (1969), one of the highlights of the collection and a personal favorite. It runs the gamut from jazzy and mellow to raucous and intense. It's psychedelic hip hop. Plant then introduces a new song, "Dancing Days," that would appear on *Houses of the Holy*. It was supposedly inspired by Indian music that Page and Plant heard while traveling.

Two more very lengthy compositions follow. "Moby Dick," from *Led Zeppelin II*, is a vehicle for an extended drum solo by Bonham, book-ended by a rapid twelve-bar blues played as a power trio without Plant. "Whole Lotta Love" also from *Led Zeppelin II*, is a twenty-five minute tour-de-force, during which the band cover a great deal of territory, including deep space. On their way, they visit "Boogie Chillen'" by John Lee Hooker, Elvis Presley's "Let's Have a Party," "Hello Mary Lou" by Ricky Nelson, and "St. Louis" Jimmy Oden's "Going Down Slow."

Bonham's crashing drum introduction ushers in the aptly titled "Rock and Roll" from *Led Zeppelin IV*. An uncompromising rocker, it features the band with some incredible high-speed ensemble playing. If anything, it's too short. "The Ocean" is next, another tune that would appear on *Houses of the Holy*. An intricate composition with several changes in time signature, the band nonetheless perform it brilliantly. *How the West Was Won* concludes with Willie Dixon's "Bring it On Home" from *Led Zeppelin II*, featuring Plant on harmonica.

"Communication Breakdown" from *Led Zeppelin*, performed on June 25 in Los Angeles but not included on the album, was one of the songs I selected to be in my book, *The 100 Greatest Rock'n'Roll Songs Ever* in 2000.

Jerry Lee Lewis & the Nashville Teens – *Live at the Star Club*

Released: 1964
Recorded: April 5, 1964, Star Club, Hamburg, Germany
Label: Philips
Producer: Sigfried Loch
Personnel:
Jerry Lee Lewis – piano, vocals
The Nashville Teens:
Johnny Allen – guitar
Pete Shannon Harris – bass
Barrie Jenkins – drums
John Hawken – piano
Art Sharp – vocals
Ray Phillips – vocals

When Jerry Lee Lewis (known as the Killer) performed the concert that was to become *Live at the Star Club* in the spring of 1964, his career was at its nadir. Following his scandalous marriage to his teenage cousin, he was blacklisted in the United States, it had been six years since he'd had a hit record, and America had fallen in love with The Beatles.

Lewis had been touring England with the Nashville Teens (who would have a hit record with "Tobacco Road" later in 1964). The Nashville Teens were booked for an extended stay at the Star Club in Hamburg, Germany, but Lewis joined them only for the one night captured on this recording. Sixteen songs were recorded over two sets, thirteen of which appear on the album. "Down the Line," omitted due to a sound fault at the start, was included on later compact disc reissues. The tapes for "You Win Again" and "I'm on Fire" were lost.

Live at the Star Club is considered by many to be among the wildest, hardest rocking concert albums ever recorded, the essence of rock'n'roll. For whatever reason, Lewis performs like a man possessed, singing himself hoarse, pounding the piano, daring the band to keep up with him, which they have difficulty doing on the first tune, "Mean Woman Blues," first recorded by Elvis Presley in 1957. Johnny Allen is featured on guitar solo.

Things get even crazier as the band shifts into "High School Confidential," a single for Lewis in 1958. Lewis bangs on the keys as if he wants to break them and performs some of his wild guttural vocalizations. The crowd chants his first name in unison. They slow things down just a tad on "Money (That's What I Want)," the Barrett Strong single from 1959, performed as a bluesy shuffle with many flourishes on the piano by Lewis and a cha-cha-cha ending.

They keep the blues thing going with a soulful rendering of Carl Perkins's 1957 single, "Matchbox." Lewis is relentless on piano and double-entendre. Allen is featured on solo guitar. Lewis then plays the familiar introductory piano notes to Ray Charles's "What'd I Say, Part 1" released as a single in 1959, and the Nashville Teens come in furiously behind him. Then they play the B-side of the same single, "What'd I Say, Part 2," basically the same tune, but a great vehicle for Lewis to stretch out on the piano. Art Sharp and Ray Phillips are featured on backing vocals, but Lewis nonetheless can be heard yelling at one of the Nashville Teens to "play that thing right, boy!"

The rhythmic German-accented shouts of "Jerry!" continue and intensify as the band begins "Great Balls of Fire," a big hit single for Lewis in 1957. This version is incendiary, to say the least, Lewis out of control at the keys, the band not really catching up with him until he segues into "Good Golly, Miss Molly," the 1958 smash single by Little Richard. Barrie Jenkins excels on drums; the crowd goes wild.

Next they launch into the obscure, previously unreleased Lewis Boogie, an up-tempo twelve bar blues, featuring Allen on guitar. This is followed by a cover of Hank Williams's ballad, "Your Cheatin' Heart," released as a single in 1953. It's a remarkable vocal and piano playing performance by Lewis, the Nashville Teens barely audible behind him. They do a hard-driving version of "Hound Dog," first released as a single by Big Mama Thornton in 1953, popularized by Presley in 1956. Lewis is an absolute madman on the piano.

At this point Lewis growls, rather than sings, "Long Tall Sally," another Little Richard single, this one released in 1956. Allen is featured on guitar solo. *Live at the Star Club* concludes with "Whole Lotta Shakin' Goin' On," Lewis's 1957 hit single. The rhythm section of Jenkins on drums and Pete Shannon Harris on bass is featured, as is Allen on guitar, but it's the Killer who has his way, on fire until the very last note.

Little Feat – *Waiting for Columbus*

Released: 1978
Recorded: August 1-4, 1977, Rainbow Theater, London, England
          August 8-10, 1977, Lisner Auditorium, Geo. Washington U.,
          Washington, DC
Label: Warner Bros
Producer: Lowell George
Personnel:
Paul Barrere – guitar, vocals
Sam Clayton – congas, vocals
Lowell George – guitar, vocals
Kenny Gradney – bass
Richard Hayward – drums, vocals
Bill Payne – keyboards, synthesizer, vocals
Mick Taylor – guitar
Michael McDonald – vocals
Patrick Simmons – vocals
Tower of Power horn section:
Emilio Castillo – saxophone
Greg Adams – trumpet
Lenny Pickett – saxophones
Stephen "Doc" Kupka – saxophone
Mic Gillette – trombone, trumpet

Waiting for Columbus is a double album, the first live recording by Little Feat, recorded in the summer of 1977 in London, England and Washington, DC. The band was backed by the Tower of Power horn section, with whom they had already recorded in the studio. Many of their well-known songs were either reworked or extended, and Little Feat additionally did a cover tune. The result was one of their biggest selling albums and a critically acclaimed live rock'n'roll album.

The album begins with a brief *a capella* cover of the traditional "Join the Band," after which local DC radio personality Don Colwell leads the audience in a F-E-A-T cheer. Drummer Richard Hayward's cowbell introduces "Fat Man in the Bathtub" from *Dixie Chicken* (1973), a personal favorite. The band immediately establishes its unique off-cadence, swampy brand of rocking out, featuring Lowell George on the vocals and Bill Payne on the synthesizer solo.

A rousing version of "All that You Dream" from *The Last Record Album* (1975) is next, featuring George on slide guitar and Payne on synthesizer. Payne's composition, "Oh Atlanta" from *Feats Don't Fail Me Now* (1974) follows, about flying into one of the band's favorite places. Paul Barrere and George engage in some inspired guitar conversations throughout.

Barrere takes over vocal duties, assisted by percussionist Sam Clayton, on his own composition, the funky "Old Folk's Boogie" from *Time Loves a Hero* (1977). Payne takes an extended keyboard solo, followed by George on guitar. The title track from *Time Loves a Hero* is next, featuring call-and-response vocals, a guitar solo from Barrere, and great drumming by Hayward. This segues into "Day or Night" from *The Last Record Album*, which features outstanding bass playing by Kenny Gradney, a quirky keyboard solo by Payne, and saxophone solos by Emilio Castillo and Lenny Pickett.

Also on *The Last Record Album*, "Mercenary Territory" is completely rearranged here to accommodate the Tower of Power horn section, notably saxophonist Stephen "Doc" Kupka. This is followed by another personal favorite, "Spanish Moon" from *Feats Don't Fail Me Now*, which features an infectious beat as laid down by the rhythm section of Gradney on bass, Hayward on drums, and Clayton on congas. The horn section plays an excellent arrangement in counterpoint to the funky jamming.

Little Feat's signature title track from *Dixie Chicken* is next. This version is greatly extended to include a piano solo by Payne, a Dixieland arrangement by the Tower of Power horn section, and a dual guitar jam between George and Barrere. This segues into an extended version of the ridiculous "Tripe Face Boogie" from *Sailin' Shoes* (1972). This is big fun in the form of nonsense lyrics and unbridled jamming.

The blatantly sexual "Rocket in My Pocket" from *Time Loves a Hero* follows, featuring George on the vocal and the guitar. George is also front and center on "Willin'," his trucker's lament that appears on Little Feat's eponymous 1971 debut album, as well as on *Sailin' Shoes*. They then perform a brief snippet of "Don't Bogart that Joint," by Elliot Ingber, who was in the Mothers of Invention with George, followed by "A Apolitical Blues" from *Sailin' Shoes*, with Mick Taylor sitting in on guitar in London.

Two studio album title tracks round out *Waiting for Columbus*. "Sailin' Shoes," one of the most covered songs in rock'n'roll, is done here in deliberate fashion, featuring George's vocal, Barrere's guitar solo, and some very funky ensemble playing. In stark contrast, the album concludes with "Feats Don't Fail Me Now" done at a frenetic pace, featuring Gradney on bass. By the end of the song, the audience is singing along enthusiastically.

In 1990, a compact disc edition of *Waiting for Columbus* was released. In order to fit the double album onto one compact disc, two tracks, "Don't Bogart that Joint" and "A Apolitical Blues," were omitted. In 2002, a deluxe two compact disc edition was released, restoring all the original tracks and including additional tracks recorded at the concert venues. "Rock and Roll Doctor" from *Feats Don't Fail Me Now*, played August 9 at Lisner Auditorium but not included on the album, was one of the songs I selected to be in my book, *The 100 Greatest Rock'n'Roll Songs Ever* in 2000.

Los Lobos – *Live at the Fillmore*

Released: 2005
Recorded: July 29-30, 2004, Fillmore Auditorium, San Francisco, California
Label: Hollywood/Mammoth
Producer: Doug Mobley
Personnel:
Steve Berlin – keyboards, saxophone, flute
Conrad Lozano – bass
Cesar Rosas – guitar, vocals
Louie Perez – guitar, drums, vocals
David Hidalgo – guitar, violin, accordion, percussion, vocals
Cougar Estrada – drums, percussion
Victor Bisetti – drums, percussion
Vincent Hidalgo – guitar

Although Los Lobos has released some live material over the years, *Live at the Fillmore* is their first live album. It was recorded at the Fillmore Auditorium in San Francisco in July 2004, on the occasion of their 30th anniversary as a band. The set-list reflects Los Lobos' long career as recording artists. It was also filmed and issued as a concert digital video disc with the same title but slightly different set list.

The concert begins with "Good Morning Aztlan" from the 2002 album of the same name. It's an absolutely infectious rocker, featuring David Hidalgo on vocal and guitar solo. Next is "I Walk Alone" from *The Neighborhood* (1990), an up-tempo blues with Cesar Rosas on vocal that features the twin guitar attack of Rosas and D. Hidalgo as well as the twin percussion attack of Cougar Estrada and Victor Bisetti.

They change things up considerably with the reggae-influenced "Maria Christina" from *Good Morning Aztlan*, which features Rosas on vocal, D. Hidalgo on accordion, and Steve Berlin on saxophone. "Charmed" is a serious blues rocker from *The Ride* (2004). It features Louie Perez on vocal and all three guitarists (Perez, D. Hidalgo, and Rosas) riffing out simultaneously. The Fillmore crowd goes wild.

"Luz de Mi Vida" is a wonderful Spanish-English hybrid song sung by Rosas, featuring Berlin on saxophone and flute and the rest of the band on backing vocals. This is followed by "Rita," a moody and complicated composition from *The Ride*. D. Hidalgo is back on lead vocal and lead guitar. Estrada's drums introduce the title track from *The Neighborhood*, Los Lobos' musical portrait of ordinary people. Berlin plays an excellent saxophone solo during this extended performance.

Rosas then steps up to the microphone to sing "Maricela" from *Colossal Head* (1996) in Spanish. It really swings, featuring Berlin on saxophone and an incredible sea of percussion by Estrada and Bisetti. They pass the vocal duties around on the beautiful and transcendent "Tears of God" from *By the Light of the Moon* (1987). D. Hidalgo once again demonstrates his virtuoso guitar playing.

"Viking" is next from *This Time* (1999), featuring Conrad Lozano on bass and David Hidalgo's son Vincent Hidalgo sitting in on solo guitar. Los Lobos then perform "How Much Can I Do?" from their debut album *And a Time to Dance* (1983). It features D. Hidalgo on vocal and accordion and Perez on drums. This is followed by the haunting and rarely played "Kiko and the Lavender Moon" from *Kiko* (1992), featuring D. Hidalgo on vocal and accordion and Berlin on keyboards.

"Cumbia Raza" from *This Time* is another Spanish language composition written and sung by Rosas. Performed in extended form, it features several cross-rhythms operating at the same time, anchored by percussionists Estrada and Bisetti. Berlin takes a solo on saxophone, followed by Bisetti on congas, D. Hidalgo on timbales, Estrada on drums, and Perez on guitar.

Live at the Fillmore concludes with a magnificent cover of "What's Going On" by Marvin Gaye, performed as an encore. It's the perfect song for Los Lobos to play, rooted as they are in rhythm and blues and with an informed political consciousness. D. Hidalgo sings an impassioned lead vocal with plenty of help from Rosas. Berlin plays an equally inspired saxophone solo.

Live at the Fillmore comes with a bonus disc containing three tracks by Los Lobos performed acoustically: "Maricela," "Saint Behind the Glass" from *Kiko*, and "Guantanamera," the classic Cuban anthem by Jose Fernandez Diaz. I was in attendance at the show on Friday, July 30.

Bob Marley & the Wailers – *Live!*

Released: 1975
Recorded: July 18-19, 1975, Lyceum Theatre, London, England
Label: Island
Producer: Bob Marley & the Wailers, Steve Smith, Chris Blackwell
Personnel:
Bob Marley – guitar, vocals
Al Anderson – guitar
Tyrone Downie – keyboards
Aston "Family Man" Barrett – bass
Carlton Barrett – drums
Alvin "Seeco" Patterson – percussion
I Threes:
Rita Marley – vocals
Judy Mowatt – vocals
Marcia Griffiths – vocals

Natty Dread (1974) is considered by many to be Bob Marley's finest recording, arguably one of the greatest reggae albums of all time. It was Marley's first album without former Wailers Peter Tosh and Bunny Livingstone and the first released as Bob Marley & the Wailers. The rock solid rhythm section of bassist Aston "Family Man" Barrett and drummer Carlton Barrett remained in place, while Marley added the I Threes, a trio of female vocalists including his wife Rita, as well as additional instrumentation.

Live! was recorded by Bob Marley & the Wailers at the Lyceum Theatre in London on the final United Kingdom leg of their tour supporting *Natty Dread*. The addition of lead guitarist Al Anderson during the recording sessions for *Natty Dread* provided just enough of a bridge to the ears of rock'n'roll music audiences. An incredible, palpable energy cycles between the band and the audience at this show, resulting in one of the most memorable and compelling concert recordings one can enjoy.

The concert begins with a new composition, "Trenchtown Rock," a song about growing up in the poorest part of Kingston, Jamaica, and about the healing power of music. Anderson's bluesy guitar is featured. The band slows it down quite a bit for "Burnin' and Lootin'" from *Burnin'* (1973). This song is about the need to break the law in order to feed one's family. Tyrone Downie is featured on keyboards as are the I Threes on vocals.

The opening notes of "Them Belly Full (But We Hungry)," written by drummer C. Barrett for *Natty Dread*, are met with a roar of approval from the London audience. Anderson's guitar is featured, as well as the author on drums and brother A. Barrett on bass. "Lively Up Yourself," also from *Natty Dread*, is next, optimistically up-tempo when compared with the tunes that precede it. Marley is clearly enjoying himself trading vocals with the I Threes.

"No Woman No Cry" from *Natty Dread* elicits a group sing-along, the sheer volume of the audience eventually overwhelming the musicians' amplified instruments. When they can be heard, Anderson and Downie take tasteful solos on guitar and organ, respectively. It is this version that would be included on the Marley greatest hits compilation, *Legend*, released posthumously in 1984. The audience reacts wildly when Downie's organ signals the start of "I Shot the Sheriff" from *Burnin'*. The I Threes also add a great deal to the performance of this popular tune. The album and the concert conclude with the militant "Get Up, Stand Up," co-written by Marley and Tosh for *Burnin'*. The rhythm section, along with percussionist Alvin "Seeco" Patterson, is featured.

A bonus track, "Kinky Reggae," was added to the 2001 re-mastered edition of *Live!*. A deluxe edition, featuring both Lyceum Theatre shows in their entirety on two compact discs, was set to be released in February 2006, then postponed to May, then September, then December, and then delayed again. As of this writing, the deluxe edition has yet to be released.

Bob Marley & the Wailers – *Babylon by Bus*

Released: 1978
Recorded: June 13, 1976, Jaap Edenhal, Amsterdam, The Netherlands
       May 22, 1977, Falconer Theatre, Copenhagen, Denmark
       June 9, 1977, Top of the Pops, London, England
       June 25-27, 1978, Pavilion de Paris, Paris, France
Label: Tuff Gong
Producer: Bob Marley & the Wailers, Chris Blackwell, Jack Nuber
Personnel:
Bob Marley – guitar, vocals
Al Anderson – guitar
Tyrone Downie – keyboards
Aston "Family Man" Barrett – bass
Carlton Barrett – drums
Alvin "Seeco" Patterson – percussion
Junior Marvin – guitar
Earl "Wire" Lindo – keyboards
I Threes:
Rita Marley – vocals
Judy Mowatt – vocals
Marcia Griffiths – vocals

Babylon by Bus, probably the most influential live reggae album ever, was mostly recorded during the European leg of Bob Marley & the Wailers' *Kaya* tour in the spring/summer of 1978. Like *Live!* released three years prior, it highlights material from the band's history to that point and captures the unique energy of a Bob Marley & the Wailers concert.

The concert begins with Bob Marley greeting the audience, getting their boisterous approval, and "Positive Vibration" from *Rastaman Vibration* (1976). It's a mellow, feel-good tune, an affirmative note with which to begin. It features the Barrett brothers, Aston "Family Man" on bass and Carlton on drums. "Punky Reggae Party" from *Exodus* (1977) is next, featuring killer bass playing by A. Barrett and outstanding keyboard accentuations by Tyrone Downie throughout.

The title track from *Exodus* takes the concert to the next level, the band taking its time in laying down an infectious, extended groove. Downie's keyboard work is once again featured, as are the I Threes on vocals. "Stir it Up," from *Catch a Fire* (1973) was probably recorded on the previous spring tour. It is a seductive love song from Marley's early rock steady period that features Marley's vocal, Downie's keyboard solo, and C. Barrett's cowbell hijinx.

"Rat Race" from *Rastaman Vibration* is a jaundiced social commentary on the race that we all seem to be running, featuring the I Threes on vocals. "Concrete Jungle" from *Catch a Fire* is similarly about the difficulties inherent in living in the big city. It is my personal favorite among all of Marley's compositions, an almost perfect song. Al Anderson is featured on guitar solo.

The social commentary continues with "Kinky Reggae" from *Catch a Fire*, likely recorded in the spring of 1976. It is an excellent example of Marley's versatile singing style, also featuring the Barrett brothers' rhythm section. "Lively Up Yourself," reprised from the *Live!* set, is an extended jam featuring Anderson's guitar solo and call-and-response between Marley and the I Threes. The female vocalists are again featured on "Rebel Music (3 O'Clock Roadblock)," written by A. Barrett. Anderson's guitar solo on this track is a highlight of the album.

Next is "War"/"No More Trouble." "War," from *Rastaman Vibration*, contains lyrics taken from a United Nations speech given in 1963 by Haile Selassie I, the Ethiopian emperor considered the father of modern Rastafarianism. The latter, from *Catch a Fire*, takes on new significance when paired with the former. "Is This Love?" is a beautiful love song from *Kaya* that's done here in extended fashion, to the uproarious approval of the audience. Probably recorded in spring 1977, it features the I Threes. Al Anderson's guitar is featured on "Heathen" from *Exodus*, an eerie song about holy war and man's redemption. This leads to the final track on *Babylon by Bus*, "Jamming" also from *Exodus*, featuring Downie's percussive keyboard riffs. It's an exuberant, celebratory song, the title of which may or may not be a euphemism for another popular physical activity.

In February 1979, my wife, Janet, and I had the privilege of vacationing in Negril, Jamaica, with two other couples. We shared a beachfront villa that belonged to the author, Alex Haley. *Babylon by Bus* had just come out the previous year. I brought the cassette with me and it will forever be the soundtrack to our memorable time together. "Is This Love?" was a special favorite of the person to whom this book is dedicated.

Curtis Mayfield – *Curtis/Live*

Released: 1971
Recorded: January 20-25, 1971, The Bitter End, NYC
Label: Curtom
Producer: Curtis Mayfield
Personnel:
Curtis Mayfield – guitar, vocals
Craig McMullen – guitar
Joseph "Lucky" Scott – bass
"Master" Henry Gibson – congas, bongos, percussion
Tyrone McMullen – drums

Curtis/Live is a double album recorded by Curtis Mayfield at The Bitter End in New York City in January 1971. Mayfield performs songs from his recent debut solo album, rearrangements of songs originally performed by The Impressions, and a cover of "We've Only Just Begun." There are twelve tracks in all and four short raps by Mayfield on the politics of the day. It is considered by many to be one of the legendary concert albums of all time.

The album begins with "Mighty Mighty (Spade and Whitey)," from *The Young Mods' Forgotten Story* by The Impressions, released in 1969. Driven by percussionist "Master" Henry Gibson, it establishes a funky groove that is maintained throughout the performance. Mayfield then speaks briefly about the need for folks to get along and the humor he sees in then Vice President Spiro Agnew.

This is followed by a new composition, "I Plan to Stay a Believer." In it, Mayfield wonders how a society as technologically advanced as ours can be so slow to achieve racial harmony. But as the title suggests, he has hope. Mayfield maintains his optimistic outlook in an inspiring version of The Impressions' "We're a Winner," a hit single in 1968, from the album of the same name. Dealing directly with issues of black pride, it features the rhythm section of Joseph "Lucky" Scott on bass and Tyrone McMullen on drums.

Mayfield then speaks extemporaneously and obliquely about being an underground artist before performing a cover of The Carpenters' "We've

Only Just Begun," offering an alternate interpretation to the lyrics. Craig McMullen is featured on guitar, as he is on the gospel-tinged "People Get Ready," a signature song for Mayfield, from The Impressions' 1965 album of the same name. It's rearranged just a little; Mayfield's vocal performance is majestic.

Mayfield then introduces the next song, another new composition, "Stare and Stare." It's a slow, bluesy commentary on the isolated nature of the human condition. C. McMullen is once again featured on guitar, this time with the wah-wah pedal in effect. This is followed by an ultra-funky performance of "Check Out Your Mind" from the 1970 album of the same name by The Impressions.

An interesting up-tempo rearrangement of The Impressions' first big hit, "Gypsy Woman," from their eponymous 1963 debut album, is next, followed by three tunes from Mayfield's 1970 solo album, *Curtis*. "The Makings of You" is a beautiful ballad and one of Mayfield's most poetic compositions. After introducing the band, Mayfield launches into a compelling version of the controversial "We the People Who Are Darker than Blue." Henry Gibson provides a dynamic solo on percussion and the band swings during the break. "(Don't Worry) If There's a Hell Below We're All Going to Go" is an extended exercise in funk, featuring C. McMullen on guitar and Gibson on percussion.

Curtis/Live concludes with "Stone Junkie," another new song that Mayfield also produced for label-mate Ruby Jones in 1971. It is his take on the widespread use of controlled substances prevalent at the time, which had already become a destructive factor in ghetto life. His stance on drugs foreshadows his breakthrough soundtrack to *Superfly* (1972).

Curtis/Live was reissued on compact disc by Rhino Records in 2000. It includes two bonus tracks: "Superfly," which would appear on *Curtis in Chicago* (1973), and the edited, single version of "Mighty Mighty (Spade and Whitey)."

MC5 – *Kick Out the Jams*

Released: 1969
Recorded: October 30-31, 1968, Grande Ballroom, Detroit, Michigan
Label: Elektra
Producer: Jac Holzman, Bruce Botnick
Personnel:
Rob Tyner – vocals
Wayne Kramer – guitar, vocals
Fred "Sonic" Smith – guitar, vocals
Michael Davis – bass
Dennis Thompson – drums

Kick Out the Jams is the debut album by MC5, recorded at their home base, Detroit's Grande Ballroom, on Halloween and the night before in 1968. While several songs begin with inflammatory rhetoric, it was the opening line to the title track that stirred up the most controversy. Elektra Records executives objected to the word, "motherfucker," printed on the original release, and soon pulled it from stores. In retrospect, *Kick Out the Jams* is considered an important forerunner to punk rock music.

The album begins with rhythmic hand clapping and an introduction by "spiritual advisor" Brother J.C. Crawford and we're straight into the barely controlled chaos that is a cover of "Ramblin' Rose" by Fred Burch and Marijohn Wilkin. A basic blues version of a country song, it is sung falsetto by vocalist Rob Tyner, and we are immediately bombarded by the twin guitar attack of Fred "Sonic" Smith and Wayne Kramer.

The title track is next, language and all, a generational call for freedom and breaking down restrictions. Smith and Kramer excel on guitars, but it is Michael Davis's monumental bass line that drives the song. This is followed by "Come Together," basically an improvised jam, evocative of "I Can See For Miles" by The Who, with Tyner riffing on the vocals and the two guitarists playing off one another brilliantly.

"Rocket Reducer No. 62 (Rama Lama Fa Fa Fa)" is named for a brand of airplane glue favored by certain band members. Tyner calls for Kramer to start the song, and we're off. After a few verses, it's a deep space jam, guitarists wailing, with Dennis Thompson doing some remarkable work on the drums. If the energy seems James Brownian, it is no coincidence. Kramer would later be quoted as saying, "Our whole thing was based on James Brown. We listened to *Live at the Apollo* endlessly on acid."

"Borderline" is a short but powerful wall of sound, the only track on *Kick Out the Jams* with a pre-existing studio version. Crawford then takes the microphone again, exhorting the crowd with, "If you ask me, THIS is high society." The band then takes it down a few notches and plays "Motor City is Burning," a twelve bar blues about one of the worst riots in American history. MC5 is locked in, Tyner is at his best on vocals, the rhythm section is rock solid, the two guitarists trade solos effortlessly.

The extended "I Want You Right Now" starts out as a guitar tour-de-force, which brings both The Troggs' "Wild Thing" and Jimi Hendrix's "Voodoo Chile" to mind. But it is really a showcase for Tyner's vocal performance, which goes from almost an unaccompanied whisper to out-and-out screaming. *Kick Out the Jams* concludes with the even longer "Starship," a complicated composition in several parts. It begins as a rocker, but quickly spirals into deep space. Tyner recites the Sun Ra poem "There," from the liner notes to *Heliocentric Worlds of Sun Ra Vol. 2* (1965). The guitarists take over, jamming furiously to several consecutive crescendos, culminating in harmonizing feedback. Sweet.

Les McCann & Eddie Harris – *Swiss Movement*

Released: 1969
Recorded: June 21, 1969, Montreux Jazz Festival, Montreux, Switzerland
Label: Atlantic
Producer: Nesuhi Ertegun, Bob Emmer
Personnel:
Les McCann – piano, vocals
Eddie Harris – saxophone
Benny Bailey – trumpet
Leroy Vinegar – bass
Donald Dean – drums

Both the Les McCann trio and the Eddie Harris Quartet performed with great success at the Montreux Jazz Festival in June 1969. Later in the week, the two headliners wanted to get together to play. The two of them asked Benny Bailey, the great expatriate trumpeter, who also was at Montreux, to join them. Neither Harris nor Bailey had ever played or rehearsed with the Les McCann Trio before. They weren't even given the music! The resultant spontaneous funk explosion was recorded and released as *Swiss Movement* that same year.

The album was a hit as was the accompanying single, "Compared to What," written by Gene McDaniels, the first song of the set. An infectious tune from the start, pianist McCann does a little introduction with his left hand, joined by drummer Donald Dean on cowbell, and we're under way. Leroy Vinegar comes in on bass and the trio states the composition's theme, with a broad allusion to "Age of Aquarius" from *Hair*.

Enter Eddie Harris on saxophone, playing off McCann's steady chording, and McCann begins singing the somewhat controversial verses. After the third and fourth verses, Bailey blows in with muted trumpet solos. Then the entire band swings until the final verse, after which McCann takes a spirited piano solo with Harris blowing complementary figures on saxophone, leading to a saxophone solo of his own and the song's conclusion.

McCann then introduces the band and the next song, Harris's "Cold Duck Time," remarking that they'd never played it before. It starts with a bass introduction by Vinegar, but Harris is immediately there on saxophone to state the theme and set the tone, augmented by McCann's chording on piano. Harris then takes off on an extended, funky, growling saxophone solo, followed by Bailey with a response in the form of a hot, atonal trumpet solo. McCann cools things down with some down home funky piano soloing, after which Harris and Bailey reenter to take the tune home.

"Kathleen's Theme" is a gorgeous slow ballad introduced by McCann on piano. The rhythm section of Vinegar on bass and Dean on drums kicks the tempo a bit, and Harris, the only soloist, does his most oblique and complicated saxophone playing of the set, loudly acknowledged by the crowd. McCann's lush piano chording indicates the start of "You Got It in Your Soulness," the title of which largely speaks for itself. McCann solos first, setting the funky groove. Then he does a thing with his left hand that Vinegar mimics on bass, ushering in Harris and his saxophone solo. Then the bass thing again, and Bailey is wailing away on trumpet, eliciting loud affirmation from the audience. McCann then performs a percussive piano solo before restating the theme and bringing the song to conclusion.

Swiss Movement concludes with "The Generation Gap," which, despite its title, is a transcendent and introspective composition. The trio sets the spiritual tone and Harris takes the first extended solo, stating idea after idea, seamlessly incorporated into Bailey's soaring trumpet solo that follows. The composition gets momentarily funkified, before McCann takes over on piano, as if to bring some order to the chaos.

Swiss Movement was reissued in 1996 with a bonus track, "Kaftan," written by Vinegar, included.

The Meters – *Uptown Rulers: The Meters Live on the Queen Mary*

Released: 1992
Recorded: March 24, 1975, Venus and Mars party aboard the Queen Mary
Label: Rhino
Producer: Allen Toussaint, Marshall E. Sehorn
Personnel:
Arthur Neville – keyboards, vocals
Leo Nocentelli – guitar, vocals
Joseph Modeliste – drums, vocals
Cyril Neville – percussion, vocals
George Porter, Jr. – bass, vocals

Paul and Linda McCartney threw a lavish party on the Queen Mary, moored off Long Beach, California, in March 1975, to celebrate the release of their album *Venus and Mars*. The performers, flown in from New Orleans, were Professor Longhair and The Meters. The Meters' set was recorded, their first live collection, but not released until 1992, entitled *Uptown Rulers: The Meters Live on the Queen Mary*.

The concert begins with an improbable introduction by television actor Gary Owens, followed by the clattering cowbells and poly-rhythms that can only mean that "Fire on the Bayou" is in full effect. The title track of The Meters' 1975 album, it is done here in extended form, featuring Leo Nocentelli on guitar and Arthur Neville on keyboards. Next up is "Africa" from *Rejuvenation* (1974), about as funky as a song can be. George Porter, Jr. is outstanding on bass and the entire band is featured on vocals.

"It Ain't No Use," also from *Rejuvenation*, is, on the one hand, an extremely effective pop love song, but also a vehicle for extended jamming by the band. It features drummer Joseph Modeliste and percussionist Cyril Neville churning up furious rhythms behind Nocentelli's lead guitar, as well as a bass solo by Porter punctuated by Modeliste's cowbell attack. They slow things down several notches with a soulful cover of "Make It With You" by Bread. While their motivation for covering this song is unknown and dubious at best, they nonetheless do a creditable job with it. Nocentelli is outstanding on the guitar, Porter on the bass.

The Meters then perform a medley. They begin with their classic instrumental, "Cissy Strut" from their eponymous 1969 debut album. They then glide effortlessly into "Cardova," also from *The Meters*, featuring fierce riffing on guitar by Nocentelli. This segues into The Isley Brothers' "It's Your Thing," featuring Modeliste on snare and cymbals. Finally, they put their own trademark sound to Stephen Stills's "Love the One You're With," featuring A. Neville on organ.

A. Neville then addresses the audience and introduces the band, after which they launch into another medley. First, they get in touch with their New Orleans roots with "Rocking Pneumonia and the Boogie Woogie Flu." Next is a cover of Huey "Piano" Smith's "Something You Got," which segues into a great interpretation of "I Know (You Don't Love Me No More)," the 1961 single by Barbara George. They end the medley with "Everybody Loves a Lover," the 1958 hit single for Doris Day, another radical selection. Nocentelli is tastefully outstanding throughout.

With "Liar," a cover of a Russ Ballard composition, a hit single for Three Dog Night in 1971, the band demonstrates its jazzier inclinations. The song is tailor made to highlight Nocentelli's guitar playing. A. Neville then dedicates "Mardi Gras Mambo" to Paul and Linda McCartney. This song was recorded in 1954 by The Hawketts, a group of New Orleans high school kids, featuring A. Neville on vocals. It was released on Chess records and became a rhythm and blues hit, a staple at the Mardi Gras in New Orleans, and the genesis of The Meters and The Neville Brothers.

Uptown Rulers: The Meters Live on the Queen Mary concludes with "Hey Pocky A-way" from *Rejuvenation*, performed as an encore. Toward the end, they break it down, doing call-and-response with the title and other invented phrases. Unfortunately, this track fades out. The Grateful Dead covered "Hey Pocky A-way" in concert twenty-five times from 1987 to 1990. Just saying.

Joni Mitchell – *Shadows and Light*

Released: 1980
Recorded: September 9, 1979, Santa Barbara County Bowl, Santa Barbara,
　　　　California
Label: Asylum
Producer: Joni Mitchell
Personnel:
Joni Mitchell – guitar, vocals
Pat Metheny – guitar
Jaco Pastorius – bass
Don Alias – drums
Lyle Mays – keyboards
Michael Brecker – saxophone
The Persuasions – vocals

Shadows and Light is a double album recorded by Joni Mitchell in Santa Barbara, California, in 1979, supporting her *Mingus* album, recorded the same year. For the concert, Mitchell assembled an all-star line-up of musicians, who bring a great deal of energy to these performances. The initial single compact disc release omitted "Black Crow," "Don's Solo," and "Free Man in Paris" due to time restrictions.

The concert begins with "Introduction," a short taped audio collage of not so random sounds, including Mitchell talking about "shadows and light," dialogue from the movie *Rebel Without a Cause*, and doo-wop singing. The first real song is "In France They Kiss on Main Street" from *The Hissing of Summer Lawns* (1975). Mitchell is in fine voice and the band sounds incredible on this tune about growing up in a small town in the '50s. Pat Metheny is featured on lead guitar.

They slow things down considerably with "Edith and the Kingpin" from the same studio release. A complicated composition, it's the story of a gangster's new moll arriving at his home town. "Coyote" from *Hejira* (1976) is next, a personal favorite. Is this one about nature vs. big city living? Or is it about Robbie Robertson or maybe Sam Shepard? I don't know, but it's a great performance of a great song, featuring Jaco Pastorius on bass.

This is followed by "Goodbye Pork Pie Hat" written by Charles Mingus in 1959 as an elegy for Lester Young, for which Mitchell composed lyrics for *Mingus*. It features Michael Brecker on saxophone. "The Dry Cleaner from Des Moines," another Mingus/Mitchell collaboration from *Mingus* features Mitchell's scat vocalizing and Brecker's dynamic extended saxophone solo.

"Amelia" is next, from *Hejira*, a beautiful song that interweaves a story of a desert journey with that of Amelia Earhart, the famous aviator. It is largely a solo performance by Mitchell, accompanying herself on guitar, with a tasteful guitar solo by Metheny at the end. This continues as "Pat's Solo," an opportunity for Metheny to further showcase his virtuoso guitar playing.

The title track from *Hejira* follows, inspired by a cross-country trip Mitchell took by herself. It is another one of her densely complicated compositions, featuring Brecker, whom she names in the song, on saxophone, but especially Pastorius on bass. "Black Crow" from *Hejira* is a sad reflection hiding in an up-tempo, feel-good song. In it, Mitchell likens herself to a ragged, black crow due to her frenetic touring schedule.

This is followed by "Don's Solo," a drum solo by Don Alias. "Dreamland" is next, from *Don Juan's Reckless Daughter* (1977). It is a lengthy poem full of historical references, which is recited by Mitchell against a sea of percussion created by Alias.

"Free Man in Paris" from *Court and Spark* (1974) is supposedly about music agent David Geffen, Mitchell's good friend. It features Lyle Mays on keyboards and Brecker on saxophone. Mitchell then introduces the band, after which they perform "Furry Sings the Blues" from *Hejira*. It concerns Mitchell's visit to Furry Lewis's apartment on Beale Street in Memphis, Tennessee, in 1976. Lewis despised the song and demanded that Mitchell pay him royalties.

The Persuasions are featured on backing vocals on the next two tunes. A cover of Frankie Lymon & the Teenagers' classic "Why Do Fools Fall in Love," a hit single in 1956, absolutely rocks out, featuring Brecker on saxophone solo. In contrast, the title track from *Shadows and Light* is transcendent in nature, with The Persuasions backing Mitchell virtually unaccompanied, save for the church-like organ played by Mays.

"God Must Be a Boogie Man" from *Mingus* is a minimalist groove featuring Metheny on guitar and Pastorius on bass and the entire band singing the song's title in call-and-response with Mitchell. *Shadows and Light* concludes with "Woodstock," Mitchell's iconic 1969 single, a favorite of aging hippies everywhere. She performs it here with a very lean arrangement, accompanied only by Metheny's guitar.

"Why Do Fools Fall In Love" was one of the songs I selected to be in my book, *The 100 Greatest Rock'n'Roll Songs Ever* in 2000.

The Thelonious Monk Quartet with John Coltrane – *At Carnegie Hall*

Released: 2005
Recorded: November 29, 1957, Carnegie Hall, NYC
Label: Blue Note
Producer: Michael Cuscuna, T.S. Monk
Personnel:
Thelonious Monk – piano
John Coltrane – saxophone
Ahmed Abdul-Malik – bass
Shadow Wilson – drums

Thelonious Monk was born in North Carolina in 1917. In 1922, the family moved to New York City, where he started paying the piano at age six, eavesdropping on his sister's lessons. In the 1940s, he was the house pianist at Minton's Playhouse, a Manhattan club that was crucial in the development of be-bop, bringing Monk in close contact with Dizzy Gillespie, Charlie Christian, Kenny Clarke, Charlie Parker, and Miles Davis.

In 1944, Monk made his first studio recording with the Coleman Hawkins Quartet. He made his first recordings as leader for Blue Note Records in 1947. Because he refused to testify against Bud Powell in a narcotics bust, Monk's cabaret card was revoked and he could not perform in New York City for a number of years. He signed with Riverside Records in 1955 and released the critically acclaimed *Brilliant Corners*, featuring saxophonist Sonny Rollins, the following year.

When his cabaret card was restored, Monk resumed his career with a landmark six-month residency at the Five Spot Cafe in New York City beginning in June 1957, leading a quartet with John Coltrane on tenor saxophone, Wilbur Ware on bass, and Shadow Wilson on drums. A recording of the quartet (with Ahmed Abdul-Malik in place of Ware) performing at Carnegie Hall in November, previously rumored to exist, was indeed recorded by Voice of America, rediscovered in the collection of the Library of Congress in 2005, and released on Blue Note Records.

At Carnegie Hall captures two sets by the quartet, an early set and an incomplete late set. The early set begins with Monk's solo piano introduction to "Monk's Mood," on which Monk and Coltrane play in duet, demonstrating their confidence and ability to communicate musically. In contrast to the somber mood set by the opener, "Evidence" simply swings. Monk's quirky intro leads to a wonderful melodic solo from Coltrane, followed by a solo of his own.

"Crepuscule with Nellie" is an incredible tune, a highlight in this collection. An introspective piano introduction is followed by unconscious interplay between the two soloists. Coltrane's fills on the melody that lead to his solo are remarkable, and his solo itself is brilliant. "Nutty," aptly titled, features great cymbal work by drummer Wilson before Coltrane and Monk trade solos. Although "Epistrophe," written with Clarke, is one of Monk's more challenging compositions, Coltrane rises to the challenge and keeps up with the author in grand style. That ends the early set.

The late set definitely has a late show feel to it. The set kicks off with "Bye-Ya," on which Coltrane and then Monk stretch out with extended solos, as the band gets more comfortable. This is followed by a lengthy cover of "Sweet and Lovely," the ballad popularized by Guy Lombardo and his Royal Canadians in 1931. The most arranged tune on the album, they start out slowly, then break into double-time, then return to the original tempo. Coltrane and Monk each get two solos along the way.

"Blue Monk," one of Monk's signature tunes, is next. Coltrane plays harmony against Monk's melody and then launches into a solo that definitely foreshadows where he was going musically. Not to be outdone, Monk follows with a dense, complicated solo of his own. *At Carnegie Hall* concludes with an incomplete alternate version of "Epistrophe."

Van Morrison – *It's Too Late to Stop Now*

Released: 1974
Recorded: May 24-27, 1973, The Troubadour, Los Angeles, California
June 29, 1973, Civic Auditorium, Santa Monica, California
July 23-24, 1973, The Rainbow, London, England
Label: Warner Bros.
Producer: Van Morrison, Ted Templeman
Personnel:
Van Morrison – vocals
Teressa "Terry" Adams – cello
Bill Atwood – trumpet, vocals
Nancy Ellis – viola
Tom Halpin – violin
David Hayes – bass, vocals
Tim Kovatch – violin
Jef Labes – piano, organ
John Platania – guitar, vocals
Nathan Rubin – violin
Jack Schroer – saxophones, tambourine, vocals
Dahaud Shaar (David Shaw) – drums, vocals

It's Too Late to Stop Now is a double live album by Van Morrison recorded during a three-month tour in 1973 with his eleven-piece band, The Caledonia Soul Orchestra. It is considered by many to represent Morrison's greatest phase as a live performer. The songs chosen go back to his days with Them, including "Gloria" and "Here Comes the Night." His first solo hit, "Brown Eyed Girl," was performed, but didn't appear until a re-mastered version of the album was reissued in 2008. Since Morrison allowed no studio overdubbing, "Moondance" is excluded due to one wrong note on guitar.

Morrison's song selection also includes covers of tunes by musicians who greatly influenced him: Bobby "Blue" Bland ("Ain't Nothing You Can Do"); Ray Charles ("I Believe to My Soul"); Sam Cooke ("Bring It On Home to Me"); two songs by Sonny Boy Williamson II ("Help Me" and

"Take Your Hands Out of My Pocket"); and Willie Dixon's "I Just Want to Make Love to You," popularized by Muddy Waters.

The album opens with the aforementioned "Ain't Nothing You Can Do," performed in a bouncy, soulful manner, featuring Jef Labes on piano, David Hayes on bass, and the horn section. "And it's ever present everywhere," chants Morrison, as the band rocks out on "Warm Love." "Into the Mystic," is a highlight, with its soothing tempo and spiritual subject matter, Morrison demonstrating incredible vocal range. The string section excels, including John Platania on guitar. This song contains the lyric that is the album's title.

The up-tempo "These Dreams of You" features Bill Atwood on trumpet and Jack Schroer on saxophone. I have always thought the latter, credited with horn arrangements, is the unsung hero of this album. Morrison and the band more than do justice to the soulful Ray Charles tune mentioned above. "I've Been Working" features an outstanding Schroer saxophone solo. "Help Me," a hit single for Williamson in 1963 and based on the instrumental "Green Onions" by Booker T. & the MG's from the year before, features Labes on piano, a guitar solo from Platania, and some scat singing by Morrison.

"Domino," a hit single for Morrison in 1970, is another highlight. A tribute to Fats Domino, it is brilliantly performed here, greater than the original in my opinion, featuring the mighty horn section and Platania on guitar. Morrison covers Willie Dixon in deliberate fashion, with plenty of stop time, featuring Platania on slide guitar solo and a little impromptu audience participation.

Morrison puts his personal stamp on Cooke's classic hit from 1962, featuring another great saxophone solo from Schroer. "St. Dominic's Preview," an intensely personal song about Morrison's life and the situation in his native Northern Ireland, features the strings. The second Williamson cover mentioned above is performed as a straight ahead blues, Hayes leading the way on bass, Schroer inspired on saxophone.

After calling out for "water," Morrison's incredible performance of "Listen to the Lion" ends in hushed quiet, the audience audibly moved. It is one of his greatest compositions, evocative of his *Astral Weeks* material. Indeed, Morrison used it as an encore at the Hollywood Bowl in 2008 at the concerts commemorating the 40th anniversary of his seminal 1968 album.

This is followed by the two Them songs. "Here Comes the Night," by Them producer Bert Berns, features the strings. "Gloria," one of Morrison's trademark tunes, a hit single in 1964 and a garage band staple ever since, is performed in rousing fashion. "Caravan," a personal favorite, features more scatting from Morrison and the ubiquitous Schroer on saxophone. After Morrison introduces the band, *It's Too Late to Stop Now* concludes with the Morrison classic, "Cyprus Avenue" from *Astral Weeks*. At song's end, Morrison announces to the audience, "It's too late to stop now!"

"Caravan" from *Moondance* (1970), was one of the songs I selected to be in my book, *The 100 Greatest Rock'n'Roll Songs Ever* in 2000.

Van Morrison – *Astral Weeks Live at the Hollywood Bowl*

Released: 2009
Recorded: November 7-8, 2008, Hollywood Bowl, Los Angeles, California
Label: Listen to the Lion
Producer: Van Morrison
Personnel:
Van Morrison – guitar, harmonica, organ, vocals
Jay Berliner – guitar
Tony Fitzgibbon – violin, viola
Roger Kellaway – piano
David Hayes – bass
Bobby Ruggiero – drums
Liam Bradley – percussion
Paul Moran – harpsichord, trumpet
Richie Buckley – flute, saxophone
Sarah Jory – guitar
Nancy Ellis – violin
Terry Adams – cello
Michael Graham – cello
John Densmore – tambourine
John Platania – guitar
Bianca Thornton – vocals

Astral Weeks Live at the Hollywood Bowl was recorded on the occasion of the 40th anniversary of the release of *Astral Weeks* in 1968. Guitarist Jay Berliner, who appeared on the original album, was a member of the band backing Van Morrison. With only one rehearsal prior to the concerts and Morrison, as producer, insisting on no post-production, the album sounds exactly as it was heard by those in attendance. Morrison has stated that he very much likes the sound of the recording.

The concerts were divided into two sets, the first half consisting of Morrison and the band performing some of his popular concert favorites, such as "Wavelength," "Moondance," "Brown Eyed Girl," and "Gloria." The second set featured the songs from *Astral Weeks*, performed in a different sequence than on the original album. On both evenings, Morrison returned to the stage for an encore of "Listen to the Lion."

The title track opens the set, a little faster, but just as beautiful as the original. Morrison allows his supporting players to shine: Berliner on guitar, Richie Buckley on flute, and Tony Fitzgibbon's violin and viola solos. After "Beside You," featuring more great guitar work from Berliner, comes "Slim Slow Slider," the last track on the original album, moved to the third spot to avoid ending on so desolate a note. The "I Start Breakin' Down" part is almost unbearable.

"Sweet Thing" is next, in an extended swinging groove, my favorite cut on the album. "The Way Young Lovers Do," on the other hand, is short and almost true to the original. "Cyprus Avenue," the centerpiece of the original studio album, struts majestically into "You Come Walkin' Down," the guitars leading the way. Morrison slows it down and delivers his best vocal performance on "Ballerina," an absolutely beautiful love song, and then closes with "Madame George," a close second. A great ending to a great performance. Morrison was a very young man when he wrote these songs. Forty years later he proves himself to be an artist who fully understands his material.

Morrison began a week of concerts and television appearances in New York City on February 27, 2009, to promote the live album. He performed songs from *Astral Weeks* as well as some of his other classic tunes at the WaMu Theater in Madison Square Garden and at the Beacon Theater. He performed "Sweet Thing" on Jimmy Fallon's first show as host of "Late Night with Jimmy Fallon" on March 2.

Astral Weeks was one of the albums I selected to be in my book, *The 100 Greatest Rock'n'Roll Albums Ever* in 2009. In retrospect, I wish I had said that it was not only one of the greatest albums ever released, it was one of the greatest artistic achievements of the latter half of the 20th century. There, I've said it. "Caravan" from *Moondance* (1970), performed on November 8 but not included on the album, was one of the songs I selected to be in my book, *The 100 Greatest Rock'n'Roll Songs Ever* in 2000.

Muddy Waters – *At Newport 1960*

Released: 1960
Recorded: July 3, 1960, Newport Jazz Festival, Newport, Rhode Island
Label: Chess
Producer: Leonard Chess
Personnel:
Muddy Waters – guitar, vocals
Otis Spann – piano, vocals
Pat Hare – guitar
James Cotton – harmonica
Andrew Stevenson – bass
Francis Clay – drums

McKinley Morganfield, known as Muddy Waters, was born on a plantation on the Mississippi Delta around 1914. He started on harmonica, but by age 17 he was playing guitar at parties, emulating Son House and Robert Johnson. In 1941, he was recorded by Alan Lomax on behalf of the Library of Congress. In 1943, he moved permanently to Chicago, where at first he backed other musicians, such as Big Bill Broonzy. He got his first electric guitar in 1945, largely to be heard above the noisy crowds in clubs.

In 1946, Muddy Waters signed with Aristocrat Records, which was to become Chess Records, and had early hits with "I Can't Be Satisfied," "I Feel Like Going Home," and "Rollin' Stone." By 1953, he was recording with one of the most acclaimed blues bands in history: Little Walter Jacobs on harmonica, Jimmy Rogers on guitar, Otis Spann on piano, Willie Dixon on bass, and Elga Edmonds on drums.

Muddy Waters's performances across the United States and Europe in the 1950s did a great deal to popularize blues music to a much broader audience, especially to white listeners. Often said to be one of the first live blues albums, *At Newport 1960* was performed and recorded by Muddy Waters and his band at the Newport Jazz Festival, further spreading the word. Although it never charted, it received critical acclaim and proved extremely influential to generations of future recording artists.

The album opens with the then-unreleased "I Got My Brand on You" written by Dixon, first recorded one month prior. A slow blues, it features Spann on piano and James Cotton on harmonica. Next is Dixon's "I'm Your Hoochie Coochie Man," one of Muddy Waters's signature tunes, a hit single in 1954, with its trademark stop time refrain. "Baby Please Don't Go," although credited to Muddy Waters on the album, is actually a cover of a Big Joe Williams tune, first recorded in 1935.

The band really cooks on "Soon Forgotten," a slow, plaintive blues by James Burke "St. Louis Jimmy" Oden. Spann, Cotton, and Muddy Waters himself excel on piano, harmonica, and guitar, respectively. This is followed by Dixon's somewhat suggestive "Tiger in Your Tank," not, strictly speaking, a blues number, but close enough, featuring Cotton's harmonica.

During the performance of Dixon's "I Feel So Good," which highlights Francis Clay on drums, Muddy Waters apparently does a series of hip swings, eliciting howls from the audience. He continues doing "Elgin movements," named for Chicago's Elgin National Watch Company, during "I've Got My Mojo Working," another signature tune, a hit single in 1957. When he does a jitterbug at the microphone, the crowd goes wild. *At Newport 1960* concludes with "Goodbye Newport Blues," spontaneously written by poet Langston Hughes and sung by Spann.

Muddy Waters was the most important blues artist to emerge in post-war America. He was a gifted singer, guitarist, songwriter, and inventor of the electric blues band. He absorbed the musical influences of the Delta and was a force in creating the Chicago blues style. The depth of Muddy Waters's influence on blues as well as rock'n'roll music is incalculable. In 2001, MCA Records released a re-mastered version of *At Newport 1960*, including three additional tracks.

Muddy Waters – *Muddy "Mississippi" Waters – Live*

Released: 1979
Recorded: March 18, 1977, Masonic Auditorium, Detroit, Michigan
           August 25-26, 1978, Harry Hope's, Cary, Illinois
Label: Blue Sky
Producer: Johnny Winter
Personnel:
Muddy Waters – guitar, vocals
Johnny Winter – guitar
Bob Margolin – guitar
Luther "Guitar Jr." Johnson – guitar
Calvin Jones – bass
Willie "Big Eyes" Smith – drums
Pinetop Perkins – piano
Jerry Portnoy – harmonica
Charles Calmese – bass
James Cotton – harmonica

Muddy Waters left Chess Records in 1975 and went looking for a new label. He signed with Blue Sky Records, home to Johnny Winter, who was eager to produce records with his hero. Muddy Waters recorded his last four albums with Blue Sky, delivering performances reminiscent of his glory days in the 1950s. *Hard Again* (1977) won him international acclaim; *I'm Ready* (1978) reunited him with early band mates; *Muddy "Mississippi" Waters – Live* (1979) testified to the brilliance of his playing and singing without studio gimmicks. All three won Grammys. *King Bee* (1981) was a fitting final album, featuring Muddy Waters in a variety of musical settings.

Muddy "Mississippi" Waters – Live was recorded in 1977 and 1978 in the Midwest with two different bands, guitarist Bob Margolin, pianist Pinetop Perkins, and drummer Willie "Big Eyes" Smith appearing in both. There are only seven tracks. The album begins with "Mannish Boy," one of Muddy Waters's signature tunes, a single in 1955. Both an arrangement of and an answer to Bo Diddley's "I'm a Man," it features Winter sharing the vocals with Muddy Waters and providing the guitar fills, as well as James Cotton on harmonica.

This is followed by "She's Nineteen Years Old," a single in 1958, a slow blues about the difficulties inherent with dating a much younger woman, which highlights Muddy Waters's vocal prowess and incredible slide guitar playing. Next is a cover of Sonny Boy Williamson's "Nine Below Zero," featuring Perkins on piano, Cotton on harmonica, and Charles Calmese, from Cotton's band, on bass. The blues can be very cold, indeed.

"Streamline Woman," another slow blues, a single way back in 1948, follows. Once again, Muddy Waters is featured on vocal and absolutely dazzles on slide guitar, blowing everyone away. The audience goes wild. "Howling Wolf" is cut from the same cloth, a slow blues showcasing Muddy Waters's vocal and slide guitar. In this instance, he trades guitar licks with Winter.

Another of Muddy Waters's signature tunes, "Baby Please Don't Go," a single in 1953, is done as a mid-tempo shuffle. It features Luther "Guitar Jr." Johnson on guitar and Jerry Portnoy on harmonica. It is actually a cover of a 1935 single by Joe Williams, from whom Muddy Waters learned the song. *Muddy "Mississippi" Waters – Live* concludes, much too quickly, with an extended performance of "Deep Down in Florida" from *Hard Again*. It's done as a loping, lazy blues, giving the musicians a chance to stretch out. It features Margolin on guitar solo, Winter on slide guitar solo, Cotton on harmonica solo, and Perkins on piano solo. Muddy Waters mentions Gainesville, Florida, where he met his third wife, Marva, in 1973.

In 2003, *Muddy "Mississippi" Waters – Live* was reissued as a two compact disc set, the first disc containing these same seven tracks. The second disc has eleven additional tracks, including Muddy Waters classics "Trouble No More," "Champagne & Reefer," Willie Dixon's "Hoochie Coochie Man," "She Moves Me," and "Got My Mojo Working," written by Preston Foster.

Nirvana – *MTV Unplugged in New York*

Released: 1994
Recorded: November 18, 1993, Sony Music Studios, NYC
Label: DGC
Producer: Alex Coletti, Scott Litt, Nirvana
Personnel:
Kurt Cobain – guitar, vocals
Krist Novoselic – bass, guitar, accordion
Dave Grohl – drums, bass, vocals
Pat Smear – guitar
Lori Goldston – cello
Cris Kirkwood – bass, vocals
Curt Kirkwood – guitar

MTV Unplugged in New York is an album by Nirvana featuring an acoustic performance taped for the television series *MTV Unplugged*, which first aired on the cable television network MTV on December 14, 1993. It was the first Nirvana album released after the death of songwriter/singer/guitarist Kurt Cobain. As opposed to the traditional practice on the television series, Nirvana played a set-list comprised mainly of lesser-known material and cover versions of songs by David Bowie, The Vaselines, and the Meat Puppets.

Nirvana is augmented by guitarist Pat Smear and cellist Lori Goldston, who had been touring with the band. Despite the premise of the television show, Cobain insisted on running his acoustic guitar through his amplifier. This can most clearly be heard during the performance of "The Man Who Sold the World." A fake box was placed in front of the amplifier to disguise it as a monitor.

The first song performed is "About a Girl" from Nirvana's first album *Bleach* (1989). It was released as a single in 1994, backed with "Something in the Way." The version here features Smear on guitar. Next is the 1992 single, "Come as You Are," the only "hit" included on *MTV Unplugged in New York*. It is one of Cobain's finest vocal performances on the album.

In light of his suicide by self-inflicted gunshot wound in 1994, hearing Cobain sing, "I swear I don't have a gun" has quite a sting to it.

This is followed by "Jesus Doesn't Want Me for a Sunbeam," a cover of a song by The Vaselines, a parody on the Christian children's hymn, "I'll Be a Sunbeam." Bassist Krist Novoselic is featured on accordion, so drummer Dave Grohl handles the bass guitar duties. "The Man Who Sold the World" is a fabulous cover of the David Bowie song from the 1970 album of the same name. It features Goldston on cello.

"Pennyroyal Tea" is from Nirvana's final studio album, *In Utero* (1993). The title refers to an ineffective herbal abortive agent. It is a very moving solo performance by Cobain on vocal and guitar. Also from *In Utero*, the melodic "Dumb" features Goldston's cello. "Polly" from *Nevermind* (1991) features Grohl on bass and backing vocal. "On a Plain" and "Something in the Way" are also from *Nevermind* and feature Goldston on cello.

At this point, Cris and Curt Kirkwood of the Meat Puppets, with whom Nirvana was touring, are called up onstage to perform three of their songs from *Meat Puppets II* (1984) with the band. "Plateau" and "Oh Me" feature the outstanding guitar interplay among Smear, Novoselic, and both Kirkwoods. "Lake of Fire" features Curt Kirkwood on guitar and Cris Kirkwood on bass and backing vocal.

"All Apologies" from *In Utero* was released as a double single, along with "Rape Me," in 1993. It is an intensely personal song, sung with much feeling, dedicated by Cobain to his wife Courtney Love and their daughter, Frances Bean Cobain. The album concludes with "Where Did You Sleep Last Night," a traditional folk song dating back to at least the 1870s and popularized by Huddie Ledbetter, also known as Lead Belly, in the 1940s. It is a remarkable performance by the band and by Cobain in particular on vocal.

MTV Unplugged in New York was released on digital video disc in 2007. It features the entire taping, including the two songs ("Something in the Way" and "Oh Me") excluded from the broadcast version. Also included are the five songs taped during the rehearsal prior to the performance: "Come as You Are," "Polly," "Plateau," "Pennyroyal Tea," and "The Man Who Sold the World."

NRBQ – *Diggin' Uncle Q*

Released: 1988
Recorded: April 16, 1987, Toad's Place, New Haven, Connecticut
    April 17-18, 1987, Lupo's Heartbreak Hotel, Providence, Rhode
        Island
Label: Rounder
Producer: Terry Adams, Joey Spampinato, Bill Scheniman
Personnel:
Terry Adams – piano, clarinet, vocals
Joey Spampinato – bass, guitar, vocals
Al Anderson – guitar, bass, vocals
Tom Ardolino – drums, vocals
Jim Hochanadel – saxophone, harmonica
Donn Adams – tambourine

Diggin' Uncle Q was NRBQ's second consecutive live release, recorded in New England in April 1987. The band went to some lengths to keep fans unaware of their intention to record live. They did no advertising, and even appeared in Providence as an opening act on the night before they were scheduled to headline. NRBQ is captured here at their best, in front of a live audience, the first seven tracks recorded in New Haven and the last seven in Providence. The set includes a couple of fan favorites, but otherwise features material that was new at the time.

The concert begins with "It Comes to Me Naturally," written and sung by guitarist Al Anderson, a personal favorite. Terry Adams performs a typically quirky piano solo. This is followed by another Anderson composition, "What a Nice Way to Go," on which he delivers an impassioned vocal performance complaining about his woman who is wearing him out. Jim Hochanadel makes a guest appearance on saxophone solo.

The jazzy, swinging "That's Neat, That's Nice," by pianist Terry Adams is next. Anderson, one of the great underrated guitarists on the planet, is featured with an understated but brilliant solo. Hochanadel sits in with another saxophone solo and Tom Ardolino excels on drums. The band does a cover of "Won't You Come Over to My House," written in 1906 by Harry Williams and Egbert Van Alstyne. Sung by bassist Joey Spampinato with help from the rest, it's got a strange nursery rhyme feel to it, just a little creepy. Anderson's guitar solo is appropriately odd.

Speaking of creepy, the title "Daddy Loves Mommy-O/Who Does Daddy-O Love?" pretty much speaks for itself. This rockabilly number features author Adams on vocal and two smoking hot guitar solos by Anderson. In honor of playing in Anderson's home town, NRBQ next perform a brief cover of "My Hometown," written in 1934 by Clara Edwards. Anderson handles the vocals while Adams carries the tune chording the piano.

The last track recorded in Connecticut is a bizarre karaoke version of Billy Joel's "Just the Way You Are," sung, in turn, by each of the band members to a prerecorded instrumental track. "You're So Beautiful" is a gorgeous love song with vocal, whistling, and guitar solo by Anderson. The popular "I Got a Rocket in My Pocket," featuring Adams on vocal and piano, is next. Anderson performs a wild guitar solo, as if he had an incendiary device in his pants.

Anderson's humorous "Macho Maria," about one tough chick, is a vehicle for him to stretch out a bit on guitar. Donn Adams is featured on tambourine. "Some Kind of Blues" is a clever composition by T. Adams that isn't quite a blues, but a close cousin, with interesting changes. It features Hochanadel sitting in on harmonica. "Crazy Eights," also written by T. Adams, is an instrumental composition featuring him on clarinet and Anderson on guitar.

On "Trouble at the Henhouse," an instrumental composition written by Spampinato, he plays guitar and Anderson picks up the bass. *Diggin' Uncle Q* concludes with yet another instrumental tune, "Scarlet Ribbons," the standard written in 1949 by Evelyn Danzig and Jack Segal. It starts with a piano introduction by T. Adams, which he hands to Anderson to continue on guitar, and who hands it back. It's a beautiful tune, and a great example of how NRBQ adapts the American songbook and makes it their own.

Graham Parker & the Rumour – *Live Sparks*

Released: 1979
Recorded: April 9, 1979, The Old Waldorf, San Francisco, California
          April 28, 1979, Park West, Chicago, Illinois
Label: Arista
Producer: KSAN-FM, San Francisco, WXRT-FM, Chicago
Personnel:
Graham Parker – guitar, vocals
Brinsley Schwarz – guitar, vocals
Martin Belmont – guitar, vocals
Bob Andrews – keyboards, vocals
Steve Goulding – drums, vocals
Andrew Bodnar – bass

In 1979, Graham Parker & the Rumour released *Squeezing Out Sparks* to critical acclaim and commercial success. To keep the interest level high, Arista Records released a limited edition promotional album called *Live Sparks*, containing the same songs in the same order plus two additional tracks, recorded on tour in April in San Francisco and Chicago. In 1996, Arista released *Squeezing Out Sparks* + *Live Sparks*, containing both.

The arrangements on *Live Sparks* are true to the studio original, with a couple of exceptions. What is immediately evident, however, is the urgency of Parker's vocal performances, and how he throws himself completely into each song. To mirror *Squeezing Out Sparks*, *Live Sparks* begins with "Discovering Japan." It's a mid-tempo rocker reflecting Parker's extensive traveling as a musician.

"Local Girls" is next, a personal favorite, an acerbic look at the women of London. Parker's vocal is appropriately biting; Brinsley Schwarz and Bob Andrews are featured on guitar and organ, respectively. In "Nobody Hurts You," Parker tells us that "Nobody hurts you harder than yourself," a profound truth. Schwarz is featured on lead guitar.

What can one say about "You Can't Be Too Strong," from which *Squeezing Out Sparks* derives its title? Whether you think Parker comes down on the wrong side of the abortion issue or not, one cannot deny the sheer power of the lyrics and the singer's artistic balladry. Each verse is more brutal than the last, even more poignant performed live. "Passion is No Ordinary Word" is Parker's commentary on the phoniness of sexual conquest, featuring passionate guitar soloing by Schwarz.

With an introduction by Parker, the band next leaps into the rocking "Saturday Night is Dead." Andrews is featured on piano, Schwarz on guitar. They slow things down on "Love Gets You Twisted," another jaundiced look at relationships. Parker warns, "Love gets you twisted, screw yourself up." Once again, Schwarz is featured on lead guitar.

"Protection" is next, an apocalyptical view of the world couched in a lilting reggae rhythm. The backing vocalists are featured as Parker delivers a lead vocal that is a precursor to rap music. This is followed by "Waiting for the UFO's," Parker's take on the inevitability of intelligent life on other planets. The last "official" track on *Live Sparks* is "Don't Get Excited," which differs from the original in that it ends with a climactic rave-up led by guitarist Schwarz which drives the audience wild.

Without missing a beat, the band goes into the first of the two additional tracks, a great cover of the Jackson 5's "I Want You Back," here entitled, "I Want You Back (Alive)." If I ever write a book about the greatest cover tunes ever recorded, this will be among them. The album concludes with "Mercury Poisoning," purportedly Parker's bittersweet farewell to his former record label. These two tracks were originally issued as a seven-inch single that was included with early copies of the album.

Squeezing Out Sparks was one of the albums I selected to be in my book, *The 100 Greatest Rock'n'Roll Albums Ever* in 2009.

Parliament – *Live: P-Funk Earth Tour*

Released: 1977
Recorded: January 19, 1977, The Forum, Los Angeles, California
            January 21, 1977, Oakland Coliseum, Oakland, California
Label: Casablanca
Producer: George Clinton
Personnel:
George Clinton – vocals
Bernie Worrell – keyboards, synthesizers
Jerome Brailey – drums, percussion
Gary Shider – guitar, vocals
Michael Hampton – guitar, snore
Glen Goins – guitar, vocals
Eddie Hazel – guitar
Cordell Mosson – bass
Bootsy Collins – bass
Fred Wesley – trombone
Maceo Parker – saxophone
Rick Gardner – trumpet
Richard Griffith – trumpet
Calvin Simon – vocals
Fuzzy Haskins – vocals
Raymond Davis – vocals
Grady Thomas – vocals
Debbie Wright – vocals
Jeanette Washington – vocals
Lynn Mabry – vocals
Dawn Silva – vocals
Gary Cooper – vocals

Parliament was originally The Parliaments, a doo-wop vocal group formed in New Jersey in the late 1950s by George Clinton. When they had a minor hit single in 1967, Clinton formed a backing band for touring. Due to a contractual dispute with his record company, Clinton lost the rights to "The Parliaments," so he signed with another label as Funkadelic. In 1970, Clinton re-launched the singing group, now known as Parliament, at first featuring the same members as Funkadelic. By 1974, Parliament and Funkadelic were touring as a combined entity known as Parliament-Funkadelic or simply P-Funk.

Live: P-Funk Earth Tour is a double album that documents the P-Funk Earth Tour of 1977. It was recorded in Los Angeles and Oakland, California, and includes songs from Parliament studio albums as well as songs from the Funkadelic repertoire. It captures leader Clinton and company in their prime and showcases their musicianship and catalogue of great tunes. It's their only officially released concert album.

The album begins with "P-Funk (Wants to Get Funked Up)" from *Mothership Connection* (1975). With an instrumental introduction featuring Fred Wesley on solo trombone and Bernie Worrell on solo keyboards, first Clinton and then the backing vocalists enter, and we're in a deep Funkadelic groove. This segues into "Dr. Funkenstein's Supergroovalisticprosifunkstication Medley," an audience participation number. Clinton leads the crowd through their paces with an enthusiastic response.

Drummer Jerome Brailey introduces "Do That Stuff" from *The Clones of Dr. Funkenstein* (1976). The backing vocalists are featured as well as Maceo Parker on saxophone. "The Landing (Of the Holy Mothership)" is a musical montage of clips from P-Funk recordings with commentary from Clinton. Technically, it is not a live track (it was the B-side of the 1977 single, "Fantasy is Reality"), but it is part of the live show nonetheless.

"The Undisco Kidd (The Girl Is Bad)" is a previously unreleased track with hilarious lyrics, a personal favorite in this collection. The backing vocalists are featured. Glen Goins takes over lead vocals on "Children of Productions" from *The Clones of Dr. Funkenstein*. It's a brief cosmic interlude amid the funk, evocative of the Sun Ra Arkestra.

"Mothership Connection (Star Child)" from *Mothership Connection* is next, presented in extended format and split into two tracks, the second entitled "Swing Down, Sweet Chariot." It's the centerpiece of the concert, on which Clinton and Goins share lead vocal duties, and after which one can hear the Mothership landing on stage to the great appreciation of the crowd.

Goins continues with the vocal on "This Is the Way We Funk with You," featuring the backing vocalists and guitarist Michael Hampton on snore. They then launch into a fifteen minute performance of "Dr. Funkenstein" from *The Clones of Dr. Funkenstein*. Admittedly it's a little self-indulgent, but the audience participation is incredible, Parker excels on the saxophone, and the aforementioned Hampton absolutely shreds his guitar solo.

"Gamin' on Ya!" is also from *The Clones of Dr. Funkenstein*. It features the horn section and the backing vocalists. The final two tracks on *Live: P-Funk Earth Tour* are from *Mothership Connection*. "Tear the Roof Off the Sucker Medley" is a P-Funk signature tune, expanded for the live performance. Worrell is featured on keyboards. The album concludes with "Night of the Thumpasorus Peoples," featuring Bootsy Collins's fabulous bass playing.

Phish – *A Live One*

Released: 1995
Recorded: July 8, 1994, Great Woods Center, Mansfield, Massachusetts
      October 9, 1994, A. J. Palumbo Center, Pittsburg, Pennsylvania
      October 23, 1994, Band Shell, U. of Florida, Gainesville, Florida
      November 2, 1994, Bangor Auditorium, Bangor, Maine
      November 16, 1994, Hill Auditorium, U. of Michigan, Ann
        Arbor, Michigan
      November 26, 1994, The Orpheum Theatre, Minneapolis,
        Minnesota
      November 28, 1994, Field House, Montana State U., Bozeman,
        Montana
      December 2, 1994, Salem Armory, Salem, Oregon
      December 7, 1994, Spreckels Theatre, San Diego, California
      December 10, 1994, Civic Auditorium, Santa Monica, California
      December 30-31, 1994, Madison Square Garden, NYC
Label: Elektra
Producer: Phish
Personnel:
Trey Anastasio – guitar, vocals
Page McConnell – keyboards, vocals
Mike Gordon – bass, vocals
Jon Fishman – drums, vocals
The Giant Country Horns:
Peter Apfelbaum – saxophone
Carl Gerhard – trumpet
Dave Grippo – saxophone
James Harvey – trombone
Michael Ray – trumpet

The Grateful Dead, whose career (1965-1995) straddled the coming
of the digital age, developed the business model of selling their archival
concert recordings to devoted fans, but Phish has turned the concept into

a cottage industry. One can download almost any Phish concert these days on one's way out of the venue, for a price. But that's neither here nor there.

A Live One was Phish's first commercially available live recording. Each track on the album was recorded at a different concert during the band's 1994 summer and fall tours through the United States. Several of the songs had never appeared on studio albums. "Montana" is not really a song, but a brief excerpt from the improvisation that followed "Tweezer" at the show in Bozeman, Montana.

The album begins with "Bouncing Around the Room" from *Lawn Boy* (1991), one of the most frequently played Phish songs. Released as a promotional single in 1995, it features guitarist Trey Anastasio, keyboardist Page McConnell, and bassist Mike Gordon singing in the round. An extended version of "Stash," from *A Picture of Nectar* (1992), a personal favorite, is next. Anastasio's guitar solo contained therein was rated one of the top one hundred guitar solos by *Guitar World* magazine in 2001. Maybe so and maybe not!

The previously unreleased "Gumbo" features The Giant Country Horns and McConnell on organ. This is followed by the aforementioned "Montana," which serves as introduction to a twenty-one-minute long "You Enjoy Myself," one of Phish's signature compositions, from *Junta* (1989). A compositional marvel, it is comprised of a composed section, then a hideous scream and some nonsense lyrics, a funky organ solo by McConnell, an extended jam led by Anastasio on guitar, a section featuring bassist Gordon and drummer Jon Fishman, and spontaneous vocal improvisation by all four that is beyond description.

"Chalkdust Torture," is another personal favorite from *A Picture of Nectar*. It's an up-tempo rocker, lyrics of which I've often posted in my university classroom when appropriate, which is often. Phish performed an abbreviated version of the song at the taping of *The Late Show with David Letterman* on December 30 before playing their concert at Madison Square Garden. "Slave to the Traffic Light," although one of the oldest Phish original compositions, was previously unreleased to this point. The jam at the end is a classic example of how Phish starts off quietly with subtle dynamics and builds gradually to a soaring climax. This represents the end of set one.

The next set starts with a bit of Miles Davis's "Right Off," simulating what is played over the public address system during set breaks. "Wilson," a song about a mythological king dating to Anastasio's college senior project, starts out with a pulse of Gordon's bass, which triggers a Pavlovian response in the audience. This is followed by the funky introduction to "Tweezer," also from *Picture of Nectar*, another of Phish's signature tunes, a favorite vehicle for extended jamming, over thirty minutes long in this iteration.

The previously unreleased "Simple," written by Gordon, was originally sung over a jam emerging from "Mike's Song," gradually evolving into a fan favorite. It features a distinctive guitar riff by Anastasio and some neat three-part harmonies. "Harry Hood," another personal favorite, had also not yet appeared on a studio recording, despite being a concert favorite. The lyrics are mostly nonsense about the Hood dairy company and Harry the animated milkman who resided in refrigerators in New England. But the jam at the end of the song is among the most beautiful and inspired in Phish's repertoire, comparing favorably with a Bach fugue.

A Live One concludes with "The Squirming Coil" from *Lawn Boy*, as if it were the encore. It is one of Anastasio's more complicated early compositions and features himself with a remarkable guitar solo, but especially McConnell on piano, who plays an extended ending, at first accompanied by his band mates, but eventually gliding effortlessly around the keyboard on his own, a superb way to end a concert.

"Stash" from *A Picture of Nectar* was one of the songs I selected to be in my book, *The 100 Greatest Rock'n'Roll Songs Ever* in 2000.

Pink Floyd – *Pulse*

Released: 1995
Recorded: August 17, 1994, Niedersachsenstadion, Hanover, Germany
September 17, 1994, Festa Nazionale dell'Unita, Modena, Italy
September 20-21, 1994, Cinecitta, Rome, Italy
October 13-15, 19-21, 23, 1994, Earls Court, London, England
Label: Columbia
Producer: James Guthrie, David Gilmour
Personnel:
David Gilmour – guitar, vocals
Nick Mason – drums, percussion
Richard Wright – keyboards, vocals
Sam Brown – vocals
Jon Carin – keyboards, vocals
Claudia Fontaine – vocals
Durga McBroom – vocals
Dick Parry – saxophones
Guy Pratt – bass, vocals
Tim Renwick – guitar, vocals
Gary Wallis – drums, percussion

Pulse was recorded during the European leg of Pink Floyd's 1994 tour in support of *The Division Bell*. The double album includes a complete live version of *The Dark Side of the Moon* (1973) as well as a rendition of "Astronomy Domine," a song written by former member Syd Barrett and not performed since the early 1970s. The album packaging is extensive and contains a booklet with many photographs from the tour.

The first album includes performances of many of Pink Floyd's hits to date. It opens with a very long and spacey version of "Shine On You Crazy Diamond," written in tribute to Barrett, and featuring Dick Parry on saxophone. It is followed immediately by the above-mentioned Barrett composition. "Keep Talking" is a highlight, featuring David Gilmour on guitar and samples of Stephen Hawking's electronic voice.

"Hey You" is interesting, as it is Gilmour's take on former band member Roger Waters's composition. As an educator, I'm keenly appreciative of "Another Brick in the Wall (Part II)," another Waters tune. It's done brilliantly here, featuring the background vocalists as school children and Gilmour's extended guitar solo. "One of These Days" is a bonus track, included on the album and cassette releases, but not on compact disc.

The second album is *The Dark Side of the Moon*, widely considered one of the great albums of all time, an estimated fifty million copies sold, in the charts from 1973 to 1988, performed live. What could be bad about that? As on the original, "Speak to Me," a series of sound effects and recorded spoken parts, segues into "Breathe," featuring Gilmour's guitar.

After racing through the instrumental "On the Run," a recorded explosion indicates that we are under the influence of "Time," one of the principle themes of *The Dark Side of the Moon*. Sam Brown, Durga McBroom, and Claudia Fontaine take over vocal duties on "The Great Gig in the Sky," also featuring Richard Wright on piano. "Money," with its signature cash register sound effect and furious bass line by Guy Pratt, is a personal favorite. As is "Us and Them," another important theme of the suite, featuring Parry on saxophone solo.

The instrumental "Any Colour You Like" segues into "Brain Damage," which flows into "Eclipse," the final track on *The Dark Side of the Moon*. These are two more examples of Gilmour interpreting Waters's compositions. *Pulse* continues with the classic, "Wish You Were Here," released as a single in 1995, from the 1975 album of the same name. This is followed by a fabulous extended version of "Comfortably Numb" from *The Wall* (1979). The album concludes with "Run Like Hell," also from *The Wall*, but the cassette release contains one more track, "Soundscape," an ambient piece that was played before the 1994 concerts.

Phish performed *The Dark Side of the Moon* in its entirety on November 2, 1998 in West Valley City, Utah. In 2006, the *Pulse DVD* was released of the entire Pink Floyd concert performed on October 20, 1994 at Earls Court. The *Dark Side of the Moon* was one of the albums I selected to be in my book, *The 100 Greatest Rock'n'Roll Albums Ever* in 2009.

The Pretenders – *The Isle of View*

Released: 1995
Recorded: May 1, 1995, Jacob Street Studios, London, England
Label: Warner Bros.
Producer: Stephen Street
Personnel:
Chrissie Hynde – guitar, piano
Adam Seymour – guitar, harmonium
Andy Hobson – bass
Martin Chambers – drums, vocals
Damon Albarn – piano
The Duke Quartet:
Louise Fuller – violin
Richard Koster – violin
Ivan McCready – cello
John Metcalf – viola

Spinal Tap may or may not have performed at the Isle of Lucy; The Pretenders definitely have *The Isle of View*. It is an acoustic album, recorded May 1, 1995, during a live televised performance at London's Jacob Street Studios. A string quartet accompanies the band for much of the concert. The Pretenders perform their hits as well as more obscure selections.

The concert opens with "Sense of Purpose" from *packed!* (1990). The mellow approach is immediately evident, Chrissie Hynde's distinctive vocal awash in acoustic rhythms and the lush string quartet. "Chill Factor" from *Get Close* (1986) is next, a personal favorite. The soulfulness and doo-wop elements of the song stand in sharp contrast to the lyrics, which are about a part-time father after a difficult divorce. Hynde's vocal performance is outstanding.

"Private Life" goes back to The Pretenders' eponymous 1980 debut album. The acoustic format works perfectly for this mysterious sounding jam, featuring Adam Seymour on guitar and Martin Chambers on drums and backing vocal. The big hit, "Back on the Chain Gang" from *Learning to Crawl* (1984), is next, featuring the string quartet. It is also very effective, and warmly received by the audience.

"Kid," also from *Pretenders*, is radically rearranged to accommodate the string quartet, not necessarily for the better. Hynde's vocal performance is nuanced and emotional as she delivers one of the classic love songs in rock'n'roll. "I Hurt You" from *Learning to Crawl*, in contrast, is an angry, vindictive tirade about the joys of getting even. It features Seymour on guitar and the string quartet.

"Criminal" from *packed!* is a beautiful ballad, performed magnificently here, Hynde's vocal weaving in and of figures played by violinists Louise Fuller and Richard Koster. The opening notes to The Pretenders' first hit single, "Brass in Pocket" from *Pretenders*, elicits applause of recognition from the crowd. Hynde does a ballsy performance of a ballsy song about a woman approaching her object of desire.

A collector of Christmas songs, I've always loved The Pretenders' classic "2000 Miles" from *Learning to Crawl*, despite its thoroughly depressing subject matter, or maybe because of it. The string quartet is very well suited for this composition. "Hymn to Her" by Meg Keene is one of the few songs by The Pretenders not written by Hynde. First appearing on *Get Close* (1986), it is an anthem of lifelong love and devotion. The version here is almost all Hynde's vocal over a drone of strings. "Lovers of Today" is another throwback to *Pretenders*. A complicated song lyrically and compositionally, the string quartet add a great deal to the overall effect.

"The Phone Call," also from *Pretenders* is next. Its bolero-like rhythm is a vehicle for some excellent jamming on guitar by Hynde and Seymour. "I Go to Sleep" is a cover of a Ray Davies song that first appeared on *Pretenders II* (1981). It is a song of unrequited love, where sleep is the only relief from the pain. Damon Albarn is featured on piano. The last real song on *The Isle of View* is "Revolution" from *Last of the Independents* (1994), about looking for a cause about which to be passionate. It is followed by a brief snippet of an unnamed instrumental track, entitled "The Isle of View" for the album.

Quicksilver Messenger Service – *Happy Trails*

Released: 1969
Recorded: June 7-8, 1968, Fillmore East, NYC
           November 7, 1968, Fillmore West, San Francisco, California
           November 19, 1968, Golden State Recorders, San Francisco,
             California
Label: Capitol
Producer: Quicksilver Messenger Service
Personnel:
John Cipollina – guitar, vocals
Gary Duncan – guitar, vocals
Greg Elmore – drums, percussion, vocals
David Freiberg – bass, piano, vocals

Happy Trails is the second album by Quicksilver Messenger Service, mostly recorded at the Fillmore East and Fillmore West in 1968. It does a good job of capturing Quicksilver's dynamic live stage performance. The first side is comprised of the "Who Do You Love Suite," a twenty-five minute homage to Bo Diddley (Elias McDaniel) and the distinctive rock'n'roll beat named after him.

The suite begins with "Who Do You Love – Part 1," a fairly straightforward, but rocking cover of Bo Diddley's classic tune. It features the psychedelic guitar playing of John Cipollina and David Freiberg's rock steady bass. This is followed by "When You Love," a guitar solo by Gary Duncan over a walking bass line by Freiberg. "Where You Love" is next, an extended improvisational piece, featuring atonal playing and audience participation in the form of clapping and shouting.

"How You Love" is a guitar solo by Cipollina, played against the rest of the band locked into the Bo Diddley beat. Freiberg takes over with a bass solo on "Which Do You Love." The suite concludes with "Who Do You Love – Part 2," a reprise of the Bo Diddley song, which starts out quiet and soft but ends up loud and raucous. The guitar interplay between Duncan and Cipollina is unconscious, while Greg Elmore excels on the drums.

Side two begins with "Mona," another classic Bo Diddley song. The band plays it in extended form, both Duncan and Cipollina taking lengthy guitar solos. This segues into "Maiden of the Cancer Moon," a short instrumental, written by Duncan, but featuring Cipollina with perhaps his best guitar solo on the album, evocative of Frank Zappa. This, in turn, segues into "Calvary," another Duncan composition, this time over thirteen minutes long, captured live in a San Francisco recording studio. It's an instrumental jam, featuring all manner of percussion, which takes us from Spain all the way into deep space.

Happy Trails concludes with the title track, a brief version of the theme from Roy Rogers's television show, allegedly written by Dale Evans. It features Elmore's drawling vocal and Freiberg on honky-tonk piano. It seems almost insignificant after such virtuoso playing, but in light of the fact that this was the last album recorded by the original quartet incarnation of Quicksilver Messenger Service, it is at once a clearing of the palette and a fond farewell.

(In 1951, Foy Willing wrote a song called "Happy Trails" for the movie *Spoilers of the Plains*, starring Roy Rogers, Willing, and the Riders of the Purple Sage. The first three notes and the title of Willing's song were used by Dale Evans in writing her version of "Happy Trails," released in 1952 as a single on RCA Records. Evans still receives credit for authorship. Go figure.)

Capitol Records released a compact disc version of *Happy Trails* in 1994. Japanese versions surfaced in 2008 and 2009. An English edition was released in 2010. Audiophile versions were re-mastered and re-released in 2012 ("mini-album" on compact disc) and 2013 (vinyl). I attended one of the concerts at the Fillmore East.

The Quintet – *Jazz at Massey Hall*

Released: 1953
Recorded: May 15, 1953, Massey Hall, Toronto, Canada
Label: Debut
Producer: Charles Mingus
Personnel:
Dizzy Gillespie – trumpet
Charles Mingus – bass
Charlie Parker – saxophone
Bud Powell – piano
Max Roach – drums

Jazz at Massey Hall is a live album recorded in May 1953 in Toronto by "the Quintet," five of the leading modern jazz players of the day, Dizzy Gillespie, Charles Mingus, Charlie Parker, Bud Powell, and Max Roach. It was the only time that the five men recorded together as a unit, and the last recorded meeting of Gillespie and Parker, who played a borrowed saxophone at the gig. For contractual reasons, Parker could not be listed on the original album cover, so he was billed as "Charlie Chan," an allusion to the fictional detective as well as to Parker's wife, Chan.

The album was released later the same year on Mingus's Debut label from a recording made by the Toronto New Jazz Society. Mingus took the recording to New York City, where he and Roach dubbed in new bass lines, which had been under-recorded, as well as a replacement bass solo on "All the Things You Are." Because the concert took place the same night as the heavyweight boxing match between Rocky Marciano and Jersey Joe Walcott, the audience was so small that the Society was unable to pay the musicians.

The concert begins with a cover of the standard, "Perdido," written by Juan Tizol and first recorded by Duke Ellington in 1941. After a brief statement of the theme, Parker is instantly soloing on saxophone to the delight of the crowd. This segues seamlessly into Gillespie's muscular trumpet solo, which, in turn, blends into Bud Powell's elegant piano solo.

This brings us to a restatement of the theme punctuated by some energetic drumming by Roach.

After a strange introduction by Parker, referring to the author as "my worthy constituent," the band launches into Gillespie's "Salt Peanuts." After an opening statement, Gillespie barks more than sings the tune's title a bunch of times and we're off. Parker goes first with a blisteringly hot saxophone solo that is hardly cooled by Powell's piano solo which follows. Roach enters the fray with an impossibly fast drum solo that takes us to the conclusion of the piece.

Next is my personal favorite in the collection, a cover of Jerome Kern and Oscar Hammerstein's "All the Things You Are." The Quintet redefines the classic ballad with some of the smoothest ensemble playing you'll ever hear. Trumpeter Gillespie and saxophonist Parker trade couplets at the start while Powell plays the melody behind them on piano. Parker steps up to solo on the saxophone as only he can, followed by Gillespie's solo on muted trumpet. Powell then delivers a deeply introspective piano solo which segues into the re-dubbed Mingus solo on bass, and a wild and wooly ending.

"Wee" is another Gillespie composition, a vehicle for unbridled jamming done at double-time. Parker solos first on saxophone, followed by Gillespie on trumpet and Powell on piano, all echoing similar ideas. Roach interjects a furious drum solo before Gillespie and Parker take us safely home. This is followed by an extended cover of Tad Dameron's bebop standard, "Hot House." The band takes its time on this one, allowing the soloists to stretch out: Parker on saxophone, then Gillespie on trumpet, Powell on piano, and finally, Mingus on bass.

Jazz at Massey Hall concludes with Gillespie's "A Night in Tunisia." On an album loaded with memorable solos, this track takes the cake. Gillespie kick starts the piece with his muted horn, but it is Parker who comes out of the shoot with a swaggering saxophone solo. This is then matched if not exceeded by Gillespie's flight into the stratosphere on the trumpet. Powell's cool piano solo brings us back to earth and to the end of the piece.

Radiohead – *I Might Be Wrong: Live Recordings*

Released: 2001
Recorded: May 28, 2001, Theatre Antique, Vaison la Romaine, France
        July 7, 2001, South Park, Oxford, England
        August 8, 2001, Blossom Music Center, Cuyahoga Falls, Ohio
        August 20, 2001, Hollywood Bowl, Los Angeles, California
Label: Capitol
Producer: Nigel Godrich, Radiohead
Personnel:
Thom Yorke – guitar, piano, vocals
Jonny Greenwood – guitar, keyboards
Colin Greenwood – bass
Phil Selway – drums, percussion
Ed O'Brien – guitar, vocals

Radiohead formed in 1985 at a school for boys in England. They released their debut single "Creep" in 1992. The song was initially unsuccessful, but it became a worldwide hit several months after the release of their debut album, *Pablo Honey* (1993). Radiohead's third album, *OK Computer* (1997), propelled them to international fame and is often acclaimed as one of the landmark records of the 1990s. *Kid A* (2000) and *Amnesiac* (2001) marked an evolution in their musical style, as the band incorporated experimental electronic music and jazz influences.

I Might Be Wrong: Live Recordings is a mini-album consisting of live performances of eight songs by Radiohead on a tour of Europe and North America in 2001. Seven of the songs are from *Kid A* and *Amnesiac*. The final track, "True Love Waits," was never released on a studio album and is performed on acoustic guitar by Thom Yorke. The arrangements of the songs differ substantially from the studio versions.

"The National Anthem" was the opening song for most Radiohead concerts in 2000-2001, and it is first up here. The song begins with the band tuning to various radio stations, then mixing the transmissions with Colin Greenwood's bass line. The song features Jonny Greenwood on the

Ondes Martenot, an electronic instrument he used on *Kid A*. However, it lacks the brass section and free-form jazz ending of the studio version.

The title track, from *Amnesiac*, one of Radiohead's more guitar-oriented compositions, is much more of a hard rocker than the original. Unfortunately, however, the sound quality on this track is poor, as the percussion is too loud and the bass is almost completely lost. "Morning Bell" features Phil Selway's drums, as opposed to a drum machine employed in the studio. "Like Spinning Plates," performed live here for the first time, is probably the most radically altered composition on the album. While the studio version featured backwards singing against an electronic background, the live version is a piano ballad sung by Yorke, accompanied by C. Greenwood on bass and J. Greenwood on synthesizer.

"Idioteque," played at nearly every Radiohead concert since 2000, is quite remarkable here, driven by a repeating electronic beat and building into crazed audience participation. It includes electronic samples credited to composer Paul Lansky. "Everything in its Right Place" is extended quite a bit in concert, and features improvisation by J. Greenwood on a KORG Kaoss Pad. Before the song begins, Yorke can be heard singing a portion of the Maniacs' "If You Tolerate This Your Children Will Be Next" so that J. Greenwood can test his technology. As the song ends, the band members leave the stage one by one until the stage is empty, but their sampled performances continue.

"Dollars and Cents" replaces studio strings with live synthesizers, played by J. Greenwood, and includes a new and interesting guitar part from Ed O'Brien at the end. *I Might Be Wrong: Live Recordings* concludes with Yorke's powerful and nuanced performance of "True Love Waits." The song was first played in 1995 when Radiohead were touring in support of their second album *The Bends*. However, despite being a concert favorite, a studio version has never been released.

Ramones – *It's Alive*

Released: 1979
Recorded: December 31, 1977, Rainbow Theatre, London, England
Label: Sire
Producer: Tommy Ramone, Ed Stasium
Personnel:
Joey Ramone – vocals
Johnny Ramone – guitar
Dee Dee Ramone – bass, vocals
Tommy Ramone – drums

It's Alive is a double album by Ramones, their first live album, recorded on the last day of 1977 in London, and drawing material from their first three studio albums. The New Year's Eve show was chosen because ten rows of seats were thrown at the stage after the concert. The performance was also filmed and later released in truncated form on a digital video disc entitled *It's Alive 1974-1996*.

Ramones perform twenty-eight songs in under an hour. The concert begins with a personal favorite, "Rockaway Beach" from *Rocket to Russia* (1977). About the summer destination in Queens, New York, it sets the tone for what is to come: Pared down three chord rock'n'roll performed at breakneck speed, no breaks between songs, insipid lyrics, and Johnny Ramone on guitar.

"Teenage Lobotomy," also from *Rocket to Russia* is next, about a young guy who is transformed into a ladies man by overexposure to DDT. Dee Dee Ramone's bass and Johnny Ramone's guitar soar above Tommy Ramone's crashing cymbals. This is followed by "Blitzkrieg Bop" from Ramones' eponymous 1976 debut album, a punk rock anthem. Joey Ramone leads the audience in the refrain of "Hey, ho, let's go," and Johnny Ramone's chording on guitar is relentless.

Joey Ramone complains about his chicken vindaloo and they actually slow things down a tad on "I Wanna Be Well" from *Rocket to Russia*. But the respite is brief, as D. Ramone counts off the frenetic "Glad to See You Go" from *Leave Home* (1977). From the same album, "Gimme Gimme

Shock Treatment" features one of Joey Ramone's more melodic vocals on the album.

"You're Gonna Kill That Girl" from *Leave Home* is a lovely misogynistic tune, rooted in 1950s doo-wop, that Ramones mash up to the delight of the London crowd. "I Don't Care" from *Ramones* features D. Ramone on backing vocals and Johnny Ramone on inventive guitar strumming. "Sheena is a Punk Rocker" from *Leave Home* is another personal favorite. It deviates from the three-chord pattern and actually is a mid-tempo pop song about a girl who breaks away from disco and surfing and embraces her true punk self.

"Havana Affair" from *Ramones* is either witty or ridiculous, depending. About a Cuban peasant turned into a CIA spy, it features D. Ramone on bass. "Commando" from *Leave Home* picks up on the war movie theme where "Blitzkrieg Bop" leaves off. Although pure punk, it's got a bouncy melody and an infectious call-and-response chorus.

They slow things down considerably to perform "Here Today, Gone Tomorrow" from *Rocket to Russia*, as close to a love ballad that Ramones have to offer. It features Joey Ramone on crooning and Johnny Ramone on killer guitar. This is followed by a crazy cover of a crazy song, "Surfin' Bird," the 1963 single by The Trashmen. "Cretin Hop" from *Rocket to Russia* is next, a loving tribute from Ramones to their devoted fans.

Did I detect a fourth chord in "Listen to My Heart" from *Ramones*? Maybe not. Johnny Ramone gets a chance, though, to stretch out a bit on guitar. This is followed by another cover, "California Sun," a hit for The Rivieras in 1964, a perfect fit for the band, which segues into "I Don't Wanna Walk Around with You" from their first album. Inspired by a scene from Tod Browning's 1939 film *Freaks*, "Pinhead" from *Leave Home* is next, a concert favorite, with it's lyric, "Gabba gabba hey," a rallying cry for Ramones fans.

They then cover "Do You Wanna Dance," a hit single for Bobby Freeman in 1958, but at double time. "Chainsaw" from *Ramones* tells the sad tale of how the Texas Chainsaw Massacre took the protagonist's love interest. This segues into "Today Your Love, Tomorrow the World" from *Ramones*. When Joey Ramone chants the song title at the end of the tune, the audience goes wild.

They then do a previously unreleased song, "I Wanna Be a Good Boy," about conforming to society after a period of institutionalization. It features T. Ramone on drums. This is followed by "Judy is a Punk" from

Ramones, another of their classic tunes, minimalism at its best, one minute and fourteen seconds. Along the same lines, "Suzy is a Headbanger" from *Leave Home* is a tribute to another worthy punk chick. T. Ramone never stops drumming as they launch into "Let's Dance," a cover of the Chris Montez hit from 1962, but nothing like the author could have imagined.

At this point, Ramones leave the stage to thunderous applause, only to return to play a three-song encore. "Oh Oh I Love Her So" from *Leave Home* is another homage to doo-wop camouflaged in a three chord barrage. "Now I Wanna Sniff Some Glue" from *Ramones* is a tongue-in-cheek tribute to getting high on inhalants. *It's Alive* concludes with "We're a Happy Family" from *Rocket to Russia*, a warped portrait of family life, another personal favorite.

"Rockaway Beach" from *Rocket to Russia* was one of the songs I selected to be in my book, *The 100 Greatest Rock'n'Roll Songs Ever* in 2000.

Otis Redding – *Live in Europe*

Released: 1967
Recorded: March 21, 1967, Olympia Theatre, Paris, France
Label: Volt/Atco
Producer: Jim Stewart
Personnel:
Otis Redding – vocals
Booker T. Jones – organ
Steve Cropper – guitar
Donald "Duck" Dunn – bass
Al Jackson, Jr. – drums
Wayne Jackson – trumpet
Andrew Love – saxophone
Joe Arnold – saxophone

The only live album released in Otis Redding's lifetime, *Live in Europe* was recorded during the Stax/Volt tour of Europe in 1967. (*Live at the Whiskey a Go Go* was recorded a year earlier, but not issued until a year later, after his death.) Redding is backed by Booker T. & the MG's and a horn section consisting of Wayne Jackson on trumpet and Andrew Love and Joe Arnold on saxophone. The audience at the Olympia Theatre in Paris is ecstatic at the rare chance to see the American soul idol in concert, and is very vocal in their enthusiasm.

The first song of the concert and album is "Respect," Redding's 1965 single that became a monster hit for Aretha Franklin in 1967. Redding's vocal is gripping, the horn section is tight, but it is Donald "Duck" Dunn's infectious bass line that drives this train. This is followed by the rocking "Can't Turn You Loose," originally the B-side to Redding's 1965 single, "Just One More Day." It, of course, was the bigger hit and became a signature tune for Redding. A personal favorite of mine, I played it dozens of times on the jukebox at the canteen at summer camp in '65. Al Jackson, Jr. excels on the drums.

The band slows it down a bit, highlighting Redding's vocal on "I've Been Loving You Too Long (To Stop Now)," the 1965 single co-written with Jerry Butler. Booker T. Jones is featured on organ. This segues into a cover of "My Girl," the 1964 single by The Temptations. The band is perfect, playing all the parts our ear is accustomed to hearing, plus some bonus riffing on guitar by Steve Cropper. This, in turn, flows into a raucous cover of Sam Cooke's "Shake," also a single in 1964. For my money, this is the definitive version of this song, featuring the mighty horn section and Jackson, Jr. on drums.

Redding then covers "Satisfaction," The Rolling Stones' 1965 smash hit, as only he can, growling out the vocal. Cropper and Dunn carry the song on bass and guitar, respectively, but it is the horn section's frenetic playing that separates this version from the rest. "Fa-Fa-Fa-Fa-Fa (Sad Song)," co-written with Cropper, turns into a sing-along with the excited crowd.

Redding's emotions nearly overflow as he addresses the audience introducing the first song he ever recorded, "These Arms of Mine." His vocal starts out softly, but he and the band build to a dynamic crescendo. They then drop into a wild cover of The Beatles' "Day Tripper," a hit single in 1965. It features Jones on organ and the great horn section. *Live in Europe* concludes with an extended version of the song most closely associated with Redding, his 1966 single, "Try a Little Tenderness." As it was originally recorded with Booker T. & the MG's, the band has no trouble adding special flourishes throughout, notably Jones on organ, Cropper on guitar, and Jackson on saxophone.

"Try a Little Tenderness" was one of the songs I selected to be in my book, *The 100 Greatest Rock'n'Roll Songs Ever* in 2000.

Lou Reed – *Rock'n'Roll Animal*

Released: 1974
Recorded: December 21, 1973, Academy of Music, NYC
Label: RCA
Producer: Steve Katz, Lou Reed
Personnel:
Lou Reed – vocals
Pentti "Whitey" Glen – drums, percussion
Steve Hunter – guitar
Prakash John – bass, vocals
Dick Wagner – guitar, vocals
Ray Colcord – keyboards

Rock'n'Roll Animal is an album recorded by Lou Reed at the Academy of Music in New York City in December 1973. The original release contains only five songs from different periods of Reed's career, including material by The Velvet Underground, radically rearranged into a hard rock set. The band includes guitarists Steve Hunter and Dick Wagner, who would later form the second Alice Cooper Band.

The concert starts with a dynamic and fabulous extended dueling guitars introduction by Hunter and Wagner, after which Reed takes the stage, to much applause, to the opening chords to "Sweet Jane," from The Velvet Underground's *Loaded* (1970). Reed delivers an inspired vocal and Hunter and then Wagner and then Hunter again play delicious guitar solos.

"Heroin" is next, from *The Velvet Underground & Nico* (1967), still controversial at the time of the recording for neither condoning nor condemning drug use. Over thirteen minutes long in this incarnation, Reed takes the song from barely accompanied spoken word to roaring crescendos and back again several times. Ray Colcord is featured on keyboards and the rhythm section of Pentti "Whitey" Glen on drums and Prakash John on bass is rock solid. Hunter and Wagner, however, steal the show with double lead guitars toward the song's conclusion.

Also about drug use, this time purportedly about the sensations derived from intravenous injection of methamphetamine, "White Light/White Heat," from The Velvet Underground's 1968 album of the same name, follows. It's a relentlessly hard rocker with great ensemble playing by all, featuring Hunter on lead guitar, a precursor of punk rock music, but with a better ending. If anything, it's too short.

"Lady Day" from Reed's solo effort, *Berlin*, is a great song and about as unsubtle as it gets. Taking its title from Billie Holiday, it is actually about Caroline, the ill-fated protagonist of the 1973 concept album. The guitarists elevate the already dramatic composition to new heights, however, with solos first by Wagner and then by Hunter. The audience responds with enthusiastic approval.

Rock'n'Roll Animal concludes, appropriately enough, with an extended version of "Rock'n'Roll" from *Loaded*. It's a magnificent live performance of a mid-tempo rocker about a girl named Jenny from New York City whose "life was saved by rock'n'roll." Wagner takes the first guitar solo, then Hunter breaks the song down with virtuoso guitar chording, soon joined first by John on bass and then by Glen on drums, eventually rejoined by Wagner with another blistering assault on guitar. Reed's final vocalizing is barely audible above the furious jamming.

Additional excerpts from the same concert were released in 1975 as *Lou Reed Live*. A re-mastered edition of *Rock'n'Roll Animal* was issued in 2000 on compact disc, including two additional tracks from *Berlin*, "How Do You Think It Feels" and "Caroline Says II." Between the two, the entire show is now available. "Sweet Jane" from *Loaded* by The Velvet Underground was one of the songs I selected to be in my book, *The 100 Greatest Rock'n'Roll Songs Ever* in 2000. Lou Reed died in October 2013 during the preparation of this project.

The Rolling Stones – *Get Yer Ya's Out!*
The Rolling Stones in Concert

Released: 1970
Recorded: November 26, 1969, Civic Center, Baltimore, Maryland
             November 27-28, 1969, Madison Square Garden, NYC
Label: Decca
Producer: The Rolling Stones, Glyn Johns
Personnel:
Mick Jagger – harmonica, vocals
Keith Richards – guitar, vocals
Mick Taylor – guitar
Charlie Watts – drums, percussion
Bill Wyman – bass
Ian Stewart – piano

I really didn't know what hit me when *Get Yer Ya-Ya's Out! The Rolling Stones in Concert* was released in 1970. I mean, I knew all about The Rolling Stones, had even seen them in concert, but the live album was such a new concept at the time, that I was nonetheless blown away. This was nothing like the Stones' studio albums; this was a rock'n'roll concert captured live. And I might add that this performance was by my favorite incarnation of the Stones, with Mick Taylor on guitar.

The title of the album derives from the song "Get Yer Yas Yas Out" by Blind Boy Fuller. The cover photograph, featuring Charlie Watts with guitars and bass drums hanging from a donkey's neck, was inspired by Bob Dylan's "Visions of Johanna," although the lyrics refer to a mule. The album was very well received critically and commercially, the first live album to reach number one on the charts in the United Kingdom. Some of the performances were depicted in the 1970 documentary film *Gimme Shelter.*

The album starts, as did all the concerts on the 1969 tour, with an introduction of "the greatest rock'n'roll band in the world" and "Jumpin' Jack Flash." Released as a single the previous year, it was seen as a departure from the Stones' acid days and a return to their bluesier roots. Next is

"Carol," the first of two Chuck Berry covers, on which Keith Richards seems to channel Berry, including *the* Chuck Berry signature guitar riff. It is also the first song on which we hear the fabulous guitar interplay between Richards and Taylor. Ian Stewart is featured on piano.

"Stray Cat Blues" from *Beggars Banquet* (1968) is done a lot slower and mellower than the studio version. Told from the perspective of a man lusting after a fifteen-year-old groupie, it features Taylor on solo guitar. "Love in Vain," a vastly rearranged cover of a Robert Johnson tune, included on the Stones' *Let It Bleed* (1969), is a highlight. It's very slow, very sad, and very much driven by Richards and Taylor on guitar, the latter taking several solos on slide guitar. Bill Wyman excels on bass on the only tune in this collection not recorded at Madison Square Garden.

"Midnight Rambler," also from *Let It Bleed*, is nothing like the original and nothing short of great. It's an extended trip that goes from a rocking shuffle to a bump-and-grind crawl and back again. Mick Jagger provides interesting harmonica fills throughout. "Sympathy for the Devil" from *Beggars Banquet* is done in a fairly straightforward manner, with a great solo work on guitar from Taylor. The controversy that would forever surround this song would originate one week later at Altamont Speedway in California.

"Live With Me" from *Let It Bleed* is done in raunchy, rocking fashion to match the song's subject matter. Richards steps out on lead guitar on his way to the second Berry cover, "Little Queenie." This one is done more deliberately, Charlie Watts rock steady on the drums, Richards uncanny on guitar, Stewart tasteful on piano. Stewart's piano is also featured on "Honky Tonk Women." Although the second verse differs completely from the single released in 1969, it is closer to that version than to the honky-tonk interpretation called "Country Honk" on *Let It Bleed*.

Get Yer Ya-Ya's Out! The Rolling Stones in Concert concludes with "Street Fighting Man" from *Beggars Banquet*. The Rolling Stones' most political song, it was supposedly written about British Pakistani journalist and activist Tariq Ali after Jagger attended an anti-war rally in London, and as a response to the movement that was fomenting in the United States and France.

In 2009, *Get Yer Ya-Ya's Out! The Rolling Stones in Concert* was reissued in a 40th anniversary boxed set. It contains unreleased songs by The Rolling Stones as well as the performances of opening acts B.B. King and Ike &

Tina Turner. It includes a digital video disc and a fifty-six page booklet. I attended one of the concerts at Madison Square Garden. "Street Fighting Man" from *Beggars Banquet* was one of the songs I selected to be in my book, *The 100 Greatest Rock'n'Roll Songs Ever* in 2000.

The Rolling Stones – *Stripped*

Released: 1995
Recorded: March 3-5, 1995, live in studio, Tokyo, Japan
       May 26, 1995, The Paradiso Club, Amsterdam, The Netherlands
       July 3, 1995, The Olympia Theatre, Paris, France
       July 19, 1995, Brixton Academy, London, England
       July 23-26, live in studio, Lisbon, Portugal
Label: Virgin
Producer: Don Was, The Glimmer Twins
Personnel:
Mick Jagger – harmonica, guitar, maracas, vocals
Keith Richards – guitar, vocals
Charlie Watts – drums
Ronnie Wood – guitar, lap-slide
Daryl Jones – bass, vocals
Chuck Leavell – keyboards, vocals
Bernard Fowler – percussion, vocals
Lisa Fischer – vocals
Bobby Keys – saxophone
Andy Snitzer – saxophone
Michael Davis – trombone
Kent Smith – trumpet
Don Was – organ

    Stripped was recorded in Europe and Japan and released in 1995 by The Rolling Stones during the *Voodoo Lounge Tour*. The album is a mixture of live recordings from smaller venues and studio recordings with no overdubs. Most of the songs are from the Stones' previous catalogue, with the exception of Bob Dylan's "Like a Rolling Stone" and Willie Dixon's "Little Baby." The album name is a play on the common title of *Unplugged*.
    The concert begins with "Street Fighting Man" from *Beggars Banquet* (1968), a personal favorite. Despite the acoustic approach, it is still a powerful song. Bernard Fowler is featured on backing vocals and percussion. This is followed by the above-mentioned Bob Dylan cover, a

very Zen choice for a band called The Rolling Stones, itself a hit single in 1995. It features Mick Jagger on harmonica and Chuck Leavell on organ.

"Not Fade Away," the Buddy Holly song covered on the Stones' 1964 eponymous debut album, is next. This one clearly benefits from the acoustic format, taking on a primitive rocking edge. Charlie Watts is outstanding on drums. Jagger is featured on harmonica and maracas. The gospel-tinged "Shine a Light" from *Exile on Main St.* is a highlight of this set. Jagger's vocal is memorable, the backing vocalists are great, Ronnie Wood's guitar solos are tight, and Don Was is featured on organ.

They dig deep again to do a bluesy rendition of "The Spider and the Fly" from *Out of Our Heads* (1965). Jagger assumes one of those affected voices of his in a tune about attracting women, but it's unclear who the spider is and who's the fly. They stick with *Out of Our Heads* to perform the optimistic "I'm Free," featuring Leavell on organ and Lisa Fischer on backing vocals.

They slow things down substantially on "Wild Horses" from *Sticky Fingers* (1971). This version, which itself became a hit single in 1996, features Leavell on backing vocals and some lovely interplay between Wood and Keith Richards on guitar. A terrific version of the title track on *Let it Bleed* (1969) follows, featuring Richards's harmony vocal, Wood's guitar solo, and Fowler on percussion.

Another highlight on *Stripped* is "Dead Flowers" from *Sticky Fingers.* This time Jagger opts for his country-western voice on this absolutely perfect performance, featuring Wood on solo guitar, Leavell on backing vocals, and Fowler on percussion. Richards takes over lead vocal duties on the bittersweet "Slipping Away" from *Steel Wheels* (1989), featuring Wood's guitar, the horn section, and the backing vocalists.

This leads to "Angie" from *Goats Head Soup* (1973), not a personal favorite, but nonetheless well performed. Jagger's plaintive vocal is nicely offset by fills on guitar by Richards and on piano by Leavell. Richards's guitar is also featured, as is Wood's, on "Love in Vain," the Robert Johnson cover included on *Let It Bleed.* This is classic Stones, recorded almost thirty years after it appeared on *Get Yer Ya-Ya's Out! The Rolling Stones in Concert.*

The raucous "Sweet Virginia" from *Exile on Main St.* is next, featuring the popular line, "Got to scrape that shit right off your shoes." Bobby Keys is featured on saxophone, as are Leavell, Fischer, and Fowler on backing vocals. *Stripped* concludes with a cover of "Little Baby" by Willie Dixon.

Avram Mednick

It's a straightforward rendition of a basic blues, featuring stop time sections, some excellent piano figures by Leavell, and a quirky guitar solo by Wood.

"Street Fighting Man" from *Beggars Banquet* was one of the songs I selected to be in my book, *The 100 Greatest Rock'n'Roll Songs Ever* in 2000.

The Roots – *The Roots Come Alive*

Released: 1999
Recorded: March 26, 1999, Roseland Ballroom, NYC
        May 6, 1999, Palais X-Tra, Zurich, Switzerland
        July 16, 1999, Montrose Jazz Festival, Montrose, Switzerland
Label: MCA
Producer: The Grand Wizards, Richard Nichols
Personnel:
Black Thought – vocals
?uestlove – drums
Rahzel The Godfather of Noyze – beatbox
Scratch – beatbox, vocals
Leonard "Hub" Hubbard – bass
Kamal – keyboards
Scott Storch – keyboards
Dice Raw – vocals
Craig Harris – trombone
Jill Scott – vocals
Jaguar – vocals
James Poyser – piano
Common – vocals
Malik – vocals

The Roots are a hip hop/neo soul band formed in 1987 by Tariq "Black Thought" Trotter and Ahmir "?uestlove" Thompson in Philadelphia, Pennsylvania. They are known for their jazzy, eclectic approach to hip hop, which includes playing instruments live on stage. The Roots have been the house band on the television program *Late Night with Jimmy Fallon* since its premier in 2009.

The Roots Come Alive was recorded at various locations in 1999. The album title is an allusion to *Frampton Comes Alive* (1976). A distinctive feature of albums by The Roots is the way tracks are numbered, using a continuous numbering system beginning with their first studio album,

Organix, in 1993. *The Roots Come Alive* has track numbers 77-86 unique to it, as well as lower numbered songs from earlier studio albums.

The first track of the album is actually a brief taped snippet of "Live at the T-Connection" by Grandmaster Flash & the Furious Five, to set the tone, as it were. This flows directly into "The Next Movement" from *The Legendary* (1999). It features Black Thought's vocal with help from Scratch. Kamal's keyboard links this song with the next, "Step Into the Realm" from *Things Fall Apart* (1999), written by Kenyatta Saunders. This is rowdy call-and-response rap, but set against a funky beat maintained by the rhythm section of ?uestlove on drums and Leonard "Hub" Hubbard on bass.

The music never really stops as the band segues into "Proceed" from *Do You Want More?!!!??!* (1995). It's your basic exercise in toasting, but so much more, as Scott Storch leads a mellow groove on the keyboards. Relentless, the band moves on to "Mellow My Man"/"Jusufckwithis" from *From the Ground Up* (1994). The former is a dense rap with Scratch supporting Black Thought on the vocals and featuring ?uestlove on drums. The latter is a super-cool, jazzy jam featuring Kamal on keyboards and Hub on bass.

The performance continues with Common doing guest vocals alongside Black Thought on his composition, "Love of My Life" from *Things Fall Apart*. It's as close to a love song as you'll find in the hip hop genre. They pause for a moment to take a breath and for Black Thought to rehearse the audience to participate appropriately in "The Ultimate" from *The Legendary*. It's a highlight of the collection.

"Don't See Us" from *Things Fall Apart* is next, featuring Scratch on turntable hijinx and one of Black Thought's strongest vocal performances on the album. A personal favorite, it puts me in mind of *Invisible Man* by Ralph Ellison. This segues into "100% Dundee," also from *Things Fall Apart*, written by Rahzel The Godfather of Noyze, although he does not appear on the track. It features Scratch's crazy turntable vocalizations and Kamal on keyboards.

"Adrenaline" is next, also from *Things Fall Apart*, featuring Dice Raw on guest vocals and an appearance by Rahzel The Godfather of Noyze on turntables and backing vocals. The rhythm section is too funky to be believed during the audience participation section of the song. And then they break it down double-time, jamming furiously, absolutely rocking the house.

After a brief pause, The Roots launch into "Essaywhuman?!??!!!" from *Organix*, written by avant-garde bassist Josh Abrams. Initially, it's a showcase for the founders, Black Thought and ?uestlove, to rock out on vocals and drums. Then they use it as a vehicle to introduce the other band members. This is followed by "Silent Treatment," a mellow groove from *Do You Want More?!!!??!*, featuring Craig Harris on trombone and Kamal on keyboards.

"The Notic," a new composition, is then dedicated to the ladies in the house, which makes sense, as it seems to be about the hypnotic effect that a woman can have on a man. Jill Scott is then introduced to deliver an unbelievable vocal performance on her composition, "You Got Me" from *Things Fall Apart*, alongside Black Thought. Scratch is featured on turntables.

Jaguar then takes the stage to perform her song, "What You Want," with Black Thought providing contrapuntal rapping behind her. Storch is featured on keyboards. Jaguar is also lead vocalist on "We Got You," featuring James Poyser on piano and ?uestlove on drums. *The Roots Come Alive* concludes with "The Lesson – Part III (It's Over Now)," featuring Black Thought, Dice Raw, and Malik on vocals, Jaguar and Scratch on backing vocals, Poyser on piano, and additional keyboards by ?uestlove.

Santana – *Lotus*

Released: 1974
Recorded: July 3-4, 1973, Koseinenkin Hall, Osaka, Japan
Label: Columbia
Producer: The New Santana Band
Personnel:
Carlos Santana – guitar, percussion
Leon Thomas – maracas, vocals
Tom Coster – keyboards, percussion
Richard Kermode – keyboards, percussion
Doug Rauch – bass
Armando Peraza – bongos, congas
Jose "Chepito" Areas – congas, timbales
Michael Shrieve – drums

Lotus was recorded by Santana in Osaka, Japan, in July 1973. It was originally released as a triple album outside of the United States and subsequently as a double compact disc. It features The New Santana Band that recorded *Welcome*, released later that year. It combines the band's jazz and spiritual influences with performances of earlier Santana Latin-flavored rock hits.

After an introduction in Japanese, the concert begins with "Going Home" from *Welcome*, soon to be released. It's a transcendent type piece, with everyone in the band playing percussion except Tom Coster and Richard Kermode on keyboards. This segues into a new track, "A-1 Funk," which is just that, a funky instrumental, still emphasizing keyboards and percussion.

This is followed by "Every Step of the Way," an extended space jam written by drummer Michael Shrieve for *Caravanserai* (1972). We finally get to hear Carlos Santana stretch out brilliantly on lead guitar. Kermode is also featured on electric piano. Peter Green's "Black Magic Woman" from *Abraxas* (1970) is next, Leon Thomas on the familiar vocal. It is slightly rearranged to give Santana even more freedom to riff out on guitar. And riff out he does in his unmistakable style.

This segues unto "Gypsy Queen," by Gabor Szabo, just like on *Abraxas*, and with equally dynamic effect. Santana takes his guitar playing to another level with special assistance from Armando Peraza on congas and Jose "Chepito" Areas on timbales. Continuing the song sequence from Santana's second album, "Oye Como Va" by Tito Puente follows, the entire band supplying the vocals, Coster the organ solo, Santana the mind-bending guitar leads.

"Yours is the Light," written by Kermode, which would appear on *Welcome*, is a jazzy instrumental featuring the author on electric piano and Santana on lead guitar, expressing one melodic idea after another. "Batuka" is a brief percussion snippet from *Santana III* (1971), which is followed by a new track, the lively "Xibaba (She-Ba-Ba)" by Airto Moreira, and another snippet, "Stone Flower (introduction)" by Antonio Carlos Jobim from *Caravanserai*.

Next is "Waiting" from Santana's eponymous 1969 debut album, featuring masterful work on the organ by Coster and a killer bass line by Doug Rauch. This is followed by a brief new track, "Castillos de Arena Part 1," written by Chick Corea and arranged by The New Santana Band. Another new track follows, "Free Angela," a complicated composition with many changes in time signature and lots of deep space jamming.

"Samba de Sausalito," destined to be on *Welcome*, is next, a dense percussion-based instrumental written by Areas and featuring Coster on electric piano. Three more new tracks follow: "Mantra," an Eastern-influenced instrumental written by Coster, Santana, and Shrieve, "Kyoto (Drum Solo)," an extended adventure in drumming starring Shrieve with noodling by Coster on electric piano, and "Castillos de Arena Part 2," picking up where they left off earlier.

They then dip back into *Abraxas* for three more tunes. "Incident at Neshabur," extended here to almost sixteen minutes in length, is a vehicle for jamming by Coster on organ, Kermode on electric piano, and, of course, Santana on guitar, who quotes liberally from "My Favorite Things." "Se a Cabo," written by Areas, is vintage Santana, guitar and organ soaring above a sea of percussion. Santana, Thomas, and Coster supply the vocals. My favorite in this collection is the gorgeous "Samba Pa Ti." Santana states the theme and then jams out endlessly and effortlessly, referencing George Benson and the Jackson 5, among others. Kermode also excels on electric piano solo.

"Mr. Udo," another new track, follows. It is a short, percussion-based jam featuring Coster on organ and Areas on timbales. *Lotus* concludes with a rousing rendition of "Toussaint L'Overture" from *Santana III*. The band states the theme and then Coster is off and running with an organ solo that bleeds into a Santana guitar solo and then a percussion jam among Shrieve, Peraza, and Areas while Santana, Thomas, Kermode, and Coster supply the vocals. Santana and Coster trade solos one last time and the song and the concert are over.

"Samba Pa Ti" from *Abraxas* was one of the songs I selected to be in my book, *The 100 Greatest Rock'n'Roll Songs Ever* in 2000.

Simon & Garfunkel – *The Concert in Central Park*

Released: 1982
Recorded: September 19, 1981, Central Park, NYC
Label: Warner Bros.
Producer: Paul Simon, Art Garfunkel, Roy Halee, Phil Ramone
Personnel:
Paul Simon – guitar, vocals
Art Garfunkel – vocals
Steve Gadd – drums
Grady Tate – drums
Anthony Jackson – bass
David Brown – guitar
Pete Carr – guitar
Richard Tee – keyboards
Rob Mounsey – synthesizer
John Gatchell – trumpet
John Eckert – trumpet
Dave Tofani – saxophone
Gerry Niewood – saxophone

The concept of a free concert in Central Park in New York City to benefit the park itself had been proposed by Parks Commissioner Gordon Davis and promoter Ron Delsener in the early 1980s. The Home Box Office channel agreed to carry the concert and worked with Delsener to decide on Simon & Garfunkel, with deep New York City roots, as the appropriate act for the event.

The concert took place on September 19, 1981, in front of more than half a million people. It was the first live recording by Simon & Garfunkel, for whom this concert and album marked the start of a short-lived reunion. Besides hit songs from their career as a duo, the set list included material from their solo careers, new songs, and covers. Despite the success of the concert and subsequent world tour, the duo decided against a permanent reunion.

The concert begins with "Mrs. Robinson," Simon & Garfunkel's 1968 hit from the soundtrack to *The Graduate* (1967) and the album *Bookends*

(1968). The crowd roars with approval. Then an acoustic rendering of "Homeward Bound" from *Parsley, Sage, Rosemary and Thyme* (1966) that shows that the duo can still make that magic sound together. Simon then addresses the crowd with, "Well, it's great to do a neighborhood concert," and they launch into a rousing version of "America" from *Bookends*. David Brown is featured on guitar.

This is followed by "Me and Julio Down by the Schoolyard," a single for Simon in 1972, done with much more of a Latin flavor and a salsa break. Gerry Niewood is featured on saxophone. They quiet things down with a gorgeous treatment of "Scarborough Fair" from *Parsley, Sage, Rosemary and Thyme*. Garfunkel then does an exquisite solo performance of "April Come She Will" from *Sounds of Silence* (1966).

Simon and Garfunkel then perform a crowd-pleasing cover of the Everly Brothers' "Wake Up Little Susie." This is followed by a solo performance by Simon of the title song from *Still Crazy After All These Years* (1975), featuring Richard Tee on keyboards and Dave Tofani on saxophone. An absolutely beautiful version of "American Tune" from *There Goes Rhymin' Simon* (1973) is next, illustrating how Garfunkel makes Simon's songs even better.

"Late in the Evening" from *One Trick Pony* is a personal favorite, performed impeccably here, the band, especially the horn section, really swinging. They bring things back down to earth with Simon's 1977 single, "Slip Slidin' Away," on which they demonstrate their uncanny harmonizing. Garfunkel then does another solo performance, "A Heart in New York" from his album, *Scissors Cut*, released the previous month. Simon follows with another solo performance of his own, "The Late Great Johnny Ace," which would appear on his 1983 album *Hearts and Bones*. "Kodachrome" from *There Goes Rhymin' Simon* is next, wildly rearranged as a rocker, and played in medley with a raucous cover of Chuck Berry's "Maybelline," featuring Brown on guitar and Tofani on saxophone.

Garfunkel then sings a nuanced and emotional version of the title tune on *Bridge Over Troubled Water* (1969) on his own, and there ain't a dry eye in the park (it rained that day). Tee is also featured on piano on what is probably the highlight of the concert. Simon does "Fifty Ways to Leave Your Lover" from *Still Crazy After All These Years* as a solo performance, with plenty of help from his friends in the horn section, not to mention Steve Gadd and Grady Tate on drums. They do a magnificent extended version of "The Boxer" from *Bridge Over Troubled Water* to the delight of the audience.

After this, Simon and Garfunkel leave the stage, only to return and do an encore of three songs, "Old Friends"/"Bookends Theme" from *Bookends*, "The 59th Street Bridge Song (Feelin' Groovy)" from *Parsley, Sage, Rosemary and Thyme*, and "The Sound of Silence" from *Sounds of Silence*. After introducing the members of the backing band, Simon & Garfunkel perform a final encore, a reprise of "Late in the Evening."

Bruce Springsteen & the E Street Band – *Live/1975-85*

Released: 1986
Recorded: October 18, 1975, The Roxy Theatre, Los Angeles, California
July 7, 1978, The Roxy Theater, Los Angeles, California
December 16, 1978, Winterland Ballroom, San Francisco, California
November 5, 1980, Arizona State U., Phoenix, Arizona
December 28-31, 1980, Nassau Coliseum, Uniondale, New York
July 6-9, 1981, The Meadowlands, East Rutherford, New Jersey
August 6, 19-20, 1984, The Meadowlands, East Rutherford, New Jersey
August 19-21, 1985, Giants Stadium, East Rutherford, New Jersey
September 30, 1985, Los Angeles Coliseum, Los Angeles, California
Label: Columbia
Producer: Jon Landau, Chuck Plotkin, Bruce Springsteen
Personnel:
Bruce Springsteen – guitar, harmonica, vocals
Roy Bittan – piano, synthesizer, vocals
Clarence Clemons – saxophone, percussion, vocals
Danny Federici – organ, accordion, glockenspiel, piano, synthesizer, vocals
Garry Tallent – bass, vocals
Steve Van Zandt – guitar, vocals
Max Weinberg – drums
Nils Lofgren – guitar, vocals
Patti Scialfa – synthesizer, vocals
Flo & Eddie:
Howard Kaylan – vocals
Mark Volman – vocals
The Miami Horns:
Stan Harrison – saxophone
Eddie Manion – saxophone
Mark Pender – trumpet
Richie "La Bamba" Rosenberg – trombone

Live/1975-85 is a compilation album by Bruce Springsteen & the E Street Band, recorded at various concerts between 1975 and 1985. It was released as a boxed set comprised of five albums, three compact disks, or three cassettes. It is a remarkable resume of Springsteen's career to that point. There are forty tracks, including seven previously unreleased songs. It is the second best selling live album in United States history, trailing only Garth Brooks's *Double Live* (1998).

The album begins quietly, with "Thunder Road," a personal favorite, from *Born to Run* (1975). Springsteen is accompanied only by Roy Bittan on piano, Danny Federici on glockenspiel, and his own harmonica on the ultimate small-town-coming-of-age anthem. There isn't a dry ear in the place. The quiet is short-lived, however, as this is followed by a raucous performance of the previously unreleased "Adam Raised a Cain," a bluesy rocker, a truly great song, featuring Steve Van Zandt on guitar and the E Street Band on backing vocals.

"Spirit in the Night" is next, from *Greetings from Asbury Park, N.J.* (1973). One of Springsteen's classic story songs about searching for freedom, it features Clarence Clemens on saxophone and the audience on backing vocals and screams. Federici's accordion introduction indicates that "4th of July, Asbury Park (Sandy)" from *The Wild, The Innocent & the E Street Shuffle* (1973) is beginning. Springsteen delivers an emotional reading of the ballad, which features Bittan on piano.

"Paradise by the 'C'" is another previously unreleased tune, an instrumental featuring Clemens on saxophone, Federici on organ, and Van Zandt on guitar. This is followed by "Fire," never before released by Springsteen but covered by a host of others. A seductive love song, it features the rhythm section of Garry Tallent on bass and Max Weinberg on drums.

The tinkling of Bittan's piano introduces "Growin' Up" from *Greetings from Asbury Park, N.J.*, during which Springsteen takes the opportunity to tell a few stories about his growing up. This segues into "It's Hard to Be a Saint in the City," also from *Greetings from Asbury Park. N.J.* It's a gloriously hard rocker about a kid growing up in the urban jungle. Toward the end Springsteen and Van Zandt audibly have fun trading guitar licks.

"Backsteets" from *Born to Run* (1975) is next, a sophisticated but heartbreaking song about life on the other side of the tracks. Springsteen sings his heart out; Federici's organ is evocative of Dylan's "Positively 4th Street." An extended performance of "Rosalita (Come Out Tonight)" from

The Wild, The Innocent & the E Street Shuffle, another personal favorite, is next. A wild and wooly tale of unrequited love, it features Clemens on saxophone. Next is a rowdy cover of Eddie Floyd's "Raise Your Hand," previously unreleased, featuring the E Street band on backing vocals, during which Springsteen admonishes the audience to get up and dance.

Some may find it corny, but I think what happens next is a classic rock'n'roll moment. As was becoming a tradition, the audience, in this case at the Nassau Coliseum, sings, and I mean really sings, the first verse and chorus of "Hungry Heart" from *The River* (1980). It gives me douche chills every time. This particular performance features Howard Kaylan and Mark Volman sitting in on backing vocals.

The next four tunes are also from *The River*. "Two Hearts" is a love song that rocks out, with blue-eyed soul overtones. "Cadillac Ranch" is a rockabilly romp that features Weinberg on drums and the E Street Band on backing vocals. "You Can Look (But You Better Not Touch)" is an infectious mid-tempo rocker with inspired vocals and guitar playing by Springsteen. "Independence Day" is a moving ballad about the parting of the ways between a father and his son, featuring Clemens on saxophone.

This is followed by "Badlands" from *Darkness at the Edge of Town* (1978). The story of a man down on his luck and angry with the world, it features Weinberg on drums and Clemens on saxophone. "Because the Night," written by Springsteen and Patti Smith, is previously unreleased by Springsteen, but recorded by Smith and others. It features Federici on organ and Springsteen on solo guitar.

The next three songs are also from *Darkness at the Edge of Town*. This performance of "Candy's Room" is remarkable in its theatrics, dynamics, and musicianship, eliciting roars of approval from the crowd. The title track is next, a slow, bluesy tune about folks living in the shadows of society. "Racing in the Street" is a great song, a dirge-like ballad about yet another guy with a dead end job who revels in racing his car. Featuring Federici on organ and Bittan on piano, the composition pays homage to Martha & the Vandellas' "Dancing in the Street" in the title and the chorus, and to The Beach Boys' "Don't Worry Baby" in the instrumental break following the second verse and chorus.

Springsteen then does an acoustic mini-set, accompanying himself on guitar and harmonica, consisting of Woody Guthrie's "This Land is Your Land" and three songs from his solo album, *Nebraska* (1982), about crime and economic depravation. The title track is about an eight-day killing spree that took place in Nebraska and Wyoming in 1958. "Johnny 99" concerns a laid off auto worker in New Jersey who commits murder and requests to be executed, juxtaposed against a rockabilly shuffle. "Reason to Believe" is a complex story song with a sarcastic title.

The E Street Band rejoins Springsteen to perform one of his signature tunes, the title track to *Born in the U.S.A.* (1984), featuring Federici on organ and Springsteen on screams. This is followed by the previously unreleased "Seeds," an infectious rocker that features Nils Lofgren on guitar. An eleven minute version of the title track from *The River* is next, a highly personal song to Springsteen, during which he talks about his relationship with his father. In this performance, he also touches on the Vietnam War, so it's appropriate that he follow with a previously unreleased cover of "War," a hit for Edwin Starr in 1970.

Live/1975-85 continues with two tracks from *Born in the U.S.A.* "Darlington County" is a raucous story song about driving down to South Carolina to look for work and meet girls. It features Clemons on saxophone and the E Street Band on backing vocals. "Working on the Highway" is a celebration of the working class life, featuring Federici on organ, Clemons on saxophone, and Patti Scialfa on backing vocals.

They dip back into *Darkness at the Edge of Town* for "Promised Land," homage to Chuck Berry's 1965 single of the same name. But unlike Berry's hero, who leaves his Virginia home to go to California, Springsteen's stays home in Utah to face the hand he's been dealt. It features Springsteen on harmonica and Clemons on saxophone. The audience goes wild.

Then four more tracks from *Born in the U.S.A.* After a psychedelic introduction with plenty of reverb, "Cover Me" turns into a gritty, bluesy rocker about loyalty. Springsteen is featured on guitar, Scialfa on backing vocals. "I'm On Fire" is a moody tune with a rockabilly beat and plenty of sexual innuendo. "Bobby Jean" is a story song about an ambiguously named character that may or may not be Van Zandt, who was leaving the band at the time it was written. It features Clemons on saxophone. "My Hometown" is a realistic glimpse at what's going on in a lot of our home towns, based on Springsteen's experiences growing up in New Jersey.

The house lights are turned fully on and the band begins the title track from *Born to Run*, featuring Clemons on saxophone and the audience singing along with Springsteen's wordless vocalizations at the end of the song. Thrilling. "No Surrender" is an up-tempo rocker on *Born in the U.S.A.*, but it is performed here acoustically, featuring Springsteen's harmonica. "Tenth Avenue Freeze-Out," about the formation of the E Street Band, is from *Born to Run*. A personal favorite, it features The Miami Horns. *Live/1975*-85 concludes movingly with a cover of Tom Waits's "Jersey Girl" from *Heartattack and Vine* (1980), performed to the delight of a New Jersey audience.

"Thunder Road" from *Born to Run* was one of the songs I selected to be in my book, *The 100 Greatest Rock'n'Roll Songs Ever* in 2000.

Steely Dan – *Alive in America*

Released: 1995
Recorded: September 6, 1993, Desert Sky Pavilion, Phoenix, Arizona
        September 10, 1993, Irvine Meadows Amphitheater, Irvine, California
        September 19, 1993, Blockbuster Pavilion, Charlotte, North Carolina
        August 19, 1994, The Thunderdome, St. Petersburg, Florida
        August 26, 1994, Poplar Creek Hoffman Estates, Chicago, Illinois
        August 27, 1994, Pine Knob Music Theater, Detroit, Michigan
        September 17, 1994, Irvine Meadows Amphitheater, Irvine, California
        September 18, 1994, Desert Sky Pavilion, Phoenix, Arizona
Label: Giant
Producer: Donald Fagen
Personnel:
Donald Fagen – keyboards, melodica, vocals
Walter Becker – guitar, vocals
Tom Barney – bass
Warren Bernhardt – keyboards
Peter Erskine – drums
Dennis Chambers – drums
Drew Zingg – guitar
Georg Wadenius – guitar
Bill Ware III – vibraphone, percussion
Cornelius Bumpus – saxophone
Chris Potter – saxophones
Bob Sheppard – saxophones
Diane Garisto – vocals
Catherine Russell – percussion, vocals, whistle
Brenda White-King – vocals

    Steely Dan toured for a couple of years after the release of their first album, *Can't Buy a Thrill*, in 1972. However, founders Donald Fagen and Walter Becker soon retreated to the recording studio and, along with producer Gary Katz, engineer Roger Nichols, and the best supporting players on the planet, created, in my opinion, some of the greatest studio albums ever recorded. Since Steely Dan attained success after they stopped touring, however, many of their dedicated fans never got the chance to see them in concert.

Following the release of their seventh album, *Gaucho*, in 1980, Fagen and Becker dissolved their partnership. They did some songwriting together in the late '80s, but with no completed work. Becker performed spontaneously with Fagen's *New York Rock and Soul Review* in 1991 and produced Fagen's 1993 second solo album *Kamakiriad*. This resulted in a reformation of Steely Dan and a tour of the United States to support *Kamakiriad*.

The following year, MCA released *Citizen Steely Dan*, a boxed set of their entire catalogue, and Becker released his first solo album, *11 Tracks of Whack*, co-produced by Fagen. Steely Dan followed with another tour in support of both releases. With Becker, originally Steely Dan's bassist, now playing guitar, both tours featured a band that included an additional keyboard player and lead guitarist, a bassist, a four-piece saxophone section, and three female backing vocalists. The bands were the same for both tours, except Dennis Chambers and Georg Wadenius replaced Peter Erskine and Drew Zingg on drums and guitar, respectively, in 1994. The band featured long-time Steely Dan collaborator, Cornelius Bumpus, on tenor saxophone.

The liner notes on *Alive in America* offer clues as to why Becker and Fagen chose to tour for the first time in almost twenty years, namely, to forestall middle age, to experience flying around in a private jet, and to hear "Babylon Sisters" live. To put it another way, that really was the question: Could Becker and Fagen even come close to duplicating their considerable studio feats live in concert. The answer, a resounding yes. "Babylon Sisters" from *Gaucho* and the other ten tracks, culled from the '93 and '94 tours, do an excellent job of presenting the recording studio perfectionists at their best.

The song selection spans their career from the first Steely Dan album to Becker's solo effort, and showcases outstanding musicianship throughout. Of particular note are "Bodhisattva" from *Countdown to Ecstasy* (1973), "Kid Charlemagne" from *The Royal Scam* (1976) and "Peg" from *Aja* (1977) featuring Wadenius on guitar solos, as well as an exquisite rendering of "Third World Man" from *Gaucho*, with Zingg on lead guitar. They even tackle their A-A-B-B-C-C-A-C opus magnum, "Aja," from the album of the same name, with Chris Potter playing Wayne Shorter's tenor saxophone part and Chambers remarkable on drums.

I attended concerts from both the 1993 and 1994 tours at the Shoreline Amphitheater in Mountain View, California. "Kid Charlemagne" from *The Royal Scam* was one of the songs I selected to be in my book, *The 100 Greatest Rock'n'Roll Songs Ever* in 2000.

Sun Ra Arkestra – *Live at Pit-Inn, Tokyo, Japan*

Released: 1988
Recorded: August 8, 1988, Pit-Inn, Shinjuku, Tokyo, Japan
Label: DIW
Producer: Kohei Kawakami, Zen Matsuura
Personnel:
Sun Ra – piano, synthesizer, vocals
Michael Ray – trumpet, vocals
Ahmed Abdullah – trumpet
Tyrone Hill – trombone
Marshall Allen – saxophone
John Gilmore – saxophone, timbales
Danny Thompson – saxophone
Leroy Taylor – clarinets
Bruce Edwards – guitar
Rollo Rodford – bass
Eric Walker – drums
Earl "Buster" Smith – drums
June Tyson – violin, vocals
Judith Holten – dance

Sun Ra was born Herman Poole Blount in Birmingham, Alabama in 1914. Nicknamed "Sonny" from his childhood, Blount was a skilled pianist by age eleven, already composing original songs. He got his first full-time musical job in 1934, working steadily around Birmingham thereafter. Blount claims that in 1936 or 1937, in the midst of deep religious contemplation, he was transported to Saturn and given the mission of speaking to the world through his music.

Blount moved to Chicago in 1945, quickly finding work with Fletcher Henderson's band. By 1952, he was leading the Space Trio with drummer Tommy "Bugs" Hunter and saxophonist Pat Patrick, who was with him, on and off, for the rest of his life. Also that year, Blount legally changed his name to Le Sony'r Ra. Soon after, saxophonists John Gilmore and Marshall Allen joined what was to become the Sun Ra Arkestra. During the late 1950s, they began wearing the outlandish Egyptian-styled and science fiction-inspired costumes and headdresses for which they would become known.

Sun Ra and his core musicians left Chicago in 1961, staying briefly in Montreal before settling in New York City. In 1966, the Arkestra got a regular weekly gig at Slug's Saloon, leading to some recognition and popularity. When the building they were living in was put up for sale in 1968, they relocated to the Germantown section of Philadelphia, where they were to become a fixture in the community.

Live at Pit-Inn, Tokyo, Japan provides the listener with a healthy combination of cosmic chaos and standard big band charts. The concert begins with "Introduction"/"Cosmo Approach Prelude." The first part is a percussion jam among drummers Eric Walker and Earl "Buster" Smith and Gilmore on timbales. Then the rest of the band comes in, first Allen taking a wild alto saxophone solo, then Gilmore and Bruce Edwards conversing on tenor saxophone and guitar, respectively, then Allen finishing with another spaced out solo.

Baritone saxophonist Danny Thompson barks out the first few notes of introduction, and we're into "Angel Race"/"I Wait For You." The first tune is a cacophonous romp, featuring the entire horn section. The second is a lilting shuffle on which Sun Ra, vocalist June Tyson, and the rest of the band do a call-and-response ode to outer space. Trumpeter Michael Ray is featured. This track fades out for unknown reasons.

"Can You Take It?" is a brilliant, short track that really swings. It features Sun Ra on piano and saxophone solos by Gilmore, Thompson, and Allen, in that order. The extended, dirge-like "If You Came from Nowhere Here" is next, a space age composition for big band. It features Sun Ra on synthesizer and the entire horn section. About halfway in, Gilmore delivers a wonderful solo on tenor saxophone. Sun Ra and Tyson chant more than sing the song's title as it concludes.

Gilmore's Coltrane-like grunting on tenor saxophone accompanied by Allen's contrapuntal squeals on alto saxophone indicate that the Arkestra has begun another extended cosmic piece, "Astro Black," one of Sun Ra's signature compositions. Vocalist Tyson sings a few choruses with help from Ray, then Allen blows his brains out for a while, Sun Ra vocalizes a bit, Ray takes a trumpet solo, Tyson performs a violin solo, and they all sing the conclusion. Guitarist Edwards is featured throughout.

A cover of Duke Ellington's "Prelude to a Kiss" is next, introduced by drummers Walker and Smith. Sun Ra plays a few choruses on piano, accompanied by the rhythm section featuring Rollo Rodford on bass, before the band comes in, led by Gilmore blowing atonal riffs on tenor saxophone. Another cover, this time Jerome Kern's "Why Was I Born" is a vehicle to showcase Sun Ra's virtuosity on piano. It also features Ray on vocal and Gilmore on tenor saxophone solo.

Live at Pit-Inn, Tokyo, Japan concludes with "Interstellar Lo-Ways," at once way out there in deep space and rooted in the blues. After Sun Ra states the theme on piano and the horn section reiterates it, the rhythm section vamps behind the soloists: Sun Ra on synthesizer, Ray on trumpet, Sun Ra on piano, Edwards on guitar, Sun Ra on piano again. The horn section reenters, restating the theme.

Sun Ra Sextet – *At the Village Vanguard*

Released: 1993
Recorded: November 15-16, 1991, The Village Vanguard, NYC
Label: Rounder
Producer: John Snyder
Personnel:
Sun Ra – synthesizer
Chris Anderson – piano
John Gilmore – saxophone
John Ore – bass
Earl "Buster" Smith – drums
Bruce Edwards – guitar

Sun Ra suffered a stroke in 1990, but kept composing, performing, and leading the Arkestra. He often pulled smaller units out of the Arkestra, as was the case when he led a sextet into the Village Vanguard in New York City in November 1991. The result was *At the Village Vanguard*, released in 1993. The album contains only five tracks, but four of them are very lengthy. We are treated, as usual, to an interesting combination of original compositions and standards, with tenor saxophonist John Gilmore the principal soloist.

At the Village Vanguard begins with a twenty-one minute version of Thelonious Monk's "'Round Midnight." After an extended introduction from Chris Anderson on piano, Gilmore initially states the theme on saxophone. Sun Ra comes in on synthesizer, accompanied by Anderson on piano. When Bruce Edwards begins his guitar solo, the whole band begins to swing, driven by the rhythm section of John Ore on bass and Earl "Buster" Smith on drums. Sun Ra takes over on synthesizer, with Ore at first playing contrapuntal bass, then taking a great solo with the bow. And, finally, here comes Gilmore's saxophone, restating the theme, with a little help from Edwards on guitar.

"Sun Ra Blues" is next, sixteen minutes long. It swings right out of the gate, Anderson on piano, Ore on bass, and Smith on drums setting the pace. Just when it seems that Ore is starting to solo, Gilmore enters on saxophone and takes over completely. Sun Ra adds some coloration to Gilmore's playing and then takes a synthesizer solo of his own, followed by an inspired extended solo on guitar by Edwards. At this point, Ore gets his obligatory bass solo, starting out skin on skin, then switching to the bow, as is his wont. Drummer Smith takes a brief but interesting solo and the rest of the band members drop back in for the conclusion of the piece.

Sun Ra's lush synthesizer introduction indicates the beginning of Vernon Duke's "Autumn in New York," appropriate to both the season and the setting. Anderson enters on piano and the two of them dance around the popular and recognizable theme. Gilmore then states the theme directly on saxophone before performing an outstanding solo. Sun Ra takes over with a staccato synthesizer solo, backed by the able rhythm section. Then it's Anderson's turn to deliver an abstract solo on piano. Sun Ra reenters on synthesizer, succinctly restating the theme, as does Gilmore on saxophone to end the composition.

Another standard, George and Ira Gershwin's "'S Wonderful" follows, my personal favorite in the collection. Anderson on piano, Ore on bass, and Smith on drums play the melody once around before Gilmore does the same on saxophone. Then it's glorious, unbridled jamming the rest of the way, with solos taken by Edwards on guitar, Sun Ra on synthesizer, Anderson on piano, Sun Ra again on synthesizer, Ore on bowed bass, Gilmore on saxophone, and Smith on drums.

At the Village Vanguard concludes with "Theme of the Stargazers." This track appears as a snippet, less than a minute in duration, on several Sun Ra albums, beginning with *Nothing Is* (1966). However, here it is played as a five-and-a-half minute song. A cross between a space age anthem and a marching band chart, it lurches along, drummer Smith driving the train, Sun Ra adding otherworldly sounds on synthesizer. Although no vocals are credited on the album, Sun Ra, nonetheless, does a little chanting about living on another world before the piece decomposes.

Sun Ra died in 1993. The Arkestra played at his funeral and the mourners left singing, "Space is the Place." Honoring Sun Ra's dying request, the Arkestra continued under Gilmore's direction until his death in 1995. The Sun Ra Arkestra continues touring under saxophonist Marshall Allen's leadership and rehearsing at the Sun Ra house in Philadelphia, which has become a music school.

Talking Heads – *The Name of This Band is Talking Heads*

Released: 1982
Recorded: November 17, 1977, Northern Studios, Maynard, Massachusetts
November 17, 1979, The Capitol Theater, Passaic, New Jersey
August 27, 1980, Central Park, NYC
November 8-9, 1980, Emerald City, Cherry Hill, New Jersey
February 27, 1981, Sun Plaza Concert Hall, Tokyo, Japan
Label: Sire
Producer: Talking Heads
Personnel:
David Byrne – guitar, vocals
Chris Frantz – drums
Tina Weymouth – bass, percussion, vocals
Jerry Harrison – guitar, keyboards, vocals
Adrian Belew – guitar, vocals
Nona Hendryx – vocals
Busta "Cherry" Jones – bass, guitar
Dolette McDonald – percussion, vocals
Steven Stanley – conga
Bernie Worrell – keyboards, clavinet, vocals
Jose Rossy – percussion

It's easy to forget what an important and influential rock band Talking Heads was in the late 1970s and on into the '80s. Their avant-guard minimalist approach to the music, based in their art school backgrounds and mentality, earned both critical and popular acclaim. Before they were done, they were to delve into everything from funk to world-beat. While there is no debating the importance of *Stop Making Sense*, the Jonathan Demme film that captured Talking Heads' 1983 tour, the soundtrack to same is uneven at best. Fact is, there's an earlier, far superior live Talking Heads album, *The Name of This Band is Talking Heads*.

The title of the double album alludes to the band's preference for having no "The" in their name. The first album features the original quartet in recordings from 1977 and 1979. The second album features the eleven-piece expanded lineup that toured in 1980 and 1981. The cassette edition of the album contained an additional track, "Cities," from *Fear of Music* (1979), subsequently included on the compact disc release.

The first series of performances is from 1977 in Massachusetts, including mostly tracks from *Talking Heads 77* (1977). "Pulled Up" is spirited and funky. "Psycho Killer" is frenetic and disturbing. "A Clean Break" is previously unreleased and an excellent surprise. Then there are songs recorded in 1979 in New Jersey, mostly from *More Songs About Buildings and Food* (1978), but including the previously unavailable "Love Goes to a Building on Fire." Among these, "Artists Only" is notable for being one of David Byrne's most outrageous vocal performances. "Stay Hungry" is prescient and ironic at the same time. And "Air" is just a great song in addition to being a cautionary tale.

The second album is taken from the *Remain in Light* (1980) tour. In order to be able to perform the music on that album, the original quartet was expanded to include two additional percussionists, two back-up vocalists, an additional bassist, none other than Bernie Worrell on keyboards, and a young Adrian Belew on lead guitar. This material absolutely exudes excitement, and the performances outdo the original versions in most cases.

"I Zimbra" is as outstanding as it is significant as a transitional composition for Talking Heads. Appearing on *Fear of Music*, it foreshadowed what was to follow on *Remain in Light*. "Drugs" is rearranged for live performance and rocks out. But the concert really kicks into high gear with "Houses in Motion," performed at greater length and much funkier than the original. "Life During Wartime," also from *Fear of Music*, a survivalist's anthem, is a personal favorite and is no disappointment here. Belew is outstanding on guitar throughout, but especially on "The Great Curve" and "Crosseyed and Painless," his wild feedback soloing never sounding more deranged.

The Name of This Band is Talking Heads concludes with "Take Me to the River," the Al Green cover that Talking Heads adapted and adopted as their own. Here it's performed with the expanded band with great results. It's been documented that I attended one of the Emerald City shows and that it was the single loudest concert of my natural life.

Ten Years After – *Undead*

Released: 1968
Recorded: May 14, 1968, Klook's Kleek, London, England
Label: Deram
Producer: Mike Vernon
Personnel:
Alvin Lee – guitar, vocals
Chick Churchill – organ
Ric Lee – drums
Leo Lyons – bass

Undead is an album recorded by Ten Years After at a small club in London in May 1968. Their eponymous debut album, released the year before, was bluesy but didn't capture their sound, so they decided to record their second album live. This album was influential on a generation of aspiring musicians in terms of the art of improvisation and breaking out of rock'n'roll boundaries. It was also very important to me, being an early example of the power of the live album, not to mention opening my ears to the amazing guitar technique and speed of Alvin Lee.

After an introduction of the band, the concert begins with A. Lee's composition, "I May Be Wrong, But I Won't Be Wrong Always," and we already know that things are radically different from Ten Years After in the studio. It's an extended composition, with much more in common with jazz than with blues or rock'n'roll. Chick Churchill is featured on organ, as is Leo Lyons on bass, but it is A. Lee who excels on guitar, with solo after lightning solo.

"At the Woodchopper's Ball" is next, another extended composition, this time a cover of an instrumental written by Woody Herman in 1939 and popularized in the 1942 movie, *What's Cookin'*. An impromptu rehearsal of this tune one afternoon at the Marquee Club, also in London, is what got Ten Years After their first break. A. Lee's guitar playing here is about the fastest you'll ever hear. In May 1969, I had the privilege of seeing Woody Herman & his Orchestra perform this tune at the Fillmore East in New York City, opening for Led Zeppelin.

"Spider in My Web" is a superbly crafted twelve-bar blues, written by A. Lee, performed in very deliberate fashion. The author delivers an emotional vocal performance, augmented by an excellent organ solo by Churchill and a frenetic guitar solo by himself. This is followed by a rearrangement of George and Ira Gershwin's "Summertime" segued into "Shantung Cabbage" by drummer Ric Lee. The former track debuted on Broadway in New York City in 1935 as part of the stage play, *Porgy and Bess*. The latter did not. Both tracks feature R. Lee on the drums.

The album concludes with the historic original recording of "I'm Going Home," the boogie that would become Ten Years After's signature tune two years later when featured in the 1970 movie, *Woodstock*, capturing the band performing it at the Woodstock Music and Art Festival in 1969. It's A. Lee's tour-de-force, taking us lyrically through the history of rock'n'roll, and shredding his guitar solos. Watermelon, anyone?

Undead was reissued on compact disc in 2002, containing four additional tracks, "Rock Your Mama," "Spoonful," "Standing at the Crossroads," and "I Can't Keep From Crying, Sometimes"/"Extension on One Chord." "I'm Going Home" from *Undead* was one of the songs I selected to be in my book, *The 100 Greatest Rock'n'Roll Songs Ever* in 2000. Alvin Lee died in March 2013 during the preparation of this project.

Traffic – *Welcome to the Canteen*

Released: 1971
Recorded: June 6, 1971, Fairfield Hall, Croydon, England
            July 3, 1971, OZ Obscenity Fund Benefit, London, England
Label: United Artists
Producer: Traffic
Personnel:
Steve Winwood – organ, piano, guitar, vocals
Jim Capaldi – percussion, tambourine, vocals
Chris Wood – saxophone, flute, piano, organ
Dave Mason – guitar, vocals
Ric Grech – bass
Rebop Kwaku Baah – congas, timbales
Jim Gordon – drums

In 1970, Traffic toured as a quartet (Steve Winwood, Chris Wood, Jim Capaldi, and Ric Grech) in support of *John Barleycorn Must Die*, recording a series of concerts at the Fillmore East for a live album that was never released for unknown reasons. By the time of their next tour, they had expanded to a septet (adding Dave Mason, Rebop Kwaku Baah, and Jim Gordon). *Welcome to the Canteen* is the fifth album by Traffic, recorded in England in 1971, during Mason's third stint with the band, which lasted only six performances.

Although regarded as a Traffic album, it was originally released without the name "Traffic" anywhere on it. Rather, it was credited to the seven individual musicians. The Traffic logo, however, did appear on the back of the album, and later compact disc releases credit the album to Traffic on the spine. There are only six tracks, three from Traffic's early albums, two from Mason's first solo album, *Alone Together* (1970), and "Gimme Some Lovin'" from Steve Winwood's former band, The Spencer Davis Group.

The album begins with "Medicated Goo" from *Traffic* (1968). It's done as a funky shuffle and features Winwood on vocal, drummer Jim Capaldi on backing vocal, great bass playing by Ric Grech, Chris Wood on saxophone, and an extended guitar solo by Mason. This is followed by

"Sad and Deep as You" from *Alone Together*. Mason takes over vocal duties on this moody tune on which Wood is featured on flute.

"(Roamin' Thro' the Gloamin With) 40,000 Headmen" known as "Forty Thousand Headmen" for short, also from *Traffic*, is next. It is a psychedelic masterpiece about escaping from reality, although often thought to be a song about drugs. The song is built around some minor chord changes with a vaguely Latin feel, but then changes to a major chord progression before a slow fade into deep space. Winwood is back on the vocal as well as on acoustic guitar. Wood is featured on flute, Rebop Kwaku Baah on congas.

Mason takes over once more on his tune, "Shouldn't Have Took More Than You Gave" from *Alone Together*. The author is featured on wah-wah pedal guitar and performs several tastefully excellent solos. Winwood is back on organ and Capaldi is outstanding on drums. This is followed by "Dear Mr. Fantasy" from *Mr. Fantasy* (1967), Traffic's signature composition. It's done here in extended fashion, featuring Winwood on vocal and both himself and Mason with some exceptional guitar playing. It's at once psychedelic rock, blue-eyed soul, and solid pop. It ends with a dynamic rave-up.

Welcome to the Canteen concludes with an extended performance of "Gimme Some Lovin," a hit single for The Spencer Davis Group in 1966 with Winwood on vocals. It is radically rearranged, however, to give it a fresh feel, with an emphasis on the percussive side of things, featuring Capaldi on drums and Baah on timbales. Mason takes the first solo on guitar, followed by Wood on saxophone, Winwood on organ, and Baah on congas.

U2 – *Under a Blood Red Sky*

Released: 1983
Recorded: May 6, 1983, The Orpheum Theater, Boston, Massachusetts
       June 5, 1983, Red Rocks Amphitheater, Denver, Colorado
       August 20, 1983, Lorelei Amphitheater, Sankt Goarshausen,
       West Germany
Label: Island
Producer: Jimmy Iovine
Personnel:
Bono – vocals
The Edge – guitar, keyboards, bass, vocals
Adam Clayton – bass, guitar
Larry Mullen, Jr. – drums

Under a Blood Red Sky is an album by U2 recorded at three shows (Boston, Denver, and Germany) on the band's *War* tour in 1983. Referred to as a mini-LP, it contains only eight tracks. An accompanying concert video entitled *U2 Live at Red Rocks: Under a Blood Red Sky*, recorded entirely at the Red Rocks Amphitheater, was released the following year. The two releases helped establish U2's reputation as a live band.

The concert begins with "Gloria" from *October* (1981). Bono's vocal features a chorus in Latin and a bunch of biblical references. He exhorts the crowd to shout rhythmically along with The Edge's slide guitar solo. Bassist Adam Clayton is also featured. This is followed by "11 O'Clock Tick Tock," U2's second single, released in 1980. A mid-tempo rocker with a staccato beat, it is a cautionary tale, desolate and desperate in viewpoint. It features The Edge with some appropriately angry guitar playing.

The audience goes wild at the first recognition of the opening notes to "I Will Follow," the opening track from *Boy*, U2's 1980 debut album. Purportedly a tribute written by Bono to his mother, who died when he was fourteen, it is U2's most frequently performed song. This performance is rocking, then spacey, then rocking again, featuring The Edge on guitar. "Party Girl," a surprise selection, was called "Trash, Trampoline and the Party Girl" when it was the B-side to "A Celebration," released as a single

209

in 1980. Bono delivers an impassioned vocal and gets the audience to chant along with him.

Bono then introduces "Sunday Bloody Sunday" from *War* with the words, "This song is not a rebel song." It is, however, a fiery rocker with drummer Larry Mullen, Jr. laying down a militaristic beat. About an infamous 1972 incident in Derry where British troops shot and killed unarmed civil rights protesters and bystanders, The Edge is once again featured on guitar.

This is followed by "The Electric Co." from *Boy*, which supposedly refers to electric convulsion therapy. It is a frenetic rocker, featuring The Edge on lead rhythm guitar. During the performance, Bono sings a snippet of "Send in the Clowns" by Stephen Sondheim, but without the permission of the author. This led to legal action resulting in U2 paying a fine and being forced to edit future editions.

The audience does that instant recognition thing again in response to the first few notes of "New Year's Day," from where the album title is derived. Written about the Polish Solidarity movement, it features Bono's vocal, Clayton's distinctive bass line, and The Edge on keyboards and guitar. *Under a Blood Red Sky* concludes with "40," the final song of every show on the *War* tour. The lyrics are a modification of Psalm 40 in the bible. This song features Clayton on guitar and The Edge on bass. Bono thanks the crowd and leaves the stage, followed by Clayton, then The Edge, and finally Mullen. The audience however, continues to sing "How long . . . to sing this song?" even after the band is gone.

Various artists – *Woodstock: Music from the Original Soundtrack and More*

Released: 1970
Recorded: August 15-18, 1969, Bethel, New York
Label: Cotillion
Producer: Eric Blackstead
Personnel:
John Sebastian – guitar, vocals
Canned Heat:
Alan "Blind Owl" Wilson – guitar, harmonica, vocals
Bob "The Bear" Hite – harmonica, vocals
Harvey "The Snake" Mandel – guitar
Larry "The Mole" Taylor – bass
Adolpho "Fito" de la Parra – drums
Richie Havens:
Richie Havens – guitar, vocals
Daniel Ben Zebulon – conga, percussion
Paul "Deano" Williams – guitar, vocals
Country Joe & the Fish:
"Country" Joe McDonald – guitar, harmonica, kazoo, vocals
Barry "The Fish" Melton – guitar, vocals
Greg "Duke" Dewey – drums
Mark Kapner – keyboards
Doug Metzler – bass
Arlo Guthrie:
Arlo Guthrie – guitar, vocals
Bob Arkin – bass
Paul Motian – drums
John Pilla – guitar
Sha-Na-Na:
Joe Witkin – keyboards
Jocko Marcellino – drums
Bruce Clark III – bass
Eliot Cahn – guitar, vocals

Henry Gross – guitar
Donald "Donny" York – vocals
Rob Leonard – vocals
Alan Cooper – vocals
Frederick "Dennis" Greene – vocals
Dave Garrett – vocals
Richard "Richie" Joffe – vocals
Scott Powell – vocals
Joan Baez:
Joan Baez – guitar, vocals
Richard Festinger – guitar
Jeffrey Shurtleff – guitar, vocals
Crosby, Stills, Nash (& Young):
Stephen Stills – guitar, organ, piano, percussion, vocals
David Crosby – guitar, vocals
Graham Nash – guitar, organ, percussion, vocals
Neil Young – guitar, organ, piano, vocals
Greg Reeves – bass
Dallas Taylor – drums
The Who:
Roger Daltrey – vocals
Pete Townshend – guitar, vocals
John Entwistle – bass
Keith Moon – drums
Joe Cocker:
Joe Cocker – vocals
Henry McCullough – guitar, vocals
Alan Spenner – bass, vocals
Chris Stainton – keyboards, vocals
Bruce Rowland – drums
Bobby Torres – congas
Santana:
Carlos Santana – guitar, maracas, cowbell, vocals
Gregg Rolie – keyboards, maracas, tambourine, jingle bells, vocals
Jose "Chepito" Areas – trumpet, percussion
Mike Carabello – congas
Michael Shrieve – drums
David Brown – bass

Ten Years After:
Alvin Lee – guitar, vocals
Chick Churchill – organ
Ric Lee – drums
Leo Lyons – bass
Jefferson Airplane:
Marty Balin – tambourine, maracas, vocals
Jack Casady – bass
Spencer Dryden – drums
Paul Kantner – guitar, vocals
Jorma Kaukonen – guitar, vocals
Grace Slick – tambourine, maracas, vocals
Nicky Hopkins – piano
Sly & the Family Stone:
Sly Stone – keyboards, harmonica, vocals
Rose Stone – keyboards, vocals
Freddie Stone – guitar, vocals
Cynthia Robinson – trumpet
Greg Errico – drums
Steve "Tiny" Kahn – drums
Larry Graham – bass
Jerry Martini – saxophone
Butterfield Blues Band:
Paul Butterfield – harmonica, vocals
Howard "Buzzy" Feiten – guitar
Rod Hicks – bass
Ted Harris – keyboards
Phillip Wilson – drums
Steve Mudalo – trumpet, percussion
Keith Johnson – trumpet, percussion
David Sanborn – saxophone, percussion
Trevor Lawrence – saxophone, percussion
Gene Dinwiddle – saxophone, percussion, vocals
Jimi Hendrix:
Jimi Hendrix – guitar, vocals
Billy Cox – bass
Larry Lee – guitar, vocals
Mitch Mitchell – drums

Juma Sultan – congas
Gerardo "Jerry" Velez – congas

The Woodstock Music and Art Fair took place on Max Yasgur's 600-acre farm near the hamlet of White Lake in the town of Bethel, New York, on August 15-18, 1969. Thirty-two acts performed to an audience of approximately 500,000 people. The documentary film *Woodstock*, directed by Michael Wadleigh, was released in 1970. Two soundtrack albums were released. The first, also in 1970, *Woodstock: Music from the Original Soundtrack and More*, is a triple album containing a sampling of one or two songs by many of the acts that performed. A year later, *Woodstock 2* was released as a double album. Both albums include recordings of stage announcements.

For reasons that defy explanation, the order of the tracks on *Woodstock: Music from the Original Soundtrack and More* is not the same as the order of the actual performances as they took place. For instance, the first track on the album, "I Had a Dream" by John Sebastian, was performed on the afternoon of the second day. Go figure. For the rest of this essay, I will use the chronology of the actual concert, rather than the order of the album tracks, as my guide.

The first artist to appear at the Woodstock Music and Art Fair was Richie Havens, who took the stage at 5:15 PM on Friday, August 15. His performance of "Freedom" is the third track on the album. Following Havens, Sweetwater, Bert Sommer, Tim Hardin, Ravi Shankar, and Melanie performed, none of whom appear on the album. (Melanie is featured on *Woodstock 2*.) Arlo Guthrie took the stage at Midnight, his rendition of "Coming into Los Angeles" appearing on side one. Joan Baez closed the Friday concert at 1:30 AM Saturday. Two of her performances appear on side two: "Joe Hill" and "Drug Store Truck Drivin' Man," with Jeffrey Shurtleff.

Quill opened Saturday's proceedings at 12:30 PM, but didn't make it onto the album. However, Country Joe McDonald, the next artist to perform, did, providing one of the album's highlights, "The 'Fish' Cheer"/"I-Feel-Like-I'm-Fixin'-To-Die Rag," on side two. At this point, the first of the heavy rainstorms came through as Santana took the stage at 2:15 PM. The first several minutes of his "Soul Sacrifice" are the "Crowd Rain Chant," started by the crowd in an attempt to stop the rain. This track appears on side four.

The aforementioned Sebastian performs next, a second song of his, "Rainbows All Over Your Blues," showing up on side five. He's followed by the Keef Hartley Band and the Incredible String Band, neither of whom are on the album. Canned Heat perform their "Goin' Up the Country" at about 8 PM, inexplicably the second track on side one. The next four performers were Mountain, Grateful Dead, Creedence Clearwater Revival, and Janis Joplin with the Kozmic Blues Band; remarkably, none appears on the album. (Mountain is featured on *Woodstock 2*.)

Sly & the Family Stone took the stage at 3:30 AM, a medley of "Dance to the Music," "Music Lover," and "I Want to Take You Higher" the centerpiece of side five. After Abbie Hoffman spoke about "The Politics of the Situation," the Who came on at 5:00 AM and performed twenty-three songs, the most by any artist. Only "We're Not Gonna Take It," the eighteenth song played, made it onto the album, interrupted by the announcement, "It's a free concert from now."

Jefferson Airplane closed the Saturday show, taking the stage at 8:00 AM Sunday. Their performance of "Volunteers" made it onto side five, famously introduced by Grace Slick with, "Okay people, you have heard the heavy groups. Now it's time for morning maniac music." At the end of the track we hear Max Yasgur himself speaking, praising the crowd for coming to the event.

Joe Cocker and the Grease Band opened Sunday's show at 2:00 PM. "With a Little Help from My Friends" appears on side three for some reason, ending with a minute-and-a-half of pouring down rain. This is appropriate, as a severe thunderstorm disrupted the concert at this point for several hours. Country Joe McDonald reappeared at 8:00 PM, this time with his band, Country Joe & the Fish, their "Rock & Soul Music," a personal favorite, appearing on side one.

Ten Years After followed, "I'm Going Home," maybe the hottest single track on the entire album, showing up on side four. The Band came on next, followed by Johnny Winter, joined by brother Edgar Winter, and then Blood, Sweat & Tears. None of these made the cut. Chip Monck then announced the next act as Crosby, Stills, Nash & Young, but Young's name was dropped from the movie soundtrack, as he skipped all but two songs of their acoustic set and refused to be filmed during their electric set. "Suite: Judy Blue Eyes" and "Sea of Madness" end side two, while "Wooden Ships" starts side three. Unfortunately, "Sea of Madness" was actually recorded a month later at the Fillmore East.

The Paul Butterfield Blues Band came on at 6:00 AM, their extended "Love March" appearing on side six. They were followed by the unlikely Sha-Na-Na, whose cover of "At the Hop" is completely misplaced on side one. Jimi Hendrix was the closing act of the Woodstock Music and Art Fair, performing the longest set of the concert, concluding at 11:10 AM Monday. A medley of "The Star Spangled Banner," "Purple Haze," and an instrumental solo entitled "Woodstock Improvisation" after the fact, all appear, as they should, at the end of side six.

In 1994, material from both albums, as well as numerous previously unreleased performances, was reissued on Atlantic Records as a four compact disc boxed set called *Woodstock: Three Days of Peace and Music*. In 2009, Rhino Records released a six compact disc boxed set, *Woodstock: 40 Years On: Back to Yasgur's Farm*, containing yet additional musical performances.

Shrouded in the folds of herstory, we see a young lad, still in his teens but of draft age, working for the summer as a member of the wait staff at a Catskill Mountain resort hotel, the last resort, as it were, suddenly disappearing for the weekend, at the height of the season, leaving his station unattended, hitchhiking then walking to Yasgur's Farm. The stuff of urban legends or mud-caked reality? Only my busboy knows for sure.

"I'm Going Home" from *Undead* (1968) was one of the songs I selected to be in my book, *The 100 Greatest Rock'n'Roll Songs Ever* in 2000. Richie Havens died in April 2013 during the preparation of this project.

The Velvet Underground – *1969: Velvet Underground Live*

Released: 1974
Recorded: October 19, 1969, End of Cole Ave. Club, Dallas, Texas
　　　　　November 23-27, 1969, The Matrix, San Francisco, California
Label: Mercury
Producer: The Velvet Underground
Personnel:
Sterling Morrison – guitar, vocals
Lou Reed – guitar, vocals
Maureen Tucker – percussion
Doug Yule – bass, organ, vocals

During 1969, The Velvet Underground toured North America. Many of the shows were taped by fans with simple hand-held recorders, with the permission of the band. In October in Dallas, a fan who was a recording engineer brought along his professional equipment, and in November in San Francisco, the band got permission to use the in-house recording deck.

Nothing was done with the tapes until 1974, after the band had dissolved and Lou Reed had become an established solo artist. They were released by Reed's management company, largely to prevent former manager Steve Sesnick from doing the same. The songs were compiled by music critic Paul Nelson, who was working at Mercury Records at the time. The result is *1969: Velvet Underground Live*.

At the time of the album's release, three of its songs ("We're Gonna Have a Real Good Time Together," "Over You," and "Sweet Bonnie Brown"/"It's Just Too Much") were previously unreleased in any form, two ("Lisa Says" and "Ocean") were previously only associated with Reed, and "New Age" and "Sweet Jane" were completely different from the versions that would appear on *Loaded* in 1970.

"Does anyone have school tomorrow?" With that considerate question, Reed kicks off the concert with "I'm Waiting for The Man," incorrectly labeled as "Waiting for My Man" on the album, in a country-rock style. "What Goes On" is an extended rave-up, featuring Doug Yule on organ and the guitar interplay between Reed and Sterling Morrison.

"Femme Fatale," sung by Nico on *The Velvet Underground & Nico* (1967), is sung much more aggressively here by Reed. He also sings the beautifully delicate "New Age," which would be later sung by Yule on *Loaded*. "Rock and Roll" is one of my all-time favorite songs, and the version here is raw and excellent, Reed and Morrison shining brightly on guitar. But the song in this collection on which the Reed/Morrison guitar collaboration is perhaps most haunting and brilliant is the magnificent "Pale Blue Eyes."

"Heroin" is very long and fairly disturbing, although not as shocking as when first heard on *The Velvet Underground & Nico*. "White Light/White Heat," only two-and-a-half minutes long on the 1968 album of the same name, is here an eight minute exercise in guitar improvisation. "I Can't Stand It" is a humorous tale of urban frustration, with a love song hidden between the lines. The album concludes with the short but exquisite "I'll Be Your Mirror," originally sung by Nico, vocal here by Yule.

1969: Velvet Underground Live is an excellent representation of The Velvet Underground's body of work and the many sides of their musical personality. It also lends credence to band's reputation for never playing a song the same way twice. When put out on compact disc by Polygram in 1988, the double album was split into two budget compact discs, with one extra track on each. "Sweet Jane" from *Loaded* was one of the songs I selected to be in my book, *The 100 Greatest Rock'n'Roll Songs Ever* in 2000.

Weather Report – *Live and Unreleased*

Released: 2002
Recorded: November 27, 1975, The New Victoria Theater, London, England
September 10, 1977, The Rainbow, London, England
November 30, 1977, Majestic Theatre, Grand Rapids, Michigan
November 28, 1978, Star Theatre, Phoenix, Arizona
July 12, 13, 1980, The Complex, Santa Monica, California
June 3, 1983, Hammersmith Odeon, London, England
Label: Columbia
Producer: Josef Zawinul, Wayne Shorter
Personnel:
Josef Zawinul – keyboards, synthesizer
Wayne Shorter – saxophone
Jaco Pastorius – bass
Alphonso Johnson – bass
Victor Bailey – bass
Chester Thompson – drums
Omar Hakim – drums
Peter Erskine – drums
Alex Acuna – percussion
Manolo Badrena – percussion
Jose Rossy – percussion
Robert Thomas – percussion

Live and Unreleased is a compilation of live recordings by Weather Report from performances that took place from 1975 to 1983, but not released until 2002. Despite being a band known for their live improvisation, it is only their third official live recording, the previous two being *Live in Tokyo* (1972) and *8:30* (1979). Although this collection is an excellent representation of Weather Report's performances over the time period, the sequencing of the tracks can be confusing for the listener, since there is little or no relationship between one track (and its associated date, venue, and line-up) and the next.

The album begins with "Freezing Fire" by Wayne Shorter from *Tale Spinnin'* (1975). It features Alex Acuna on percussion, Alphonso Johnson on bass, and Chester Thompson on drums. This is followed by Shorter's "Plaza Real" from *Procession* (1983), featuring Victor Bailey on bass and Omar Hakim on drums. Then comes "Fast City" by Josef Zawinul from *Night Passage* (1980), with Jaco Pastorius on bass and Peter Erskine on drums. See what I mean?

The next two tracks were actually played at the same concert in Grand Rapids, Michigan, in 1977. Both also first appeared on *Montreux Jazz Festival, 1976*. "Portrait of Tracy," by Pastorius, is a vehicle for the author to take an extended, inventive bass solo. "Elegant People" by Shorter, likewise gives its composer an opportunity to stretch out on the saxophone, to the delight of the crowd.

This is followed by an extended performance of "Cucumber Slumber" by Johnson and Zawinul from *Mysterious Traveler* (1974), the band's first full-fledged foray into funk. That's alliteration. It's a great track and a highlight of the collection. Shorter takes the first solo on saxophone, followed by Zawinul on electric piano and then synthesizer. The two of them continue to trade solos while the rhythm section of Acuna, Johnson, and Thompson rocks out.

"Teen Town," written by Pastorius, first appeared on *Black Market* (1976). It's a space jam in double time, featuring Manolo Badrena on all manner of percussion. Zawinul's "Man in the Green Shirt" from *Tale Spinnin'* is another extended track, a wonderful journey down any number of improvised pathways. Shorter and Zawinul trade soaring solos on saxophone and keyboards, respectively.

The joyous title track from *Black Market*, written by Zawinul, opens with the taped noises of a street market. One can hear bassist Pastorius conversing musically with both saxophonist Shorter and keyboardist Zawinul. "Where the Moon Goes" from *Procession*, also by Zawinul, is a complicated, extended composition, featuring the author on vocalizations run through his synthesizer.

Pastorius's "River People" from *Mr. Gone* (1978) features Erskine with some triple time drumming between Zawinul's electric piano solo and Shorter's on saxophone. "Two Lines" from *Procession* is written by Zawinul and features Joe Rossy on percussion. "Cigano" is a previously unreleased composition by Shorter. It's a mellow, soulful tune, featuring the author with some bluesy saxophone solos.

The next three performances flow together best on the album, being performed by the same line-up, the latter two at the same concert in Santa Monica, California. "In a Silent Way"/"Waterfall" by Zawinul, also previously unreleased, is a showcase for its author's keyboard prowess. "Night Passage," from the album of the same name, features the rhythm section of Pastorius on bass and Erskine on drums. Shorter's "Port of Entry" from *Night Passage* is an elegant exercise in syncopation, with the members of Weather Report passing the riff around, as it were.

"Rumba Mama" is a short snippet of a percussion-based jam, with chanting, written by Acuna and Badrena for *Heavy Weather* (1977). *Live and Unreleased* concludes with "Directions"/"Dr. Honoris Causa," a new composition by Zawinul. It captures the essence of the Weather Report sound, Zawinul and Shorter trading ideas in front of the killer rhythm section, in this case, Acuna, Johnson, and Thompson.

Ween – *Live in Chicago*

Released: 2004
Recorded: November 8-9, 2003, Vic Theatre, Chicago, Illinois
Label: Sanctuary
Producer: Ann Bailz, Travis Boyle, Sara Maher
Personnel:
Dean Ween – guitar, vocals
Gene Ween – guitar, vocals
Glen McClelland – keyboards, vocals
Dave Dreiwitz – bass, vocals
Claude Coleman, Jr. – drums, vocals

Packaged alternately as a compact disc with a bonus digital video disc or as a digital video disc with a bonus compact disc, *Live in Chicago* documents two nights that Ween performed in Chicago in support of their 2003 album, *Quebec*. The digital video disc features a wide variety of songs, covering nearly every Ween album. The compact disc, by comparison, contains a different track list and fewer songs.

The concert starts, in typical Ween fashion, with "Take Me Away," an up-tempo number, which could have been sung by Bill Murray's lounge lizard character on *Saturday Night Live*. Dean Ween immediately illustrates why he is one of the great, unknown, underrated guitar players on the planet. "The Grobe" is next, Gene Ween changing voices entirely to match the mood of the piece, which is sort of heavy metal meets twisted chamber music.

The apocalyptic "Transdermal Celebration" from *Quebec* is next, featuring D. Ween on guitar. "Even if You Don't" from *White Pepper* (2000) is a personal favorite, the version here featuring Glen McClelland on piano and D. Ween on guitar. "Voodoo Lady," a long-time Ween concert favorite, is then done in extended form to the delight of the audience. Ween is an acquired taste and not for everyone, as evidenced by "The HIV Song," which could hardly be more politically incorrect.

The lovingly titled "Baby Bitch" is a wicked hate ballad, delivered in appropriately acerbic fashion by G. Ween. "Roses Are Free," as performed here, is one of my favorite versions of one of my favorite Ween tunes. The entire band excels, most notably Dave Dreiwitz on bass and the ubiquitous D. Ween on solo guitar. "Mutilated Lips" from *The Mollusk* (1997) features a remarkable vocal performance, in fact several electronically enhanced vocal performances, from G. Ween.

"Chocolate Town" from *Quebec* is one of Ween's beautifully melodic pop tunes, seemingly out of place among the bizarre, but a showcase, nonetheless, of the band's chops. The frenetic "I'll Be Your Jonny on the Spot" is next, returning us to the land of the bizarre. D. Ween is relentless on guitar, bending down, I'm certain, as is his wont, all the way to the floor as he delivers his solo. "Buckingham Green" from *The Mollusk* is another concert favorite, performed here masterfully. It features D. Ween and G. Ween on guitars and outstanding drumming from Claude Coleman, Jr.

"Spinal Meningitis (Got Me Down)" is about as strange as it gets, the similarity between the title and the lyric, "Smile, All Mighty Jesus" being just the beginning. The crowd chants every line of the song and D. Ween is at it again on guitar. "Pork Roll Egg and Cheese" is a throwback to Ween's earliest days and an absolutely ridiculous song, but in a good way! "The Argus" from *Quebec*, about a mythological all-seeing creature, features interesting interplay between D. Ween on guitar and Dreiwitz on bass.

An extended version of "Zoloft" is next, a not-so-subtle commentary on prescription drug abuse. The tune drifts along, like many among us drift through the days, D. Ween's guitar playing hypnotic in nature. *Live in Chicago* concludes with the popular and rousing "Ocean Man" from *The Mollusk*. The too-short nautical themed tune features some inspired guitar work from D. Ween.

In May 2012, G. Ween (Aaron Freeman) announced the end of Ween and his desire to pursue a solo career. D. Ween (Mickey Melchiondo) was apparently unaware of the decision. Later on, Freeman confirmed that his departure from Ween was triggered by his desire to remain sober. In April 2013, during the preparation of this project, the former members of Ween, minus G. Ween, performed a set at John & Peter's in New Hope, Pennsylvania.

The Who – *Live at Leeds*

Released: 1970, 1995
Recorded: February 14, 1970, U. of Leeds, Leeds, England
Label: Decca, MCA
Producer: Jon Astley, Kit Lambert, The Who
Personnel:
Roger Daltrey – harmonica, tambourine, vocals
Pete Townshend – guitar, vocals
John Entwistle – bass, vocals
Keith Moon – drums, percussion

In my Foreword, I state that my focus here is on original recordings, not expanded, re-mastered later versions, with one exception, *Live at Leeds* by The Who. The original album, released in 1970 with only six tracks, was a truly great album, one of the best, very important to me at the time. Little did I know that it didn't really represent The Who live onstage at the time, when they were at the peak of their power and popularity following the release of *Tommy* the previous year. Only when the album was reissued as a remixed compact disc in 1995 were we treated to the concert the way it was performed and meant to be heard.

The concert begins with "Heaven and Hell," written and sung by bassist John Entwistle. It was the B-side to the live "Summertime Blues" single in 1970. It is immediately apparent that The Who are at the top of their game, jamming furiously from the outset. Pete Townshend is featured on guitar solo. They next do a dynamite version of their hit single from 1964, "I Can't Explain," Roger Daltrey permanently assuming lead vocal duties. Next is a cover of "Fortune Teller," written by Allen Toussaint under the pseudonym Naomi Neville. It features great harmony vocals by Daltrey and Townshend.

This segues into "Tattoo" from *The Who Sell Out* (1967). About two brothers who decide to get tattoos in their efforts to achieve manhood, it features an outstanding nuanced vocal by Daltrey. A cover of "Young Man Blues" by Mose Allison is next, one of the six tracks on the original album. It features a stop-time section where Daltrey sings unaccompanied between bursts of bluesy jamming. Keith Moon is monumental on drums; Townshend and Entwistle engage in some brilliant interplay between guitar and bass.

Townshend then announces that the band would play "three selected hit singles," all from 1966, the first of which is "Substitute," another of the original tracks. Then comes "Happy Jack," featuring Entwistle on vocals on the first verse and some fabulous bass playing. One wonders how The Who captured their live sound so well on even their earliest studio tracks. This is followed by "I'm a Boy," one boy's lament at his mother's refusal to acknowledge his gender, often cited as a precursor to The Who's rock operas.

Speaking of which, Townshend introduces the next song, "A Quick One, While He's Away" from *A Quick One* (1966) as a mini-opera and as *Tommy*'s parents. A composition in six distinct movements, it features Entwistle in the role of Ivor the Engine Driver. Continuing along these lines, the band next plays "Amazing Journey"/"Sparks" from *Tommy*. The former is about Tommy's revelatory psychedelic trip featuring Daltrey on the vocal; the latter an instrumental featuring some of *Tommy*'s signature themes and some of the fiercest jamming on the album.

The final four tracks on the expanded 1995 *Live at Leeds* were also included on the original 1970 release. Eddie Cochran's "Summertime Blues" is the first of these, the single from the album. It features vocal contributions from Daltrey, Townshend, and Entwistle. "Shakin' All Over" is next, a cover of the 1960 single by Johnny Kidd & the Pirates. It features Entwistle on the bass and Townshend on the guitar.

What can you say about a fifteen-minute performance of "My Generation?" Released as a single in 1965, it never sounded like this! After delivering the standard version of the tune, we're treated to a glorious jam session, including a bunch of themes from *Tommy*, lead bass playing by Entwistle, and many interesting guitar solos by Townshend. Both editions of *Live at Leeds* end with an extended performance of the 1968 single, "Magic Bus," featuring the Bo Diddley beat, Moon on claves, and Daltrey on harmonica.

Widespread Panic – *Light Fuse, Get Away*

Released: 1998
Recorded: 1997, various venues
Label: Capricorn
Producer: John Keane
Personnel:
John Bell – guitar, vocals
Michael Houser – guitar, vocals
John Hermann – keyboards, vocals
Todd Nance – drums, percussion, vocals
Domingo S. Ortiz – percussion
Dave Schools – bass, percussion, vocals
Branford Marsalis – saxophone

Light Fuse, Get Away is a double album released by Widespread Panic. It was recorded during 1997 at concerts at various venues. Despite my best efforts, I cannot ascertain the exact dates and sites of these concerts beyond September 7, 1997 at the Harbor Lights Pavilion in Boston, Massachusetts, and the following night at Club Soda in Montreal, Quebec.

The album features concert favorites and album tracks, many in extended form, showcasing Widespread Panic's legendary onstage ensemble jamming. The album begins with "Porch Song" from their first album, *Space Wrangler* (1988). It may start out as a mellow back porch tune, but it soon evolves into a bluesy rocker, driven by underrated Michael Houser on guitar and John Hermann on piano.

A bass solo by David Schools takes us into the next song, "Disco," a funky instrumental featuring Hermann on piano and a guitar solo by Houser. This is followed by a fourteen minute performance of "Diner" from *Everyday* (1993). It's a mid-tempo groove that features John Bell's nuanced vocal, spinning out vignettes of diner life. Houser plays a couple of inspired guitar solos.

"Wondering" is next, a feel-good rocker that has to make you smile. Todd Nance is featured on drums as is Hermann on piano. "Love Tractor," from their eponymous second album, is an infectious rocker with interesting changes in time signature and plenty of distortion in Houser's guitar solo. "Pilgrims" from *Everyday* is a complicated composition, a history lesson of sorts on which Widespread Panic distinguish themselves with fabulous ensemble playing.

This segues into the title track from *Space Wrangler*. It also has several interesting changes and features Hermann on organ and Houser on guitar. This is followed by a cover of J.J. Cale's "Travelin' Light" from *Troubadour* (1976). It features Nance on drums and Domingo S. Ortiz on percussion. Houser and Hermann take solos on guitar and piano, respectively.

"Pickin' Up the Pieces" from *Everyday* has a mellow, jazzy feel to it, underlined by the presence of Branford Marsalis, who sits in on saxophone. An extended performance of "Conrad" follows, apparently about a caterpillar. It's a bluesy jam that features dynamic bass playing by Schools and solos by Hermann on piano and Houser on guitar. "Papa Legba" is an interesting cover of a Talking Heads song from *True Stories* (1986). Bell is outstanding on vocals, Hermann anchors the tune on piano, and Houser rocks out mightily on solo guitar.

A nifty bass introduction by Schools kick starts "Rebirtha" from *Bombs & Butterflies* (1997), a very funky groove of a song. Houser's guitar solo leads the band temporarily into deep space, but they return to the planet successfully. "Rock" from *Widespread Panic* begins with a percussion introduction from Nance and Ortiz, but it quickly evolves into a country-ish rocker with contrapuntal riffs being played by Houser on guitar and Hermann on keyboards.

The following three tracks are all extended performances, each exceeding ten minutes in length. "Greta" from *Bombs & Butterflies* is an interesting composition that reminds me of both "Jack Straw" by the Grateful Dead and "Split Open and Melt" by Phish. Houser gets the chance to stretch out with a long and excellent guitar solo. "Barstools & Dreamers" captures that live sound that is unique to Widespread Panic, featuring Houser on slide guitar and Hermann on organ. As if all this free-form jamming weren't sufficient, the next song is "Impossible"/"Jam," the former from *Widespread Panic* with heavy metal overtones, the latter a purely improvisational composition.

"Drums" is next, featuring Nance and Ortiz, followed by "Gimme," on which the rest of the band falls in. *Light Fuse, Get Away* concludes with "Pigeons" from *Widespread Panic*, a personal favorite. Bell's vocal performance is outstanding, but the highlight is the jam at the end, featuring Schools on bass, Hermann on piano, and the ubiquitous Houser on guitar.

In April 1998, Widespread Panic played a free live show in home town Athens, Georgia, as part of the release party for *Light Fuse, Get Away*. Attendance was estimated at 100,000 people, breaking Metallica's record for the largest such party. The concert was filmed and released later in the year on video. J.J. Cale died in July 2013 during the preparation of this project.

Johnny Winter – *Live Johnny Winter And*

Released: 1971
Recorded: November 27, 1970, The Capitol Theater, Port Chester, New York
        January 1-2, 1971, Pirate's World, Dania, Florida
Label: Columbia
Producer: Johnny Winter, Rick Derringer
Personnel:
Johnny Winter – guitar, vocals
Rick Derringer – guitar, vocals
Randy Jo Hobbs – bass, vocals
Bobby Caldwell – drums, percussion

    Johnny Winter was born in 1944 in Beaumont, Texas. Both he and his brother, Edgar, both of whom suffer from albinism, began performing at an early age. His recording career began at the age of fifteen, when his band Johnny and the Jammers released "School Day Blues' on a Houston record label. In 1968, he released his first album, *The Progressive Blues Experiment*, on Austin's Sonobeat Records.
    Winter's first eponymous album on Columbia Records was recorded and released in 1969. It featured selections that became his signature songs, including his composition "Dallas," Sonny Boy Williamson's "Good Morning Little School Girl," and B.B. King's "Be Careful with a Fool." With brother Edgar added as a member of his band, Winter recorded his third album, *Second Winter*, in Nashville in 1969.
    Winter released his fourth album, *Johnny Winter And*, in 1970. It was his first album with Rick Derringer as a sideman. It was also briefly the name of his band. That fall and winter, Winter's band was recorded live at various locations, with Derringer as sideman and co-producer. The result is *Live Johnny Winter And*. The studio album contains the original version of "Rock and Roll, Hoochie Koo," a hit for Derringer in 1973, but otherwise sounds a bit dated these days. The live album still kicks ass, and with no filler.
    This is straight ahead, no bullshit, take no prisoners, rock and blues. The band is relentless, Winter's signature growling vocals leading the

charge. From the first note of the Sonny Boy Williamson classic, "Good Morning, Little Schoolgirl," we know we're in for a treat. Winter and Derringer are clearly enjoying themselves as they trade complementary guitar solos.

They slow things down significantly with a marathon version of "It's My Own Fault." It's a twelve-bar blues to be sure, but about as funky as can be, the two guitarists having the opportunity to really stretch out. The cover of The Rolling Stones' "Jumpin' Jack Flash" is nothing short of brilliant. It got a great deal of airplay on FM radio, at the time a medium in its formative stages.

The so-called "Rock and Roll Medley" is wildly raucous. It's like a Little Richard sandwich on toasted Jerry Lee Lewis, complete with audience participation. Specifically, they play "Great Balls of Fire," the 1957 hit single for Lewis, "Long Tall Sally," Little Richard's 1956 smash, and "Whole Lotta Shakin' Goin' On," another hit in 1957 for Lewis. Bobby Caldwell is outstanding on drums. I'm sure it made The Killer proud.

"Mean Town Blues" is the only Winter original tune on *Live Johnny Winter And*. It features the author on a couple of extended guitar solos. The album concludes with a cover of Chuck Berry's "Johnny B. Goode." Other than the original, I have always considered this to be the definitive version of this tune, no matter how many times I heard it performed by the Dead. Winter seems to personify the title character in every way, from his given name to his remarkable, prodigious guitar playing.

The Youngbloods – *Ride the Wind*

Released: 1971
Recorded: November 26-29, 1969, Fillmore East, NYC
Label: Warner Bros.
Producer: Charlie Daniels
Personnel:
Jesse Colin Young – bass, guitar, kazoo, vocals
Joe Bauer – drums
Lowell "Banana" Levinger – guitar, piano

The Youngbloods were one of the better bands to emerge from the East Coast in the mid-1960s. When they relocated to the San Francisco Bay Area, they traded in their blues and jug band influences for a gentle psychedelic sound. "Grizzly Bear" was a minor hit in 1967, as was "Get Together," a Dino Valenti song previously recorded by Jefferson Airplane.

Following the success of *Elephant Mountain* in 1969 with its hit single, "Darkness, Darkness," The Youngbloods followed up with two live releases, the disappointing *Rock Festival* in 1970 and *Ride the Wind* the following year. After the departure of original band member, guitarist Jerry Corbitt, The Youngbloods found themselves a trio, with the versatile Banana and a rhythm section.

Boy, did I listen to this album a lot! And practice bass guitar along with it all the time. Too much information? Probably so. Simply put, *Ride the Wind* by The Youngbloods is one of my most listened to albums ever. It's got a certain mellow jamming groove to it that I have always found pleasing and somewhat mesmerizing. Although Jesse Colin Young is the namesake and founder and leader and singer and principal songwriter of the band, Banana is the star of this album.

There are only six tracks on the album, but not unlike their Marin County contemporaries, the Grateful Dead, the band stretches out and takes their improvisational play up several notches as compared with their studio work. The album opens with an almost ten minute version of the title track, from *Elephant Mountain*, with Banana brilliant on electric piano. The extended groove ebbs and flows and builds to a crescendo.

"Sugar Babe" is fun, fairly true to the original on *Earth Music* (1967), and likewise featuring Young on kazoo. What's not to like about that? "Sunlight," an absolutely beautiful song, also from *Elephant Mountain*, is enhanced by the improvisational interplay between Banana and Young, both here on guitar. They then cover Fred Neil's "The Dolphin," getting very jazzy in their jamming, Banana back on electric piano.

"Get Together," from their 1967 eponymous debut album, was The Youngblood's biggest hit and best-known track, further popularized by its use in a public service advertisement on television in 1969. It is presented here with great spirit and with just enough rearrangement to keep it interesting, Banana on guitar. *Ride the Wind* concludes with "Beautiful," co-written by Young and Carole King for *Elephant Mountain*. It's a positive hippy anthem if there ever was one, performed here at length and with quite a bit of funky guitar playing by Banana.

The Youngbloods disbanded in 1972, each of the members pursuing solo careers. In 1984, the band briefly reunited for a club tour. The lineup included Young, Banana and Corbitt, in addition to new members David Perper on drums and Scott Lawrence on keyboards and woodwinds. Once the tour was completed in early 1985, the group called it quits once again.

I attended one of the concerts represented here, probably November 28, the day after Thanksgiving, 1969. The Youngbloods were opening for Jefferson Airplane. "Sunlight" from *Elephant* Mountain (1969) was one of the songs I selected to be in my book, *The 100 Greatest Rock'n'Roll Songs Ever* in 2000.

Frank Zappa/Mothers – *Roxy & Elsewhere*

Released: 1974
Recorded: December 10-12, 1973, The Roxy Theatre, Hollywood, California
        May 8, 1974, Edinboro State College, Edinboro, Pennsylvania
        May 12, 1974, Auditorium Theater, Chicago, Illinois
Label: Barking Pumpkin
Producer: Frank Zappa
Personnel:
Frank Zappa – guitar, vocals
Tom Fowler – bass
Chester Thompson – drums
George Duke – keyboards, vocals
Napoleon Murphy Brock – saxophone, flute, vocals
Bruce Fowler – trombone
Walt Fowler – trumpet
Ruth Underwood – percussion
Don Preston – synthesizer
Jeff Simmons – guitar, vocals
Ralph Humphrey – drums

Roxy & Elsewhere is a live album released by Frank Zappa & the Mothers in 1974, mostly recorded in Los Angeles. It is a great example of a live set by one of the most celebrated incarnations of the Mothers. It features several seemingly impossible-to-play instrumental compositions, re-workings of earlier tracks, as well as "Cheepnis," Zappa's tribute to low-budget monster movies, and "Penguin in Bondage," his take on toys in the bedroom and bdsm.

The album begins with a lengthy introduction by Zappa, in which he attempts to talk around the subject matter of the first song, the aforementioned "Penguin in Bondage," for a television broadcast that never took place. This song is the perfect juxtaposition of Zappa's penchant for outrageous lyrics and his compositional genius. It features the horn section of Napoleon Murphy Brock on saxophone, Bruce Fowler on trombone and Walt Fowler on trumpet, as well as one of Zappa's signature guitar solos.

This segues seamlessly into "Pygmy Twylyte," a brief tune with nonsense lyrics that features Brock's wide vocal range. This, in turn, segues into "Dummy Up," co-written by Zappa with Brock and guitarist Jeff Simmons. The three of them improvise a bunch of lyrics about the negligible benefits of "higher" education while the band vamps behind them.

"Village of the Sun" is about Sun Village, California, near Palmdale, twin city to Lancaster, Zappa's hometown. Brock is featured on vocals, singing about living under the influence of the stench of turkey farms. Before you know it, the band is into "Echidna's Arf (Of You)," an incredibly intricate composition with numerous changes in meter. Ruth Underwood is featured on percussion on this and the next, even more bizarre, instrumental number, "Don't You Ever Wash That Thing?" It also features solos by B. Fowler on trombone, George Duke on piano, Chester Thompson on drums, and, of course, Zappa on guitar.

Zappa then gives the audience an explanation of his motivation for writing the very funny "Cheepnis." Brock does the singing while Zappa plays narrator to the worst movie ever made. Individuals named Debbie, Lynn, Ruben, and "Frog" are credited with backing vocals. "Son of Orange County" is excerpted from "Oh No" from *Weasels Ripped My Flesh* (1970) and augmented with a remarkable extended guitar solo by Zappa.

This builds to a jam that becomes "More Trouble Every Day," a reprise of "Trouble Every Day" from *Freak Out* (1966), the debut album by The Mothers of Invention. Slowed down a bit from the original, the tune is no less powerful, predicting revolution in the air and rioting in the streets. As if to underline his point, Zappa absolutely shreds his guitar solo.

Roxy & Elsewhere concludes with "Be-Bop Tango (of the Old Jazzman's Church)," introduced by Zappa as "a perverted tango." It's a vehicle for the band to show off their chops as well as an opportunity for audience participation, a staple at most Zappa concerts. While the band plays "sort of jazz" and Duke sings nonsense lyrics, audience members are invited up on stage to dance the be-bop tango. Underwood is featured on percussion and B. Fowler lays down an excellent trombone solo.

Frank Zappa – *Zappa in New York*

Released: 1978
Recorded: October 29-31, 1976, Felt Forum, Madison Square Garden, NYC
          December 26-29, 1976, Palladium, NYC
Label: DiscReet
Producer: Frank Zappa
Personnel:
Frank Zappa – guitar, keyboards, vocals
Ray White – guitar, vocals
Eddie Jobson – keyboards, synthesizer, violin, vocals
Patrick O'Hearn – bass, vocals
Terry Bozzio – drums, vocals
Ruth Underwood – synthesizer, percussion
Dave Samuels – timpani, vibraphone
Randy Brecker – trumpet
Mike Brecker – saxophone, flute
Lou Marini – saxophone, flute
Ronnie Cuber – saxophone, clarinet
Tom Malone – trombone, trumpet, piccolo
Don Pardo – voice

Frank Zappa had an affinity for New York City ever since 1967 when he and his Mothers of Invention arrived in March of that year for an Easter gig at the Garrick Theater on Bleeker Street. The engagement was so successful that the promoter decided to hold them over through the summer. After expenses they each received about two hundred dollars a week, which was good money at the time and it was steady. Zappa and his wife Gail took an apartment on Thompson Street and the rest of the band migrated between the Chelsea Hotel on West 23rd Street and the Zappas' living room floor.

Zappa started a tradition of playing on Halloween in New York City in 1972 (if you count New Jersey, or 1974 if you don't) that lasted until 1984. In 1976, the band played a series of shows around Halloween at the Felt Forum and a follow-up series at the end of the year at the Palladium.

These concerts resulted in *Zappa in New York*. Zappa states on the original album cover: "In 1976 we played for a group of deranged lunatics in New York City, some of the nicest people we have had the experience of playing for. New York is what made this album possible."

Zappa, of course, was a staunch defender of the First Amendment to the Constitution of the United States and free speech advocate. *Zappa in New York* has no shortage of language and subject matter that some might find obscene, whatever that means. I personally find it obscene that in 2013, even on community supported, listener sponsored radio stations, on-air personalities may not say the word "piss" for fear of sanctions by the Federal Communications Commission.

In Terry Bozzio, Zappa found a great drummer with massive stage presence who could sing, so he wrote material to highlight Bozzio. One such example is the first song on the album (I warned you!), "Titties and Beer." It's an extended dialogue between a guy (Zappa) and the Devil (Bozzio), with whom he must make a deal in order to have his fill of titties and beer, with the band in a groove behind them. Despite Zappa's reputation as a taskmaster and perfectionist, he's loose enough to interrupt the song to read a message on microphone from a woman in the audience who is missing her brother.

And then there's "Punky's Whips," sung by Bozzio, an ode to a photo of Punky Meadows, lead guitarist of Angel. It's bizarre, it's offensive, it's sexually ambiguous, and it's great. They do "Big Leg Emma," an inappropriate and chauvinistic love song, which was regularly performed by the Mothers of Invention at the Garrick Theater in 1967. They also do "Honey, Don't You Want a Man Like Me?" about a pick-up in a singles bar.

There are several instrumental tunes on *Zappa in New York*, typical for a Zappa concert. "I Promise Not to Come in Your Mouth" features Zappa on guitar and Eddie Jobson on Moog synthesizer. "Sofa" is a fairly straightforward rendering of the version on *One Size Fits All* (1975). "Manx Needs Women" is an arrangement of an exercise published in *Guitar Player Magazine*.

"Black Page #1" is a drum improvisation by Bozzio, joined by Ruth Underwood and Dave Samuels on percussion; "Black Page #2" is one of Zappa's signature themes. "The Purple Lagoon" was performed on "Saturday Night Live" the previous September, with John Belushi as a Samurai be-bop musician. It features solos by Michael Brecker on tenor saxophone, Zappa on guitar, Ronnie Cuber on baritone saxophone, Patrick O'Hearn on bass, and Randy Brecker on trumpet, in that order.

But the centerpiece, the highlight, my favorite piece on *Zappa in New York* is "The Legend of the Illinois Enema Bandit," the true story of Michael H. Kenyon, who terrorized coeds at the University of Illinois at Urbana. Zappa takes the basic story and let's his imagination and creativity run wild. It's like a perverted mini-opera, complete with an introduction by announcer Don Pardo, inspired singing by Ray White, another great guitar solo from Zappa, and a call-and-response courtroom scene. Great stuff.

I attended shows at both runs in 1976. Please don't expect me to remember which ones. I didn't keep a journal and I never collected ticket stubs. It is difficult to imagine that Frank Zappa will soon be dead twenty years.

The Zombies – *Odessey & Oracle (Revisited)*: The 40ᵗʰ Anniversary Concert

Released: 2009
Recorded: March 7-9, 2008, The Shepherd's Bush Empire Club, London,
      England
Label: Redhouse
Producer: Al Kooper
Personnel:
Rod Argent – keyboards, vocals
Jim Rodford – bass
Chris White – bass, vocals
Colin Blunstone – vocals
Hugh Grundy – drums
Steve Rodford – drums
Keith Airey – guitar
Darian Sahanaja – keyboards

Odessey & Oracle (1968) by The Zombies is considered by many, including myself, to be one of the most influential rock'n'roll albums ever. However, because the band broke up before the album was released, they never performed any of the songs live. The five original members reformed briefly in 1997 for the launch party of the *Zombie Heaven* boxed set, performing "She's Not There" and "Time of the Season" at a London club. Colin Blunstone and Rod Argent reunited in 2001, touring and recording with ex-Argent bassist Jim Rodford, his son Steve Rodford on drums, and Keith Airey on guitar.

There was one final reunion of the five at a benefit for Paul Atkinson in 2004. He died later that year. In March 2008, on the occasion of the 40ᵗʰ anniversary of the release of *Odessey & Oracle*, the four surviving original members reunited for a series of three concerts in London. The result is *Odessey & Oracle (Revisited): The 40ᵗʰ Anniversary Concert*.

The show is divided into two sets, the first featuring The Zombies' touring band and a string quartet. Early Zombies songs like "I Love You" from *The Zombies* (1964) and Argent hits like "Hold Your Head Up," released as a single in 1972, are mixed together nicely, along with great covers of "What Becomes of the Broken Hearted," a hit single in 1966 for Jimmy Ruffin and "Misty Roses" by Tim Hardin, also a hit in 1966. Argent and Blunstone seem to be having a blast trading vocals backed by outstanding musicianship.

The second set is the performance by Argent, Blunstone, Chris White, and Hugh Grundy of *Odessey & Oracle*. They are supported by Airey on guitar and Darian Sahanaja on keyboards. As soon as they begin "Care of Cell 44," with its complicated harmonies, we know we're in for a treat. The band lovingly recreates each of the tracks, effectively performed for the first time in public. They are clearly gratified to be so warmly received.

It's difficult to pick a favorite here. "A Rose for Emily" is simply brilliant. The harmonies on "Maybe After He's Gone" remind us of why the original album was compared favorably with The Beatles and The Beach Boys. Great vocals also on "Hung Up on a Dream." The *Odessey & Oracle* section of the show ends with a rocking version of "Time of the Season," maybe stronger than the original. The Zombies end the concert with encore performances of "Tell Her No" and "She's Not There," both from their 1964 eponymous debut album.

The concerts were sell-outs and highly critically acclaimed. One of the shows was filmed and released on digital video disc. The reunion was so successful that The Zombies reprised the show for four dates in April 2009, playing in Glasgow, Bristol, Manchester, and London. At the last show on April 25 at the Hammersmith Apollo, Argent announced that it would be the last time the album would be performed on stage. *Odessey & Oracle* was one of the albums I selected to be in my book, *The 100 Greatest Rock'n'Roll Albums Ever* in 2009.